Ann Arbor's Cookin' II

Proceeds benefit the Ronald McDonald House®

Additional copies may be obtained by filling out the order blank in the back of the book or write directly to:

ANN ARBOR'S COOKIN' II
Ronald McDonald House
1600 Washington Heights
Ann Arbor, MI 48104
(313-994-4442)

Please include a check made payable to Ronald McDonald House for $15.00 (Michigan residents add .60 sales tax per book), plus $2.00 for postage and handling per book.

Printed by
Thomson-Shore
Dexter, MI

ISBN 0-9618208-1-0

COOKBOOK COMMITTEE

Ann Betz, Chairman
Kristi Stutz, Chief Editor
Tissy Ansbacher
Aileen Clark
Susan Hurwitz
Mary Johnson
Jeri Kelch
Kay Moler
Mariel Peck
Helen Woodke

Our gratitude is extended to Blixt Associates, an Ann Arbor-based marketing, advertising and public relations firm, who donated the time and talents of its creative staff in the design of this cookbook. In particular, we wish to thank Heather Wall, Junior Art Director and Catherine Powers Hunter, Vice President, Creative Services, for the cookbook cover design and Lois Diehl, Agency Administrator, for her assistance. We also wish to acknowledge members of the Service Department, Kelly Services Headquarters, for editing and proofreading services. A special thank you to Lorris Betz who helped in so many different ways in the completion of this cookbook.

Ann Arbor's Cookin' II is a collection of 700 all new, prized recipes selected from over 1,000 submitted. We regret that some had to be omitted because of space and duplications. A warm thank you to all of the busy Ann Arbor cooks (many affiliated with The University of Michigan and Ronald McDonald House) who submitted their ideas and recipes and gave unselfishly of their time. We also wish to express our appreciation to the area restaurants and shops for freely sharing some of their kitchen secrets.

FOREWORD

When I began work on *Ann Arbor's Cookin'!* in 1985, I hoped that, in some small way, this project would bring much-needed revenue to the Ann Arbor Ronald McDonald House which was then under construction. The first printing was 5,000 copies, an intimidating number to our committee, but economical in terms of printing costs. We soon realized with elation that we had grossly underestimated the appeal of both our cookbook and the cause that it supported because, within four months, we had sold our entire first printing. To this date, nearly 17,000 copies of *Ann Arbor's Cookin'!* have been sold and more than $150,000 has been provided to support our local Ronald McDonald House.

As Anne M. Duderstadt, wife of the President of The University of Michigan, stated: "A seriously ill, hospitalized child is most in need of love, comfort, and reassurance. Both parents and children experience profound anguish when they must be apart at such a time. We are fortunate to have the Ronald McDonald House on our Medical Campus to enable parents to be near their children during these painful and distressing times. The House fills a vital need in the lives of families whose children are treated at Mott Children's Hospital."

I would like to take this opportunity to express my gratitude to all those who contributed recipes, purchased the first cookbook, and told their friends about it. *Ann Arbor's Cookin'!* is a well used and valued addition to many kitchen libraries both locally and across the country. We are pleased to respond to the many requests for a sequel with the publication of *Ann Arbor's Cookin' II*, a completely new collection of wonderful recipes that have been passed from neighbor to neighbor and friend to friend. *Ann Arbor's Cookin' II* features a selection of over 100 recipes from many of Ann Arbor's noted restaurants and shops, and we are grateful that they have so generously shared their culinary secrets.

So cook, eat, and enjoy! From healthy to sinful, from simple to complicated, the recipes in *Ann Arbor's Cookin' II* will delight your entire family. At the same time, your purchase of this cookbook will provide much needed sustenance and comfort to the families who stay at the Ann Arbor Ronald McDonald House.

Ann Betz
Chairman

TABLE OF CONTENTS

Appetizers

APPETIZERS

Anchovy and Pimento Spread

11/2   2-ounce cans flat fillet anchovy, drained and finely
       chopped
2   pimentos, finely chopped
1/2   cup finely-chopped Spanish onions
1   tablespoon minced parsley
       Freshly-ground pepper
1   tablespoon olive oil
11/4   teaspoons red wine vinegar
1   6-ounce box Melba rounds
       Parsley leaves for garnish

Mix together in a small bowl, anchovy, pimentos, onions, parsley and pepper. Add olive oil and vinegar. Refrigerate several hours or overnight. Spread on Melba rounds. Garnish with parsley leaf. (6-8 servings)

MIDGE WAKEFIELD AND KAREN STEWART

Shrimp Dip

1/4   pound butter
1   8-ounce package cream cheese, room temperature
1/4   cup mayonnaise
1   small onion, chopped
1   tablespoon lemon juice
1   41/4-ounce can shrimp

Blend all ingredients together. Serve with crackers. *"This dip is even better the next day."* MARY DOYLE

Betsy's Seafood Dip

1   pound frozen shrimp (thawed)
1   6-ounce can crabmeat
1   8-ounce jar chili sauce
1   pint jar mayonnaise
1/4   cup pickle relish
1   onion, chopped
3   hard-boiled eggs, chopped

Mix all ingredients and serve with crackers. BETSY WITLIN

Smoked Salmon Spread

1	pound cream cheese, room temperature
1/2	cup heavy cream
2	green onions, chopped
1/4	cup minced fresh parsley
2	tablespoons minced fresh dill (or 2 teaspoons dried)
2	teaspoons fresh lemon juice
1	clove garlic, minced
	Dash hot pepper sauce
	Salt and pepper to taste
8	ounces smoked salmon or lox trimmings, shredded
	Vegetables, crackers or French bread

Beat cream cheese and cream in large bowl until smooth. Stir in green onions, parsley, dill, lemon juice, garlic and hot pepper sauce. Season with salt and pepper. Fold in smoked salmon. Serve with vegetables, crackers or slices of French bread. (10 servings) JANET GILSDORF

Caviar Plus

4	hard-boiled eggs
2	medium onions
	Mayonnaise
1/2	pint sour cream
1	8-ounce package cream cheese, room temperature
1	envelope green onion dip
1	3-ounce jar black or red caviar
3/4	cup chopped parsley
	Crackers

Chop eggs and onions lightly in food processor, mixing with a little mayonnaise to hold together. Layer in a pie plate. Mix sour cream, cream cheese and dip; spread on egg mixture. Top with caviar (all black or mix black and red). Decorate edge with parsley. Refrigerate at least 4 hours or a day ahead. Serve with crackers. DOROTHY WARDELL

Smoked Oyster Spread

1	31/2-ounce can smoked oysters, drained and minced
1/2	cup cream cheese, room temperature
1	green onion, minced
1	tablespoon chili sauce
	Cucumber slices or crackers

Mix oysters, cream cheese, onions and chili sauce in small bowl. Cover and refrigerate overnight to blend flavors. Serve with cucumber slices or crackers. JANET GILSDORF

Lo-Cal Dip

1	61/2-ounce can minced clams
1	pint large curd cottage cheese
1	small package Good Seasons Italian dressing mix
1	teaspoon dill
11/2	teaspoons Beau Monde seasoning
11/2	teaspoons dried onion flakes

In blender, mix clams and cottage cheese. Add remaining ingredients and blend well. (6-8 servings) MRS. DONALD SMITH

Mexican Triangles with Salsa

1	package flour or corn tortillas
1/2	pound Provolone, sliced thin
1/2	pound salami, sliced thin

SALSA:

2	large fresh tomatoes, diced
10	green onions, sliced (include some green part)
5	cloves garlic, minced
1/4	cup chopped fresh basil
3-4	dashes hot sauce, or to taste
1	teaspoon dried cilantro
1	tablespoon sugar

Combine all salsa ingredients at least 4 hours prior to serving. Cut tortillas into triangles. Alternate tortilla, salami and cheese in a circle on a large platter. Serve with bowl of salsa placed in middle. *"This garlicky salsa is addictive. Improves with age."* ANN BETZ

Taco Salsa Dip

1	8-ounce container sour cream
1	16-ounce jar chunky salsa (mild or hot)
1	8-ounce package cream cheese, room temperature
1	4-ounce can jalapeño slices/pieces (optional)
1/2	cup shredded cheddar cheese
1/2	cup shredded Monterey Jack cheese

Mix ingredients together in large bowl. Chill about 1/2 hour. Serve with chips. (6-8 servings) KATHRYN SULLIVAN

Guacamole Dip

1/2	cup mayonnaise
1	large avocado, peeled and mashed
1	small tomato, peeled and chopped
1/4	cup minced onions
1/4	cup chopped green chiles, drained
1	tablespoon lemon juice
1/2	teaspoon salt

Stir all ingredients together; cover and chill. (2 cups) PRUE ROSENTHAL

Guacamole - Avocado Dip

4	large avocados
	Juice from 1 lemon
2-3	canned green chiles, chopped
2	medium ripe tomatoes, chopped
1/2	cup chopped onions
2	cloves garlic, minced
1	teaspoon Worcestershire sauce
1/4	teaspoon hot pepper sauce
1/4	teaspoon ground coriander

Use a stainless steel spoon to mix and mash ingredients. Cover and refrigerate until used. KATHERINE HAY

6

Cucumber Dill Dip

1	8-ounce package cream cheese, room temperature
1	cup mayonnaise
2	medium cucumbers, peeled, seeded and chopped
1/8	cup sliced green onions
1	tablespoon lemon juice
2	tablespoons snipped fresh dill (or 1/2 teaspoon dried)
1/2	teaspoon hot pepper sauce

Beat cream cheese until smooth. Stir in remaining ingredients and mix. Cover and chill. (Makes 21/2 cups) PRUE ROSENTHAL

Stuffed Eggplant Dip

1	large eggplant
1	tablespoon lemon juice
1/4	cup olive oil or vegetable oil
1	green pepper, diced
2	celery stalks, diced
1	onion, diced
1	carrot, finely chopped
1	garlic clove, minced
1	tablespoon red wine vinegar
2	tomatoes, peeled, seeded and chopped
2	tablespoons chopped cilantro leaves
1/4	teaspoon dried basil leaves
1	teaspoon salt
1/8	teaspoon cayenne pepper
	Pita bread or sourdough bread

Cut eggplant in half lengthwise. Use a spoon to scoop out pulp, leaving a 1/2-inch shell (reserve pulp). Brush inside of eggplant shells with lemon juice to prevent browning; set aside. In a medium saucepan, cook reserved pulp in boiling water until tender, about 8 minutes; set aside. In a large skillet, heat oil. Add green pepper, celery, onions and carrot. Saute until vegetables are tender, 3-4 minutes. Stir in garlic, vinegar, tomatoes, cilantro, basil, salt, cayenne pepper and cooked eggplant pulp. Stir and cook over medium heat, 10-15 minutes or until vegetables are tender. Cut pita bread into wedges; set aside. Spoon cooked vegetable mixture into eggplant shells. Serve warm or refrigerate 1 hour. Serve as a dip with pita bread or sourdough bread. (Makes 31/2 cups)

COOK'S TIP: The eggplant shell makes a good container for vegetable dip. CHRIS IMAZUMI-O'CONNOR

Mock Oysters Rockefeller

1	onion, minced
2	tablespoons butter or margarine
1	8-ounce can minced mushrooms
1	can mushroom soup
1	package frozen chopped broccoli (thawed and cooked)
1	4-ounce roll or jar of Kraft garlic cheese (or like substitute)
	Hot sauce to taste

Sauté onions in 2-quart saucepan. Add remaining ingredients and simmer until cheese is melted and well blended. Serve with toasted French bread chunks as dippers. PAT HEUTER

Pesto Dip

1	cup mayonnaise
1	cup sour cream
1	10-ounce package frozen chopped spinach (thawed and squeezed)
1/3	cup grated Parmesan cheese
1/4	cup walnuts
1	teaspoon dried basil
1/4	teaspoon salt
1	clove garlic, minced

In blender or food processor, blend all ingredients until almost smooth. Cover and chill. (Makes 2 cups) PRUE ROSENTHAL

Cute and Sassy Dip

1	cup sour cream
1	cup mayonnaise
1	package smoked, dried or chipped beef
	Lawry's salt to taste
	Dill to taste
1	small onion, minced
1	loaf pumpernickel bread (unsliced)
	Fresh parsley for garnish

Combine sour cream, mayonnaise, beef, salt, dill and onion. Cut out the center of loaf of bread. Cut extracted bread into cubes. Fill shell with dip and use bread chunks for dipping. DOROTHY WARDELL

Chunky Onion Dip

1	8-ounce package cream cheese, room temperature
1/2	cup chopped onions
1/2	cup chili sauce
3	tablespoons mayonnaise
1/2	teaspoon Worcestershire sauce
	Vegetables

Mix all ingredients together. Let stand at least 24 hours, then serve with vegetables. MELISSA SNAVELY

Indonesian Peanut Dip

1/2	cup crunchy peanut butter
1/4	cup Kecap Manis (see recipe below)
2	tablespoons hot water
1	tablespoon fresh lemon or lime juice
1	teaspoon sugar
1	teaspoon crushed red chili
1	garlic clove, minced
	Vegetables

Combine all ingredients in a food processor and purée coarsely in pulses. Transfer to serving bowl. Serve at room temperature with fresh vegetable dippers. (Makes 1 cup)

KECAP MANIS:

1 1/2	cups sugar
2	cups soy sauce
1/4	cup water
3 - 4	lemon grass stalks
2	garlic cloves, minced
2	Chinese star anise

Melt sugar in medium saucepan over low heat until dissolved and light caramel color. Stir in soy sauce, water, lemon grass, garlic and star anise, blending well. Bring to boil over low heat stirring constantly, about 10 minutes. Cool 1 hour. Strain through several layers of cheesecloth into jar with tight lid. "*Keeps forever.*" (Makes 3 cups) JANET GILSDORF

APPETIZERS

Curry Dip

1	cup mayonnaise
1	teaspoon grated onions
1	teaspoon horseradish
1	teaspoon tarragon vinegar
1/4	teaspoon curry powder
	Dash garlic powder

Blend all together and refrigerate a few hours before serving. (Makes 1 cup) RUTH BEAN

"Philly" Cheese Balls

1	package Cracker Barrel cold-pack cheese
1	8-ounce package cream cheese, room temperature
2	teaspoons minced pimentos
2	teaspoons minced green pepper
2	teaspoons minced onions
1	teaspoon Worcestershire sauce
1/2	teaspoon lemon juice

Blend all ingredients together. Form into balls with plastic wrap. Chill until firm. MELISSA SNAVELY

Chutney-Cheese Spread

1	8-ounce container sharp cheddar cheese spread
1	8-ounce package cream cheese, room temperature
2-3	tablespoons dry sherry
1/2-1	teaspoon curry powder
	Dash garlic salt
1	12-ounce jar chutney (mango or apple)
2-3	green onions, chopped

With electric mixer, combine cheeses, sherry, curry powder and garlic salt. Spread in glass pie plate; refrigerate. When ready to serve, spread with chutney and sprinkle with green onions. Serve with crackers.

ANDREA WOO

Liptauer Cheese Spread

1   8-ounce package cream cheese, room temperature
1/2 cup butter, room temperature
1   tablespoon French's yellow mustard
1/2 teaspoon Hungarian paprika
1   tablespoon chives
1/2 teaspoon caraway seeds
1   inch anchovy paste from tube (optional)

Mix all ingredients well in bowl. Serve at room temperature for best spreadability. Good on rye or pumpernickle party bread or crackers.

BARBARA COLWELL

Stinky Cheese

2   pounds sharp cheddar or Tillamook cheese, shredded
1   pound Monterey Jack cheese, shredded
1   4-ounce can whole green chiles
1   4-ounce jar pimentos
10-14 cloves fresh garlic
1/2   cup dried minced onions
1/8   teaspoon ground pepper
       Garlic powder
3/4   cup mayonnaise
1   cup water (approximately)

Shred all cheese into shallow pan or mixing bowl. Dice chile peppers and pimentos and sprinkle over cheese. Press garlic cloves adding both juice and pulp to cheese. Add onions and pepper. Generously sprinkle powdered garlic over all. Thoroughly mix together; then add mayonnaise and blend, adding water as needed to attain a smooth mixture. Store in airtight container at least 2 days before using. (Makes about 8 cups) *"Easy to make, this excellent cheese spread is good to have on hand to stuff celery, spread on crackers, for grilled cheese sandwiches, or as a topping for toasty French bread."* LYNN SORRELLS

11

Pâté with Olives, Pine Nuts and Prosciutto

1	pound pork
1/2	pound veal
1/4	pound pork fat
1/3	cup chopped black olives
1/4	cup chopped pine nuts (lightly toasted)
1/4	cup chopped prosciutto
1/4	cup fresh white bread crumbs
2	tablespoons dry vermouth
11/2	teaspoons chopped fresh basil
1/2	teaspoon thyme
1/4	teaspoon pepper
1	small garlic clove, peeled
1/2	teaspoon salt
1	egg, lightly beaten
1/2	pound bacon, sliced thin
	Dark bread

Preheat oven to 350°. Grind together pork, veal and fat. In a large bowl, combine meat with olives, pine nuts, prosciutto and bread crumbs (moistened in vermouth). Add basil, thyme and pepper. In a mortar, crush garlic with salt. Add it to meat mixture and blend thoroughly. Add egg and mix again. Line the bottom of a 10-inch loaf pan with half the bacon. Turn meat mixture into pan and press down firmly. Cover top of mixture with the remaining bacon. Bake pâté 11/2 hours. Weight the pâté, allow to cool and chill 12 hours. Unmold onto a serving dish and remove bacon. Serve at room temperature on thinly-sliced dark bread with thinly-sliced dill pickles. ANN SCHRIBER

Cindy's Wine Liver Pâté

3/4	cup margarine
1	pound chicken livers
1/2	pound mushrooms
1/3	cup chopped onions
1/2	cup dry white wine
1	garlic clove, minced
1/8	teaspoon dill

In a medium saucepan, melt 1/4 cup margarine. Add chicken livers, mushrooms and onion. Simmer 10 minutes. Add wine, garlic and dill. Cover and cook 10-15 minutes until tender. Process in blender adding the last 1/2 cup melted margarine. Pour into bowl and chill. (Makes about 3 cups) *"Great served on sourdough rounds."* CAROLINE BLANE

Mexican Fondue

1	onion, chopped
5	tablespoons butter
2	16-ounce cans stewed tomatoes, drained
	Salt to taste
6	drops Tabasco sauce
2	tablespoons flour
1/2	cup evaporated milk
1/2	cup shredded cheddar cheese

Sauté onions in 3 tablespoons butter. Add tomatoes and simmer one hour. Add salt and Tabasco. Mix 2 tablespoons butter and flour together and drop by spoonfuls into tomatoes; mix. Add evaporated milk and stir over low heat until thick. Just before serving add cheese. Let this melt, but don't boil. Serve in a fondue pot with nacho chips. *"This is wonderful on a cold, snowy evening or after a football game!"* BARB LANESE

Chili Con Queso

1	pound ground beef
1/4	cup chopped green onions
1	8-ounce can tomato sauce
1	4-ounce can chopped green chile peppers
1	teaspoon Worcestershire sauce
1	pound American cheese, cut into pieces
	Dash garlic powder

In a large skillet, brown meat. Add green onions; cook over low heat until tender but not brown. Add tomato sauce, chile peppers, Worcestershire and cheese. Cook, stirring occasionally, until all cheese melts. Stir in garlic powder. Serve in a chafing dish over low heat with corn chips. (Makes 1 quart)

VARIATION: Serve flour tortillas with Chili Con Queso. Cut tortillas into quarters and fry in 2-3 inches vegetable oil until puffed and light brown. Drain and sprinkle with salt. (Can be fried ahead and warmed when needed.) Be careful not to burn. ANN SCHRIBER

Hot Artichoke Cheese Dip

1   81/2-ounce can artichoke hearts packed in water, drained
1   6-ounce jar marinated artichoke hearts, drained
1   4-ounce can diced green chiles
6   tablespoons mayonnaise
11/2-2 cups (6-8 ounces) shredded cheddar cheese

Preheat oven to 325°. Grease shallow baking dish. Chop artichoke hearts. Distribute evenly in dish. Scatter chiles on top and spread mayonnaise carefully over all. Top with cheddar cheese. Bake 20 minutes or until bubbly. Serve with tortilla chips. (6-8 servings) CHRIS IMAZUMI-O'CONNOR

Cheese Spread

Take cheddar cheese and put milk in it. Melt the cheese and milk on the stove for 10 minutes. Stir the cheese while it's melting. You can eat this with a spoon or pour it on bread, crackers or noodles. COREY, AGE 6

Hot Cheese Appetizers

1/2   cup sliced green onions
1/2   cup grated Parmesan cheese
1/2   cup mayonnaise
        Melba toast rounds

Mix onions, Parmesan and mayonnaise well. Spread onto Melba toast and broil until golden and bubbly. Serve hot. CHRIS IMAZUMI-O'CONNOR

Deliciously Easy Dip

1   cup mayonnaise
1   cup chopped onions
1   cup shredded mild cheese (Muenster)

Mix all ingredients well. Heat in oven until bubbly and serve with Triscuits. DOROTHY WARDELL

Eggplant and Sesame Paste Dip

1	eggplant
2	teaspoons minced garlic
2	tablespoons lemon juice
1/4	cup sesame paste (tahini)
1	tablespoon olive oil
3	tablespoons chopped parsley

Preheat oven to 350°. Bake eggplant until it wilts, about 25 minutes; cool. Scrape flesh from skin. (There should be 1 cup of flesh.) Blend smooth and add garlic, lemon juice, sesame paste, oil and parsley. Continue blending to make a fine purée. (Makes about 11/2 cups) PRUE ROSENTHAL

Mrs. Campbell's Clam Dip

1	61/2-ounce can minced clams (reserve juice)
1	8-ounce package cream cheese, room temperature
2	teaspoons lemon juice
1/2	teaspoon Worcestershire sauce
	Dash garlic salt
2	dashs hot sauce
3	tablespoons reserved clam juice

Preheat oven to 350°. Drain clams and combine with all ingredients. Place in baking dish; bake 15 minutes. Serve with your favorite crackers or toasted bread. SARA HICKEY

Shrimp Dip

1	8-ounce package cream cheese, room temperature
2	tablespoons mayonnaise (do not use salad dressing)
2	tablespoons minced onions
1	hard-boiled egg, finely chopped
1	7-ounce can tiny shrimp ("broken pieces" can is fine)

Preheat oven to 350°. Blend cream cheese and mayonnaise. Add onions, egg and shrimp; stir well. Place in small dish and bake, covered, 30 minutes or until heated through. Stir mixture; serve immediately. Can be served hot or cold, but is really best served hot. It goes well with any cracker, especially Triscuits or a butter-flavored cracker. KATHY WARNER

Crab Appetizer

1	pound crab (fresh, frozen or canned and picked over)
1/2	green pepper, minced
1/2	pimento, minced
1	tablespoon lemon juice
1	teaspoon Worcestershire sauce
1/2	cup mayonnaise
3	drops Tabasco sauce
1/2	teaspoon dry mustard
1/4	teaspoon salt
1/4	teaspoon white pepper
4	tablespoons bread crumbs
2	tablespoons butter

Preheat oven to 375°. Combine all ingredients except last two. Arrange 8 scallop shells on a baking sheet. Divide mixture onto shells or casserole dish. Rub butter into crumbs with fingers. Top with bread crumb mixture. Bake 15 minutes. BRIDGET MCGILLICUDDY

Clam Dip Pie

1/2	cup butter or margarine
1	medium onion, chopped
1	bunch fresh parsley, chopped
1	tablespoon oregano
1	tablespoon lemon juice
	Garlic powder to taste
2	drops Tabasco sauce
2	6 1/2-ounce cans minced clams (with juice)
3/4	cup Italian bread crumbs
	Grated Parmesan cheese

Preheat oven to 350°. Sauté onions and parsley in butter until soft. Add oregano, lemon juice, garlic powder and Tabasco, combining well. Add clams with juice and bread crumbs. Spread mixture in a buttered pie or quiche pan. Cover top of mixture with a generous coating of Parmesan cheese, approximately 1/4 inch. Bake until golden brown and bubbling. Serve with Ritz or Townhouse crackers. SARA HICKEY

Hot Seafood Cocktail

1/4	pound butter or margarine
4	garlic cloves, minced
4	shallots, minced
1/2	pound fresh mushrooms, sliced fine
	Juice from 1/2 lemon
1	31/2-ounce can Demings cocktail shrimp, drained
1	61/2-ounce can Doxsee chopped clams, drained
1	61/2 -ounce can Demings crabmeat, drained and deboned
1/2	teaspoon chervil
1/2	cup fresh bread crumbs
1/2	cup freshly-grated Parmesan cheese
	Paprika
1/2	teaspoon thyme
1/4	cup finely-chopped parsley
	Salt and pepper to taste

In large frying pan, melt butter. Add garlic and shallots; sauté until soft. Add mushrooms and lemon juice; sauté until mushrooms are cooked. Add all seafoods and stir. Add all seasonings. (May need salt and pepper.) Mix lightly until hot. Place in baking dishes. (Large clam shells work great.) Top with crumb-cheese mixture and dash of paprika. Broil until crumbs are brown and mixture is bubbly. Serve with small slices of French bread. (8 or more servings) This can be made ahead and frozen.

ROBERTA LAPIDES

Hot Mushroom Dip

4	slices bacon
1/2	pound fresh mushrooms, sliced
1	clove garlic, minced
1	medium onion, finely chopped
	Salt and pepper
2	teaspoons flour
1	8-ounce package cream cheese
2	teaspoons Worcestershire sauce
2	teaspoons soy sauce
1/2	cup sour cream

Fry bacon until crisp (reserve 2 tablespoons of fat). Sauté mushrooms, garlic and onions until most of liquid has evaporated. Mix in salt, pepper and flour. Add cream cheese, Worcestershire sauce and soy sauce. Heat on low until cheese is melted. Stir in sour cream and crumbled bacon. Serve warm with assorted crackers. LYNN SORRELLS

Dried Beef Treats

Garlic powder
Sour cream
Dried beef slices
Large dill pickles

Season sour cream with garlic powder. Spread this combination on slices of dried beef. Cut a large dill pickle in quarters lengthwise. Roll a beef slice around the quartered pickle. Secure with a toothpick. Cut each rolled treat into bite-size pieces.

COOK'S TIP: Season a small amount of sour cream at a time because it goes a long way. CAROL ZIEGLER

Mexican Roll-Ups

1   8-ounce package cream cheese, room temperature
1   4-ounce can of chopped olives
1   4-ounce can of diced chiles
    Green onions, chopped (optional)
12 flour tortillas
1   12-ounce jar salsa sauce

Mix cream cheese, olives, chiles and onions. Spread mixture on flour tortillas; roll up. Refrigerate overnight. Slice each tortilla into bite-size pieces. Serve either at room temperature or warmed in oven. Use salsa sauce for dipping. MICHELE KARLE

Party Pinwheels

2   8-ounce packages cream cheese, room temperature
1   package Hidden Valley Ranch original salad dressing mix
2   green onions, minced
4   12-inch flour tortillas
1/2   cup diced red pepper
1/2   cup diced celery
1   21/4-ounce can sliced black olives, drained

Mix first three ingredients. Spread mixture on tortillas. Sprinkle on remaining ingredients; roll and wrap tightly. Chill 2 hours. Cut off roll ends. Cut rolls into one-inch slices. (Makes 3 dozen) *"Everyone always asks for this recipe after tasting them. Even men!"* JILL WEBER

Camembert in an Apple

4   ounces Camembert cheese, room temperature
3   8-ounce packages cream cheese, room temperature
1-2   tablespoons white wine
1   large beautiful apple
       Chopped walnuts

Mix together Camembert, cream cheese and white wine until smooth. Core apple and make a hole large enough to stuff. Spoon cheese into hole and cover top with walnuts. To serve, cut apple into wedges. Serve with crackers. ANN SCHRIBER

Dried Beef Circles

1   8-ounce package cream cheese, room temperature
11/2   teaspoon extra-hot horseradish
1   glass jar dried beef

Blend cream cheese and horseradish until smooth. Spread onto dried beef. Roll up and chill. MARY DOYLE

Mushroom Sandwiches

1   loaf of thinly-sliced Pepperidge Farm bread
4   tablespoons butter
1/2   pound mushrooms, finely chopped
1   medium onion, finely chopped
1/4   teaspoon thyme
1/4   teaspoon pepper
1/2   teaspoon salt
1   tablespoon flour
1   cup sour cream

Preheat oven to 450°. Cut crusts off bread. Lightly brown onion in butter. Add mushrooms, thyme, pepper and salt. Sauté 5-6 minutes. Add flour; add sour cream and cook until thick. Cool in refrigerator. Spread on slices of bread and top with another slice. Cut into quarters. Bake until done. *"You may freeze these and then toast when needed."* SALLY KENNEDY

Steve's Shrimp and Dip

SAUCE:

2	12-ounce bottles chili sauce
1	cup ketchup
1	cup finely-chopped celery
1/2	cup finely-chopped green pepper
2/3	cup finely-chopped onions
2	cloves garlic, minced
1/4	teaspoon salt
1/4	teaspoon freshly-ground black pepper
3	tablespoons lemon juice (fresh squeezed)
1	tablespoon dry mustard
2	tablespoons pure horseradish (more or less to taste)
1	teaspoon Tabasco sauce
2	teaspoons Worcestershire sauce
1	tablespoon dried chopped parsley

Mix all ingredients well and chill for 4-6 hours. (Makes 1 quart) Serve with the following:

SHRIMP:

5	pounds or more large (21-26 count) shell-on shrimp (frozen ok)
11/2	bottles pickling spice
4-6	celery tops
2	quarts water
3	beers of choice (the cheaper, the better!)
	Romaine lettuce

Divide shrimp in half. In a large stockpot, bring next 4 ingredients to a boil. Add one portion of shrimp, cover and boil approximately 4 minutes, stirring once. (Shrimp is done when it turns bright red - do not overcook.) Repeat with remaining shrimp. Place shrimp on top of a bed of Romaine lettuce on a serving platter. Peel, dip and enjoy! (Serves 8) *"These are fantastic! Everyone asks for the recipe"* STEVE COMSTOCK

Dried Beef Cheese Ball

1	8-ounce package plus 1, 3-ounce package cream cheese, room temperature
1	21/2-ounce jar dried beef, chopped
1	small onion, finely chopped
11/2	teaspoons Accent

Mix all ingredients well. Roll into a ball and serve. KAREN RITZ

Mardi Gras Shrimp

8-12	fresh shrimp, peeled
1	tablespoon butter
1	tablespoon Worcestershire sauce
1	teaspoon minced garlic
1/8	teaspoon crushed red pepper
1	teaspoon Paul Prudhomme's seafood seasoning

Sauté shrimp in butter until cooked. Add remaining ingredients and blend. Serve warm with toothpick in each shrimp. JANET GILSDORF

Seafood Appetizer Cheesecake

1	cup crushed buttery crackers
3	tablespoons margarine, melted
2	8-ounce packages cream cheese, room temperature
3	eggs
3/4	cup sour cream
1	73/4-ounce can salmon, drained and flaked (or tuna)
1	teaspoon lemon juice
1/2	teaspoon onion powder
1/8	teaspoon pepper

Preheat oven to 350°. Combine crumbs and margarine in food processor or mixer. Press onto bottom of 9-inch springform pan. Bake 10 minutes. Combine cream cheese, eggs and sour cream. Stir in remaining ingredients and mix well. Pour mixture over crust. Bake at 325° 45 minutes. Loosen cake from rim of pan. Cool before removing rim. DENISE PROCHOWNIK

Crabbies

1	6-ounce can crabmeat
1	jar Kraft English cheddar cheese (or like substitute)
1/2	cup softened butter (or margarine)
2	tablespoons mayonnaise
1/2	teaspoon garlic salt
1/2	teaspoon seasoned salt
	Dash Tabasco sauce (optional)
	English muffins

Combine all ingredients and spread on English muffins; quarter muffins into bite-sized pieces and place on a cookie sheet. Put under broiler 8 minutes, or until cheese melts. Serve hot. SARA HICKEY

Latvian Piragi

5	egg yolks
3/4	cup sugar
1	cup whipped vegetable shortening
	Grated lemon peel
2	cups milk
3	packages dried yeast or cake yeast
3	tablespoons sugar
1	teaspoon salt
6	cups flour (approximate)
2	pounds bacon, chopped
2	medium onions, chopped
	Pepper
1	pound boiled ham, chopped

COATING:

1	egg
2	tablespoons sugar

Cream egg yolks with 3/4 cup sugar. Add shortening and blend in food processor. Add grated lemon rind. Slightly warm milk in a large bowl. Place yeast into a small bowl and add 3 tablespoons of sugar and 3 tablespoons of warm milk and mix. Place yeast mixture into remaining warm milk. Add salt. Combine shortening mixture and milk mixture. Add flour gradually (two cups at a time). Ideally, use a food processor as kneading becomes more difficult and the lightness of the dough is increased. Use all flour until dough "clears" from one's hands and the bowl so it does not stick. Let dough rise (covered) in a warm place for 1 hour. Combine bacon, onions and pepper in a sauté pan. Sauté until crisp; drain fat. Chop ham and combine with bacon mixture. Roll out the dough 1/4-inch thick (use extra flour if dough sticks to the table). Cut a round shape with the edge of a glass. Place 1 teaspoon of meat mixture inside each round shape. Fold dough in half over mixture. Pinch edges of round together (now called pirags) with forefinger and thumb. Be firm. Turn pirags over with pinched side on the bottom. Place about 24-30 pirags on one cookie sheet (using foil makes cleaning easier). Let pirags rise in a warm place at least 20 minutes. Preheat oven to 400-425°. Blend one egg with 2 tablespoons sugar. Brush mixture on top of each piragi. Bake 10 minutes. Take pan out of the oven and cover with a clean towel. Serve hot for best enjoyment. *"Excellent appetizer. Worth every bit of effort. Not hard, but definitely time-consuming."*

COOK'S TIP: Freezing pirags after baking is best. Warm before serving.

MAYA SAVARINO

Pull-Apart Bacon Cheese Wreath

3	tablespoons butter-flavored Crisco
1	5-ounce jar cheese spread with bacon
1	10-count package refrigerated flaky biscuits
4	slices bacon, cooked and crumbled
2	tablespoons chopped fresh parsley

Preheat oven to 450°. Cut a 12-inch square of aluminum foil and press on bottom and sides of a 9-inch round cake pan. Place inverted 31/2 inch custard cup in center of pan. Lightly grease foil and sides of custard cup. Set aside. Melt Crisco and cheese in a small saucepan on low heat (mixture may appear curdled). Remove from heat and stir vigorously until smooth and creamy. Spread to cover bottom of pan around custard cup. Cut each biscuit into quarters and fit pieces into pan around custard cup to form a "wreath". Bake 14 minutes (top will be brown). Turn over onto serving platter. Remove foil and custard cup. Sprinkle with crumbled bacon and parsley. Serve warm. (About 40 appetizers or 6 servings) DEBBIE ZIES

Teriyaki Chicken Wings

3	pounds chicken wings
1/3	cup fresh lemon juice
1/4	cup soy sauce
1/4	cup vegetable oil
3	tablespoons chili sauce
2	cloves garlic, minced
1/4	teaspoon pepper
1/4	teaspoon celery seed
	Dash dry mustard

Cut chicken wings at the joints, remove wing tips and place wings in a shallow baking dish. Combine rest of ingredients and stir to blend. Add marinade to chicken, cover and refrigerate at least 4 hours. Drain and save marinade to use as basting liquid. Place wings on a broiler pan approximately 7 inches from heat source and broil 10 minutes on each side, brushing occasionally with marinade. Serve with hot, cooked rice as a main dish or wings alone as an appetizer. *"These freeze well in a Ziplock bag to be served at a later date."* (Makes about 40) CAPRICE WARREN

Chinese Chicken Wings and Drumsticks

1 0   chicken wings and 6 drumsticks
1   clove garlic, minced
2   green onions, chopped
1/4   cup soy sauce
1   tablespoon vermouth
1/2   cup water
1/4   cup honey
2   tablespoons sugar
3   tablespoons oyster sauce

Cut each wing into two parts. Place remaining ingredients in a large saucepan. Stir and mix well. Add wings and drumsticks. Bring to boil and simmer, covered, about 40 minutes.   Shake pan and baste occasionally. Uncover pan and simmer an additional 15 minutes, stirring and basting frequently. Remove wings and drumsticks from pan and reserve liquid. When ready to serve, sprinkle with reserved liquids and broil until brown and crispy. Turn once. (4 servings) JEANNINE CHARRON

Sesame Chicken Wings

1 2   chicken wings
2   tablespoons oil
2   cloves garlic, minced
3   slices ginger, grated
3   tablespoons soy sauce
4   tablespoons toasted sesame seeds
1   bunch green onions, chopped

Cut off bony tips of chicken wings and discard. Cut remainder of each wing into two pieces at the joint. Heat oil in a wok or skillet. Add garlic and ginger. Stir briefly and add chicken wings. Brown wings lightly. Add soy sauce and cook, stirring for a minute or two. Cover and simmer about 10 minutes. Uncover, raise heat, continue cooking until sauce is almost evaporated and chicken wings are glazed. Remove from heat, season to taste. Just before serving, add sesame seeds and chopped green onions. (8 servings) SUSAN KULICK

Grace's Dilly Meatballs

1	pound ground beef
2	slices white bread
1/3	cup milk
1	egg, slightly beaten
1/4	cup chopped onions
2	tablespoons parsley
1	teaspoon salt
1/4	teaspoon pepper

SAUCE:
1	can Campbell's potato soup
1/2	cup milk
2	teaspoons dill

Mix all meatball ingredients and form into balls. Cook in oil until browned. Mix sauce ingredients together and heat. Add meatballs.

ANN SCHRIBER

Mexican Meatballs

3	pounds ground beef
2	envelopes dried onion soup mix
3/4	cup salsa
1/2	cup pickle relish
1/2	teaspoon garlic powder
1	teaspoon pepper
1	tablespoon soy sauce
1	tablespoon Worcestershire sauce
3	tablespoons grated Parmesan cheese
3	tablespoons brown sugar
4	eggs, well beaten
1	small can evaporated milk
6	cups bread crumbs

SAUCE:
1/2	cup barbecue sauce
11/2	cups salsa
21/2	cups tomatoes
1/2	cup jelly (any kind, but I usually use grape)
1/4	cup chili sauce
3	tablespoons molasses

Preheat oven to 375°. Combine all meatball ingredients; mix well. Shape into 1-inch balls and bake on cookie sheet until brown. Combine all sauce ingredients and heat in a pan. Pour over meatballs. KATHERINE HAY

Spinach Balls with Spicy Mustard Sauce

SPICY MUSTARD SAUCE:

1	cup (4-ounce can) dry mustard
1	cup tarragon or cider vinegar
3	eggs
1	cup sugar

Blend dry mustard and tarragon vinegar together. Let stand overnight. Beat eggs and add sugar. Mix together with mustard mixture. Cook over low heat until thick, stirring constantly. Set aside. Serve hot or cold with Spinach Balls. (Keeps well in refrigerator.)

SPINACH BALLS:

6	eggs
2	10-ounce packages frozen chopped spinach (thawed, drained and squeezed)
2	cups herb stuffing mix
1	large onion, grated
1	cup grated Parmesan cheese
3/4	cup (11/2 sticks) butter, room temperature
1	teaspoon poultry seasoning
	Salt and pepper

Preheat oven to 350° Beat eggs lightly in large bowl. Add remaining ingredients and blend well. Roll into walnut-size balls. Transfer to baking sheet. Bake 20 minutes, or until golden. (Makes 6 dozen) Serve hot with Mustard Sauce.

COOK'S TIP: Spinach Balls can be partially baked for 10 minutes, cooled and frozen. Reheat thawed balls in 350° oven for about 10-15 minutes.

CHRIS IMAZUMI-O'CONNOR

Sue's Cheerios Snack

	Pam cooking spray
1	cup brown sugar
1/2	cup margarine
1/4	cup light corn syrup
1/2	teaspoon salt
1/2	teaspoon soda
6	cups Cheerios cereal
1	cup Spanish peanuts
1	cup raisins

Preheat oven to 250 degrees. Spray a 9 x 13-inch pan with Pam. Combine Cheerios, peanuts and raisins in pan. In a saucepan, heat sugar, margarine, corn syrup and salt stirring until bubbly around the edges. Cook 2 minutes more (do not stir). Remove from heat; stir in soda. Pour over cereal mixture. Mix well. Bake 20 minutes. Turn immediately onto waxed paper. Let cool. *"Wonderful snack for those tailgate parties!"*
ANDREA WOO

Salami Chips

Salami, sliced thin
Parmesan cheese, finely grated

Preheat oven to 350°. Separate salami slices and put in a single layer on a cookie sheet. Sprinkle with Parmesan cheese. Bake about 5 minutes, or until slightly browned. (Do not let burn.) Drain and serve. ANN SCHRIBER

Different Peanuts

Chili powder
Spanish peanuts

Shake chili powder on peanuts and heat in oven. *"Nifty variation."*
DOROTHY WARDELL

Chinese Fried Walnuts

4	cups walnuts
6	cups water
1/2	cup sugar
	Oil
	Salt

Boil walnuts in water for one minute. Rinse walnuts under hot water for one minute. Drain and place in bowl. Sprinkle with sugar and stir gently until sugar is dissolved. Deep fry in oil (350°) until golden, about 3-5 minutes. Drain well in colander and spread on foil. Sprinkle very lightly with salt.

COOK'S TIP: I would suggest you not try this recipe unless you have a thermostatically-controlled deep fat fryer. I burned my walnuts to a crisp the first time I tried this on a stove-top burner! MARJORIE BEST

Cinnamon Sugar Pecans

1	pound shelled pecans
4	tablespoons sugar
11/2	teaspoons cinnamon
1/4	teaspoon nutmeg
2	tablespoons butter or margarine

Arrange pecans in a 9 x 12-inch glass baking dish. Microwave on high 5 minutes, stirring after 3 minutes. Toss pecans with butter. Stir until butter is melted and pecans are evenly coated. In a bowl, combine sugar and spices. Add sugar mixture to pecans and stir well. Microwave another 3 minutes. Stir once to coat. Set aside to cool. JEAN WEAVER

APPETIZERS

Soups

SOUPS

32

White Gazpacho

3   medium cucumbers
1   clove garlic
3   cups chicken broth
2   cups sour cream
1   cup yogurt
3   tablespoons vinegar
2   teaspoons salt
2   teaspoons white pepper

GARNISH:
4   medium tomatoes, peeled and chopped
1/2   cup chopped green onions (including tops)
1/2   cup chopped fresh parsley
3/4   cup toasted almonds or sunflower seeds

Peel and dice the cucumbers. Place in a blender with garlic and a small amount of chicken broth; purée mixture. Add remaining broth and thoroughly blend ingredients. Mix sour cream and yogurt in a medium-sized bowl and thin with about 1/3 cucumber mixture. Add remaining cucumber mixture to the bowl. Season with vinegar, salt and pepper. Chill 6-8 hours. Serve in chilled bowls with tomatoes, green onions, parsley and almonds in smaller bowls. (6-8 servings) ANN SCHRIBER

Asparagus Soup

3	pounds asparagus
1/2	cup plain yogurt
4	tablespoons sour cream
1	cup (1/2 pint) heavy cream
4	tablespoons lemon juice
	Garnish: Chopped cucumbers and parsley

Trim white part from asparagus. Cook until green (save 2 cups of the broth). (Do this in two batches.) Cut asparagus in 1-inch pieces (save the tips) and process in blender 1 minute. Add broth and process 5 seconds. Add yogurt, sour cream and heavy cream. Add the tips and refrigerate at least two hours. Right before serving, add lemon juice. Garnish with cucumbers and parsley. (8 servings) PRUE ROSENTHAL

Cream of Curried Pea Soup

1	cup fresh peas
1	medium onion, diced
1	small carrot, sliced
1	stalk celery with leaves, sliced
1	medium potato, sliced
1	clove garlic, minced
1	teaspoon salt
1	teaspoon curry (or more to taste)
2	cups chicken stock
1	cup heavy cream

Place vegetables, seasoning and one cup of chicken stock in pan and cook 15-20 minutes. Blend in food processor, and with motor running, add second cup of stock and cream. Chill. PRUE ROSENTHAL

Vichyssoise à la Ritz

4	leeks (white part only), sliced
1	medium onion, sliced
1/4	cup butter
5	medium potatoes, thinly sliced
1	quart chicken broth
	Salt to taste
11/2	cups milk
1	cup heavy cream
	Chopped chives

Brown leeks and onions lightly in butter. Add potatoes, broth and salt. Boil for 35 minutes. Purée mixture in blender. Return to pot and add milk and cream. Bring to a boil. Cool and blend. Chill. Garnish with chives.

PRUE ROSENTHAL

Cold Tomato Soup

3	cups tomato juice
2	tablespoons tomato paste
4	green onions, minced
	Salt and pepper to taste
	Pinch thyme
1/2	teaspoon curry powder
	Grated rind of 1/2 lemon
2	tablespoons lemon juice
	Sugar to taste
1	cup sour cream
	Chopped parsley

Mix all ingredients except sour cream and parsley. Add sugar to taste. Chill. Just before serving, blend in sour cream and sprinkle with parsley.

PRUE ROSENTHAL

35

Avocado Soup

2	cans Madrilène (consommé)
1	large avocado, peeled and puréed
1	cup sour cream
2	tablespoons grated onions
	Dash dill
	Salt to taste
	Chili powder or cayenne pepper to taste
	Garnish: Fresh dill

Combine consommé with avocado and sour cream. Season with salt, chili powder and pepper. Chill thoroughly until soup thickens. Garnish with dill. PRUE ROSENTHAL

Cold Curried Cream of Chicken Soup (Créme Senegal)

2	tablespoons butter
1/2	cup chopped onions
1/2	teaspoon curry powder
1	cup chopped leeks
1	clove garlic, minced
11/2	cups peeled diced apples
1	cup peeled, diced tomatoes
1	cup peeled, diced potatoes
	Salt and pepper to taste
4	drops Tabasco sauce, or to taste
31/2	cups chicken broth
1/2	cup heavy cream
1/2-1	cup finely-chopped or diced cooked chicken

In a heavy skillet, heat butter and add onions. Sauté, stirring for one minute. Add curry powder, leeks, garlic, apples, tomatoes, potatoes, salt, pepper and Tabasco. Stir. Add broth and simmer 20 minutes. Process half of mixture at a time in food processor to make smooth. Pour into a bowl and chill. Add heavy cream and chicken. Serve cold.

PRUE ROSENTHAL

Leek and Asparagus Chowder

3	cups sliced mushrooms
3	large leeks, sliced in rounds
1	10-ounce package frozen cut-up asparagus (thawed)
6	tablespoons butter
3	tablespoons flour
1/2	teaspoon salt
	Pepper to taste
2	cups chicken broth (2 cans)
2	cups half-and-half cream
1	12-ounce can white whole kernel corn
1	tablespoon chopped pimentos

Sauté vegetables 10 minutes in butter. Stir in flour, salt and pepper. Add broth and cream. Cook and stir until thick and bubbly. Stir in corn and pimentos and heat through. (6 servings) *"This is very filling; can be served with just a salad and rolls!"* ELAINE SCHWARTZ

Leek Stew

	Salt and pepper to taste
4	tablespoons flour
4	tablespoons corn oil
1/2	pound mushrooms, sliced
1	medium onion, chopped
3	large leeks, white part only, sliced 1/4-inch thick
1/2	cup red wine
1	pound inexpensive cut of beef, cut into bite-size pieces
3/4	cup water or beef broth
3	tablespoons Kitchen Bouquet*
1/4	cup chopped parsley

Preheat oven to 350°. Salt and pepper meat, dust with flour and brown in oil 5 minutes. Put into baking dish. Add mushrooms, onion and leeks to pan and cook in remaining oil 2 minutes. Add rest of flour mixture onto onions. Add red wine and stir 4 minutes. Add water, stir and cook until thickened. Add Kitchen Bouquet seasoning and parsley and pour all into baking dish. Mix with meat. Cook covered 1 hour. (4 servings) *"This goes well with thick bread, noodles or rice."*

*COOK'S TIP: Browning sauce available in grocery stores.

CAROLINE BLANE

37

Minestrone

3/4	cup dry Great Northern white beans
11/2	quarts water
1	teaspoon salt
3	tablespoons olive oil
1/8	pound dried salt pork, coarsely chopped (or bacon)
6	sprigs parsley, chopped
1	onion, chopped
1	stalk celery, chopped
2	tomatoes, peeled and coarsely chopped*
1	carrot, chopped
2	cups beef broth
2	cups chopped cabbage
2	zucchini, chopped
2	leaves Swiss chard, chopped
1	teaspoon basil
1/2	teaspoon thyme
	Salt and pepper to taste
1	cup grated Parmesan or Romano cheese

Soak beans overnight in enough water to cover. Drain and put beans in soup pot with 11/2 quarts water and salt. Simmer until tender, about 1 hour. Drain and purée in blender or food processor; set aside. Heat olive oil in frying pan and sauté pork, parsley, onion and celery. Cook until onions and celery are tender. Add tomatoes and carrots; cook about 3 minutes, stirring constantly. Add beef broth and bean purée; stir. Cover and simmer 15 minutes. Add cabbage, zucchini, Swiss chard, basil and thyme. Stir to mix and gently simmer 15 more minutes; add more broth if too thick. Season with salt and pepper. Serve with cheese to sprinkle on top.

*COOK'S TIP: You may use only the juice from tomatoes. (Cut tomatoes in half, squeeze and strain.) CHRIS IMAZUMI-O'CONNOR

Nine Bean Soup

1	cup garbanzo beans
1	cup pinto beans
1	cup white navy beans
1	cup black beans
1	cup lentils
1	cup lima beans
1	cup kidney beans
1	cup barley
9	hot chile peppers

Combine all beans and divide into nine (1 pound) bags and add hot chile pepper. Give to 9 friends with the recipe below.

1	pound of beans
2	quarts water
	Meat of choice: beef, ham, turkey
1	medium onion, chopped
1	28-ounce can tomatoes
2	tablespoons fresh lemon juice
1	tablespoon cumin or chili powder
1-2	tablespoons brown sugar
1/2	cup pasta of choice
	Optional: hot chile pepper

Soak beans overnight in water. Cook beans in 2 quarts water, 2 turkey legs or uncooked chuck roast or ham bones with meat for 2 hours. Remove meat and cut up. Place beans in food processor and process to desired consistency. Process onions and tomatoes and add to beans. Add lemon juice, cumin or chili powder, brown sugar and pasta. Simmer 1 hour and then add chopped meat. DEBBIE LOWN

Winter Borscht

2	pounds shin of beef with bone
6	cups water (or stock)
1	onion, cut in large pieces
2	carrots, diced
3	beets (11/4 pounds)
4	garlic cloves, minced
1/2	pound cabbage
1	pound tomatoes, peeled and seeded
6	tablespoons tomato paste
1	bay leaf
2	tablespoons red wine vinegar
2	tablespoons plus 2 teaspoons sugar
2	potatoes, cooked and cubed
	Pepper to taste
1/3	cup fresh dill
	Salt to taste
	Garnish: Sour cream and dill

In large pot, combine beef with water, onions and carrots. Boil, skimming the froth and simmer, covered, 11/2 hours. Strain and reserve beef; discard vegetables. Add beets and cook 20 minutes. Remove the beets, peel and grate. Add beets, garlic, cabbage, tomatoes, tomato paste, bay leaf, vinegar and sugar; simmer 30 minutes. Cut reserved beef into 1/2-inch cubes. Add beef, potatoes, pepper and dill; boil for 2 minutes. Add salt. Divide among bowls adding sour cream and dill. PRUE ROSENTHAL

Cucumber Soup

2	tablespoons butter
1/4	cup chopped onions or leeks
2	cups chopped, unpeeled cucumber
1/4	teaspoon each salt and pepper
1/2	cup finely-diced raw potato
1/4	teaspoon dry mustard
1	cup watercress leaves
2	sprigs parsley
2	cups chicken broth
1	cup heavy cream
	Garnish: Chives

In a saucepan, melt butter and cook onions until transparent. Add remaining ingredients except cream and chives. Bring to a boil, simmer 15 minutes until potatoes are tender. Purée in blender. Before serving, stir in cream. PRUE ROSENTHAL

Broccoli Cheese Soup

1/2	cup chopped onions
4	tablespoons margarine
4	cups frozen corn
2	cups chopped broccoli
2	cups shredded carrot
1	cup water
4	cans cream of potato soup
4	cups milk
1	cup shredded Monterey Jack cheese
4	ounces Provolone cheese, cut up
1/2	teaspoon pepper

In large kettle, sauté onions in hot margarine until tender. Add corn, broccoli, carrot and water. Bring to a boil. Reduce heat, cover and simmer 10 minutes. Stir in soup, milk, cheeses and pepper. Heat over medium heat until cheeses melt. Stir frequently. (6-8 servings)

JERRI JENISTA AND BARBARA JENSEN

Elizabeth's Favorite Broccoli Soup

2	bunches fresh broccoli, cut into bite-size pieces
3/4	cup butter or margarine
1/3	cup flour
2	cans chicken broth
3	cups warm milk
2	cans cream of mushroom soup
1/2	teaspoon white pepper
5	tablespoons lemon juice
2	tablespoons Worcestershire sauce
1/4	teaspoon Tabasco sauce

Sauté broccoli in 1/2 cup of margarine until tender. Heat milk and remaining 1/4 cup margarine in microwave until hot. Whisk flour into milk until dissolved. Add flour/milk mixture to broccoli. Add all other ingredients. Warm to desired temperature on low heat. (10-12 servings)

COOK'S TIP: Do not allow this to come to a boil; it will separate. If frozen, this soup will change texture. CATHY MALETTE

Zucchini Soup

1	cup fresh basil leaves
2	cloves garlic, minced
1	tablespoon pine nuts
2-3	tablespoons grated Parmesan cheese
	Olive oil
6-8	cups chicken stock
2	small zucchini, cut in 1/4-inch slices
1	cup broken vermicelli
	Salt and pepper to taste

Blend basil, nuts, garlic and cheese in food processor. Add enough olive oil so to become a thick paste. Heat chicken stock. Add pasta and zucchini; cook 10 minutes more. Season with salt and pepper; whisk paste into soup and serve. PRUE ROSENTHAL

French Onion Soup au Gratin

4	large onions, thinly sliced
4	tablespoons butter
4	cans beef broth
1/2	cup dry sherry
2	teaspoons Worcestershire sauce
	Dash pepper
6	slices French bread (toasted and sliced 1/2-inch thick)
3/4	cup grated Parmesan cheese
6	slices Gruyère or Swiss cheese

Preheat oven to 375°. In large saucepan, sauté onions in butter until tender, but not brown, about 20 minutes. Add beef broth, sherry, Worcestershire sauce and pepper; bring to a boil. Pour into 6 individual casseroles or ovenproof bowls. Float a slice of bread in each; sprinkle generously with Parmesan. Top each with a slice of cheese. Bake 15-20 minutes, or until cheese is bubbly. (6 servings) MARY LOUISE GOOD

Carrot Soup with Curry

4	cups vegetable stock
1/2	pound carrots, sliced
2/3	cup chopped onions
2	teaspoons ginger
2	teaspoons curry powder
1	clove garlic, minced
1/2	cup low-fat milk
1	tablespoon unsalted butter
	Salt and pepper
	Garnish: 1 tablespoon chopped mint

Combine vegetable stock, carrots, onions, ginger, curry and garlic in a Dutch oven. Cover and simmer 20 minutes, until carrots are tender. Purée mixture in blender until smooth. Return mixture to the pot and stir in milk and butter. Season with salt and pepper. (4 servings) PRUE ROSENTHAL

Cheddar-Corn Chowder

1	can chicken broth
11/2	cups chopped potatoes
1	cup sliced carrots
1/2	cup sliced celery
1/4	cup chopped onions
11/2	teaspoons salt
1/4	teaspoon pepper
1/4	cup margarine
1/4	cup flour
1	cup milk
21/2	cups (10 ounces) shredded sharp cheddar cheese
1	16-ounce can cream-style corn (or 2 cups fresh)

Combine broth, potatoes, carrots, celery, onions, salt and pepper in a large saucepan. Cover; bring to a boil. Simmer 10 minutes or until vegetables are tender. Melt butter in a saucepan. Stir in flour; cook until bubbly. Gradually add milk, stirring constantly. Bring to a boil, cook 1 minute. Add cheese; stir until melted. Gradually add cheese sauce to soup, stirring constantly. Stir in corn. (6 servings) ANN BETZ

Corn and Mushroom Chowder

4	slices bacon
1/2	cup chopped onions
1/2	green or red bell pepper, chopped (optional)
1	can cream-style corn
1	can condensed mushroom soup
11/4	cups milk
1/4	teaspoon curry powder

Sauté bacon until crisp; drain on paper towel. Use 2 tablespoons bacon drippings to sauté onions and bell pepper (if used). Mix corn, soup, milk and curry in saucepan. Add onions and pepper. Heat to simmer. Crumble bacon and add to soup; heat and serve. DR. AND MRS. CHARLES SHIPMAN

Lentil Soup I

3	cups raw lentils, washed
7	cups water or stock
2	teaspoons salt
2	teaspoons minced garlic
1	cup chopped onions
1	cup minced celery
1	cup chopped carrots
11/2	cups chopped tomatoes
4	tablespoons butter
	Lots of black pepper
2	tablespoons dry red wine
2	tablespoons lemon juice
11/2	tablespoons molasses or brown sugar
1	tablespoon wine vinegar
	Optional: Fines herbes, thyme, oregano or basil

Place lentils, water and salt in a large Dutch oven. Simmer, covered, for 3-4 hours. Steam or sauté vegetables in butter. Add to lentils. Continue to simmer over low heat. 30 minutes before serving, add rest of the ingredients. May sprinkle extra vinegar and scallions onto each serving.
AUDREY CURTIS

Mushroom Soup

1	pound mushrooms
4	cups chicken broth
4	tablespoons butter
1/4	teaspoon dry mustard
3	tablespoons flour
1/2	cup heavy cream
1/4	cup sherry

Separate mushroom stems from caps, then chop stems and add to chicken broth. Simmer 30 minutes; strain. In sauté pan, melt butter and sauté mushroom caps; add mustard and flour; stir. Gradually add to broth until mixture thickens. Cook 20-30 minutes. Stir in sherry and cream. Cook 2 minutes, stirring. ALICE VINING

Lentil Soup II

2	cups dried lentils
21/2	cups beef stock
3/4	cup chopped carrots
3/4	cup chopped onions
3/4	cup chopped celery
1	clove garlic, minced
	Beef bones
1	bay leaf
2	whole cloves
	Dash cayenne pepper
11/2	teaspoons salt
1/4	teaspoon pepper
	Chopped parsley
	Curry to taste
	Garnish: Celery, carrots, onions

Combine lentils and beef stock. Add vegetables, garlic, beef bones, bay leaf, cloves, curry, salt and pepper. Simmer gently 2 hours. Strain out the vegetables, purée or discard as desired. Garnish with finely-chopped celery, carrots and onions. PRUE ROSENTHAL

Pioneer Potato Soup

2	cans chicken broth
4	potatoes, chopped
2	cups sliced carrots
1/2	cup sliced celery
1/4	cup chopped onions
1	box frozen chopped spinach, thawed and squeezed dry
1	teaspoon salt
1/8	teaspoon white pepper
1	cup milk or half-and-half cream
2	tablespoons flour

Combine all ingredients except milk and flour in a large Dutch oven. Bring to a boil; reduce heat and simmer 30 minutes. Gradually add milk to flour, stirring until smooth. Stir into soup. Bring soup to boiling; boil 1 minute, stirring constantly. (4-6 servings) ANN BETZ

Potato Cheese Soup

4	tablespoons unsalted butter
2	cups chopped onions
2	cups chopped carrots
6	parsley sprigs, chopped
1	cup chopped fresh dill
11/2	pounds potatoes, peeled and cubed (4-5 cups)
5-6	cups chicken stock
1/2-1	cup heavy cream (or milk)
1/2	teaspoon salt
1/4	teaspoon pepper
2-3	cups shredded cheddar cheese

Melt butter; add onions and carrots. Cook over medium heat for 3-5 minutes. Add parsley, 1/2 cup of dill, potatoes and chicken stock. Bring to a boil, reduce heat and simmer for 10-15 minutes until potato is soft. Put in food processor or blender in batches (pulse if you want small chunks of potato). Return to pan, simmer, gradually add heavy cream, salt and pepper, cheese and remaining dill. Serve warm. (6-8 servings)

DEBBIE LOWN

Italian Wedding Soup

1/2	pound ground veal
1/4	cup Italian bread crumbs
4	teaspoons grated Parmesan cheese
1	teaspoon minced parsley
1	small clove garlic, minced
1/2	large egg, beaten
1/4	teaspoon freshly ground pepper
3	tablespoons olive oil
4	quarts chicken stock, homemade preferred
1	cup orzo*
1/2	pound fresh spinach, julienned

Combine veal, bread crumbs, cheese, parsley, garlic, egg and pepper (mixture will be moist). Roll into 3/4-inch balls. Heat oil in sauté pan until hot. Sauté a few balls at a time until browned on all sides; drain. Bring broth to a boil. Add orzo and simmer 10 minutes. Add meatballs and simmer 10 minutes more. Add spinach and cook 5 more minutes. Serve with additional Parmesan cheese. (12 servings)

*COOK'S TIP: Orzo is rice-shaped pasta, available at most grocery stores. SANDY MERINO

Hearty Italian Vegetable Soup

1	large onion, chopped
1	tablespoon olive oil
2	small zucchini, sliced
2	small yellow squash, sliced
1/2	head cauliflower, broken into flowerets
1	28-ounce can Italian tomatoes with juice
1	bunch fresh spinach
2	teaspoons salt
1	teaspoon coarsely-ground black pepper
1	tablespoon chopped fresh oregano
4	basil leaves, chopped
1	tablespoon fresh thyme
1	tablespoon balsamic vinegar

Sauté chopped onions in olive oil in a large Dutch oven. Add all remaining ingredients and cook on medium heat for one hour. Reduce heat and simmer at least 6 hours to blend flavors. (6 servings) JANET GILSDORF

SOUPS

Beef-Barley Stew

3   tablespoons salad oil
2   pounds beef cubes
2   large onions, diced
6   cups water
1/2 cup medium barley
1   teaspoon salt
1   teaspoon oregano leaves
1/2 teaspoon pepper
2   10-ounce packages Brussels sprouts
2   medium tomatoes, cut into 8 wedges each

Preheat oven to 350°. About 3 hours before serving, in 12-inch skillet over medium high heat in hot salad oil, cook beef, half at a time, until browned on all sides. Remove pieces to 4-quart casserole as they brown. In remaining drippings in skillet over medium heat, cook onions until tender stirring occasionally. Add water. Over high heat, heat to boiling, stirring to loosen brown bits. Pour onion mixture over beef in casserole; stir in barley, salt, oregano and pepper. Cover casserole and bake 11/2 hours, stirring occasionally. Stir in Brussels sprouts. Bake 30 minutes. Add tomato wedges; continue baking 10 minutes longer or until meat and vegetables are fork-tender. (Makes 8 servings) NORAH KARSCH

Hamburger Kniffle Soup

21/2 pounds ground beef
1 2   cups water
3   medium potatoes, cubed
4 - 5 carrots, sliced
2   beef bouillon cubes
3   small onions, sliced
1   package au jus gravy mix (dry)
1   10-ounce package frozen peas

KNIFFLES:
1   cup flour
1/2 teaspoon salt
3   eggs

Brown ground beef lightly; drain grease. Combine rest of soup ingredients in large soup pot. Simmer 1 hour. While soup is simmering, beat flour, salt and eggs together (or use kniffle press). Drop by small spoonfuls into boiling salted water; cook until done, about 3-4 minutes. Add to soup. *"Kniffle press available at Hertler's in Ann Arbor."* MARGARET TAPPING

48

Chicken and Sausage Jambalaya

4	chicken breast halves, skinned and boned
1	stalk celery, sliced with leaves
1	onion, quartered
3	clove garlic, minced
1	cup uncooked rice
1	pound smoked sausage, sliced into 1/2-inch pieces
1	pound ham, cubed
4	tablespoons margarine
1	cup chopped yellow onions
3/4	cup chopped green pepper
1/4	cup chopped parsley
1	6-ounce can tomato paste plus 1 can water
1	bay leaf
1/4	teaspoon thyme
2	teaspoons salt
1/2	teaspoon pepper
1/4	teaspoon Tabasco sauce

In a large pot, cover chicken with water; add celery, onions and 1 clove minced garlic; boil until tender, about 1/2 hour. Reserve stock. Cut chicken into small pieces. Cook rice using reserved stock and enough water. In a skillet, fry sausage and ham until lightly browned. Remove meat. Add margarine to pan and sauté onions, pepper and parsley until tender. Add chicken, sausage, and ham. Stir in remaining 2 cloves minced garlic, tomato paste and water, bay leaf, thyme, salt, pepper and Tabasco. Add rice and mix thoroughly. Cook over low heat 15 minutes, stirring frequently. Remove bay leaf and serve. (6-8 servings) ANN BETZ

Sausage Soup

1	pound pork sausage, cooked and drained
1	19-ounce can red kidney beans
1	141/2-ounce can tomatoes
3	medium potatoes, diced
1/2	green pepper, chopped
1	onion, chopped
2	cups water
	Salt and pepper
	Ground celery seed or celery salt to taste
2	bay leaves
1/2	teaspoon thyme

Combine all ingredients in 3-4 quart saucepan. Cover and cook about 50 minutes or until tender. (4 servings) MARY ANN ROLOFF

Mardi Gras Gumbo

1	medium onion, chopped (1/2 cup)
1	clove garlic, minced
4	tablespoons butter or margarine
2	envelopes instant vegetable broth (or 2 vegetable bouillon cubes)
1	1-pound can tomatoes
2	14-ounce cans minced clams
1	12-ounce can mixed vegetable juice
1	teaspoon salt
1	teaspoon sugar
1/4	teaspoon bottled red pepper seasoning
1	tablespoon cornstarch
1/2	cup cold water
2	10-ounce cans shrimp, rinsed (or fresh)
2	packages frozen cut okra
	Buttered hot rice

In a large pan, sauté onions and garlic in butter just until soft. Stir in vegetable broth, tomatoes, clams, vegetable juice and seasoning; heat to boiling. Simmer 10 minutes. In a cup, blend cornstarch into cold water until smooth. Stir into soup mixture. Cook, stirring constantly, until soup thickens slightly and boils 3 minutes. Stir in shrimp and frozen okra; cook 2-3 minutes longer or just until heated through. Spoon mounds of buttered hot rice into heated soup plates or bowls. Ladle hot soup around rice dividing evenly. (6 generous servings) LOLA PAULUS

Jean's New Brunswick Fish Chowder

1	pound white saltwater fish (cod, haddock, scrod or pollock)
1	medium onion, chopped
4-5	medium to large potatoes, finely sliced
4	cups milk (approximately)
	Salt to taste

Steam fish until opaque. Break up and remove bones. Sauté onions in large soup pot. Add potatoes and cover with water. Bring to a boil and boil 20 minutes. Add cooked fish. Boil another 15-20 minutes, stirring occasionally. Add milk and water as needed to keep covered. Add salt and pepper. Heat until steaming, but do not boil. (4-6 servings)

COOK'S TIP: For variety, add other cooked seafood in addition to the fish (lobster, crab, scallops, oysters or clams). JOHN BARKS

Tomato Fish Soup

1	pound fish (cod, orange roughy or whitefish)
5	medium potatoes, cooked and diced
2	small onions, diced
1	tablespoon minced garlic
1-2	tablespoons olive oil
1	15-ounce can clam chowder
1	28-ounce can crushed tomatoes with juice
1/2	cup white wine
2	teaspoons dill
2	teaspoons celery flakes
	Salt and pepper to taste
4	cups water

Poach fish. In poaching liquid, cook potatoes. Brown onions and garlic in small amount of olive oil in Dutch oven or soup pot. Add rest of ingredients and about 4 cups of water. Cook 20 minutes. Serve as main dish, or omit potatoes and serve as first course. Garnish with fresh dill or parsley. CHARLENE HANCOCK

SOUPS

Salads

SALADS

Lime Jell-O Salad

1   3-ounce package lemon Jell-O
1   3-ounce package lime Jell-O
1   15-ounce can crushed pineapple
1   16-ounce carton large curd cottage cheese
1   cup Miracle Whip salad dressing
1   10-ounce can evaporated milk
1   tablespoon horseradish
1   tablespoon vinegar
1   cup chopped nuts

Drain pineapple, reserving juice. Add water to juice to make 2 cups liquid. Heat liquid to boiling; mix in Jell-O; cool. Mix together pineapple together with all remaining ingredients. Add this mixture to cooled Jell-O. Refrigerate overnight (in 9 x 13-inch pan or gelatin mold). *"A favorite at family gatherings, often requested as 'Grandma's Green Salad'."* (12 servings) MOLLY GATES

Frozen Jell-O Salad

1   3-ounce package cherry or strawberry gelatin
1   cup boiling water
1   6-ounce can frozen concentrated lemonade
3   cups non-dairy whipped topping, thawed
1   16-ounce can fruit of choice, or fresh
1/2 cup chopped pecans

Dissolve gelatin in boiling water. Add frozen lemonade and stir until melted. Chill until slightly thickened. Fold in whipped topping; then fold in fruit. Freeze until firm. Slice and serve. MELISSA WILLIAMS

Cranberry Salad Mold

1   8-ounce can crushed pineapple, drained (reserve liquid)
2   3-ounce packages lemon Jell-O
1/2 cup sugar
1   cup finely-chopped celery
1   pound raw cranberries, ground or finely chopped
1/2 cup chopped nuts

Add enough water to pineapple syrup to make 3 cups. Heat liquid and pour over Jell-O. Add sugar and stir until thoroughly dissolved. Chill. When mixture is slightly thickened, fold in pineapple, celery, cranberries and nuts. Pour into shallow pan. Chill until firm. Cut into squares and serve on lettuce with mayonnaise as dressing, if desired. DIANE WOLFF

Pretzel Salad

FIRST LAYER:
2   cups crushed pretzels (small pieces, not crumbed)
3   tablespoons sugar
3/4   cup margarine

SECOND LAYER:
1   8-ounce package cream cheese, room temperature
1   cup sugar
1   8-ounce container Cool Whip

THIRD LAYER:
1   6-ounce package strawberry or raspberry Jell-O
2   cups boiling water
2   10-ounce packages frozen strawberries or raspberries
     (don't thaw)

Preheat oven to 450°. Combine ingredients for first layer; spread in a 9 x 13-inch pan and bake 8 minutes. Cool. Beat together cream cheese and sugar; fold in Cool Whip. Spread over pretzel layer and refrigerate 15-20 minutes to set. Mix together ingredients for third layer and allow to set in refrigerator 10-20 minutes to soft-set. Pour over cream cheese layer, then refrigerate overnight. *"You can also combine strawberry and raspberry flavors. This is a very favorite recipe for potlucks and family dinners."*

KATHY D. FINGER

Cucumber Mold Salad

1   3-ounce package lime Jell-O
1   cup hot water
1   medium-sized cucumber
1   teaspoon vinegar
1   cup sour cream
1/2   cup mayonnaise

Dissolve Jell-O in hot water. Grate cucumber (or chop in blender) and mix with vinegar. Add cucumber to dissolved Jell-O. When cool, add sour cream and mayonnaise. Wet ring mold with cold water; pour mixture in and chill in refrigerator. *"This is good with crab, shrimp or chicken."*

TAMAE YOKOYAMA

Crunchy Tomato Aspic

2	envelopes unflavored gelatin
1	cup cold water
1	small clove garlic, peeled and minced
2	cups tomato juice
1/4	cup lemon juice
1	tablespoon sugar
1	teaspoon salt
	Dash hot pepper sauce
	Dash pepper
1	medium stalk celery, chopped
1	small onion, chopped
1/2	green pepper, chopped
1/2	cucumber, chopped

Sprinkle gelatin over cold water in 1 1/2-quart saucepan; dissolve over low heat. Stir in garlic, tomato juice, lemon juice, sugar and seasonings. Chill gelatin mixture until partially set; about 40 minutes. Stir chopped celery, onion, pepper and cucumber into partially set gelatin. Pour into 5-cup mold. (8 servings) SUE CHANDLER

Chutney Aspic

1	3-ounce package lime Jell-O
1	cup hot water
1	cup drained pineapple tidbits (save liquid)
1/2	cup drained chutney (save liquid)

Dissolve Jell-O in hot water. Add pineapple and chutney liquids (and enough water to make 1 cup) to Jell-O. Chill until syrupy. Fold in chutney and pineapple. Turn into mold. (4-6 servings) MARGARET SMITH

Orange Fluff

1	small container cottage cheese
1	small container Cool Whip
1	flat can crushed pineapple
1	small can mandarin oranges, well drained
1	box orange Jell-O

Combine cottage cheese, Cool Whip, pineapple and oranges. Pour into large bowl and sprinkle dry Jell-O mix on top. Refrigerate. FRANCES CASEY

Pink Cloud Salad

1	21-ounce can cherry pie filling
1	20-ounce can crushed pineapple, drained
1	8-ounce carton sour cream
1	41/2-ounce carton whipped topping
1	11-ounce can mandarin oranges
2	bananas, peeled and sliced

Mix together the first five ingredients and chill. Just before serving, add two sliced bananas. (12 servings) CAROL ZIEGLER

Fruit Salad

Take a big bowl of water. Put in half a watermelon. Then put in some apple slices, cherries, then some other fruits that you like. Then you freeze it for one year and a half. Then you have a fruit salad. JAYONNE, AGE 7

Glazed Fruit Salad

SALAD:

1	20-ounce can unsweetened pineapple chunks (save juice)
1	11-ounce can mandarin oranges (or fresh)
2	cups seedless green grapes, halved
2	large bananas, sliced 1/2-inch thick

GLAZE:

1	cup liquid (from drained pineapple, plus water, if needed)
1/4	cup sugar
1	tablespoon plus 1 teaspoon cornstarch
1	teaspoon almond extract

Drain pineapple and oranges thoroughly for several hours or overnight in refrigerator. (Leave pieces whole.) Save pineapple juice for glaze. Do not slice bananas until 1/2 hour before serving, when adding glaze. Stir cornstarch into a small amount of juice in a small saucepan. Stir until smooth. Add rest of juice and sugar. Cook over low heat until clear and thickened. Remove from heat. Add almond extract. Chill. (Glaze can be made ahead and refrigerated.) Add glaze to fruit 1/2 hour before serving. Stir gently with a wooden spoon. For a more tart glaze with fewer calories, sugar may be omitted or decreased. *"This is a very colorful salad since the glaze does not color the natural fruit colors. Serve in a clear glass bowl. Other fruits may be added or substituted. Can also be served as a dessert."* CAROL ZIEGLER

Neo-Classic Waldorf Salad

1	large Granny Smith apple, diced
2	medium McIntosh apples, diced
1 5	dried apricots, diced
1/2	cup golden raisins
1	cup pecans
1	large orange (optional)
1	cup small marshmallows (optional)
2	tablespoons sugar
1	8-ounce container lemon or vanilla yogurt

Mix the first seven ingredients in a medium bowl. If using an orange, cut each section into thirds after peeling. Mix sugar with yogurt. Fold yogurt into apple mixture and chill. *"Possible additional natural sweeteners: 1/4 cup dates, 1 cup grapes, 1/2 cup shredded coconut, 1 teaspoon vanilla. This is nice served at brunch with pancakes or French toast."* (6 servings)
CHRIS BLACK

Cranberry Salad

1	cup ground cranberries
3/4	cup sugar
1	cup red seedless grapes
1	cup walnuts
1	8-ounce container Cool Whip

Mix ground cranberries with sugar. Let mixture stand overnight or approximately 8 hours. Add grapes, walnuts and Cool Whip; mix and serve. (8-12 servings) NADINE KORC

Frozen Cranberry Salad

1	14-ounce can sweetened condensed milk (not evaporated)
1	16-ounce can whole cranberry sauce
1	20-ounce can crushed pineapple, drained
1/2	cup chopped walnuts
1	8-ounce container whipped topping

In a large bowl, combine sweetened condensed milk, cranberry sauce, pineapple and nuts. Fold in whipped topping. Spread in a 9 x 13-inch pan. Freeze until firm. Remove 10 minutes before serving. Serve on lettuce leaves. This can also be frozen in individual aluminum tart pans or foil baking cups. (12 servings) BARBARA WRANESH

SALADS

24-Hour Fruit Salad

2	eggs, beaten
4	tablespoons vinegar
1/4	cup plus 4 tablespoons sugar
2	tablespoons butter
21/2	cups plus 1 cup miniature marshmallows
1	16-ounce can fruit cocktail, drained
1	20-ounce can pineapple chunks, drained
1	cup heavy cream

Combine eggs, vinegar and 4 tablespoons sugar; cook over low heat until thickened. Add butter and 1 cup marshmallows; stir until melted. Cool. When partially set, add fruit and remainder of marshmallows. Whip cream with 1/4 cup sugar and fold into salad mixture. Chill overnight.

MAGGIE BROWNRIDGE

Watergate Salad

1	3-ounce package pistachio instant pudding mix
1	8-ounce can crushed pineapple (drained)
1	8-ounce container Cool Whip
1/2	cup chopped nuts
1	cup miniature marshmallows

Mix dry pudding mix into pineapple and Cool Whip. Add nuts and marshmallows. Chill 4-6 hours. HOWARD CRIMMINS

Dressing for Fruit Salad

1/2	cup orange juice
1/4	cup lemon juice
1/2	cup sugar
3/4	cup pineapple juice
21/2	tablespoons cornstarch

Combine all ingredients in a medium saucepan. Cook over medium heat until thick. Cool and pour over any variety of canned or fresh fruit such as pineapple, grapes, kiwi, mandarin oranges, apples or bananas.

MARIAN JOHNSON

Cranberry Relish

1	pound cranberries
2	unpeeled oranges, seeded and quartered
2	cooking apples (tart are best)
1	whole lemon
21/2	cups sugar

Grind all ingredients in blender or food processor. Refrigerate. May be frozen. (8 servings) *"Absolutely delicious with turkey."* JERRI JENISTA

All-Season Wild Rice Salad

2	cups cooked wild rice
2	cups cooked brown rice
2	medium carrots, diced
2	stalks celery, diced
2	green onions, thinly sliced
1	cup broccoli flowerets
2	tablespoons olive oil
2	tablespoons low-sodium soy sauce
2	tablespoons red wine vinegar
	Dash black pepper
1	clove garlic, minced
1/2	teaspoon freshly-grated ginger
	Dash hot sauce
	Greens

Place all ingredients (except greens) into a bowl; toss well and allow to marinate 2 hours. Serve on bed of kale, red cabbage or some attractive greens to complement the salad. (6 servings) Reprinted with permission, MedSport, High Fit-Low Fat™, REGENTS OF THE UNIVERSITY OF MICHIGAN

Beet and Pea Salad

SALAD:
2   14-ounce cans cubed beets, drained (or sliced, then cubed)
1   10-ounce package frozen green peas (cooked)
1   medium onion, chopped

DRESSING:
3-4   tablespoons chopped green onions
4   tablespoons (or more) mayonnaise
4   tablespoons (or more) sour cream
3   tablespoons fresh dill (or dried)
2-3   tablespoons lemon juice
3/4   teaspoon salt
      Dash pepper

Combine all dressing ingredients; toss with vegetables and refrigerate 1 hour. LARISSA GHISO

Broccoli Salad

SALAD:
1   bunch broccoli, separated into flowerets
6   slices bacon, cooked and crumbled
1   cup raisins
3/4   cup chopped onions
1   ounce diced pimentos
1/4-1/2 cup chopped almonds (or other nuts)

DRESSING:
11/2   cups mayonnaise
3   tablespoons sugar
2   tablespoons vinegar

Mix dressing ingredients with wire whisk until smooth. Combine broccoli, bacon, raisins, onion, pimento and nuts. Add dressing and toss gently. (6-8 servings) KAREN BARKS AND OLGA STAUDT

Cauliflower Salad

SALAD:
1   head cauliflower, separated into flowerets
8-10 spears asparagus, cut into 1-inch pieces
4   slices dill pickles, chopped coarsely
1   red bell pepper, chopped coarsely

DRESSING:
1/2   cup mayonnaise
2   tablespoons dill pickle juice
     Salt and pepper to taste

Steam cauliflower and asparagus until moderately soft. Mix vegetables together. Combine mayonnaise, pickle juice, salt and pepper; pour over vegetables. Let sit at room temperature 1-2 hours or in refrigerator for 4-6 hours to blend flavors. JANET GILSDORF

Broccoli Salad Snack

1   large bunch broccoli, separated into flowerets

DRESSING:
1/2   cup cider vinegar
2   tablespoons sugar
1   teaspoon salt
     Freshly-ground pepper to taste
1/2   cup vegetable oil

Mix dressing ingredients in a jar or blender and pour over broccoli. Toss and mix well. Marinate 24 hours and serve chilled. Also can be made with cauliflower or mushroom caps. (4-6 servings) LIN OSBORN

Cucumber Salad

3   tablespoons sugar
1/4   cup fresh lemon juice
1   8-ounce carton sour cream .
1   teaspoon salt
1/2   teaspoon dill
1   cucumber, sliced

Dissolve sugar in lemon juice. Add sour cream, salt and dill. Mix with cucumbers and refrigerate. MARY DOYLE

Cauliflower and Broccoli Marinade

1   head cauliflower, separated into flowerets
1   large head broccoli, cut into pieces or flowerets
      Fresh mushrooms, optional
      Black olives, optional

MARINADE:
11/2   cups oil
1   cup wine vinegar (may be with garlic)
1   tablespoon Accent
1   teaspoon salt
1   tablespoon dill
1   tablespoon sugar
1   teaspoon pepper
1   teaspoon garlic salt (less if you use garlic vinegar)

Mix marinade well with whisk or blender. Pour over vegetables; cover and refrigerate 12 hours (or a minimum of 4-5 hours). Mix again when serving. LINDA FAY

Do-Ahead Zucchini Salad

SALAD:
3   medium zucchini, shredded
1/2   cup finely-chopped green pepper
1/2   cup finely-chopped celery
1/2   cup finely-chopped onions

DRESSING:
1/4   cup salad oil
1/4   cup dry white wine
2   tablespoons (or more) white wine vinegar
1/3   cup sugar
1   teaspoon salt
1/2   teaspoon freshly-ground pepper

Toss vegetables together. Combine oil, wine, vinegar, sugar, salt and pepper in a jar with a good lid. Cover and shake well, until sugar is dissolved. Pour dressing over vegetables; toss well. Cover and refrigerate at least 6 hours before serving. *"Salad will keep up to 2 weeks in refrigerator."* (6 servings) CHARLOTTE BETZ

German Potato Salad

6	red potatoes
1/2	pound bacon
1	cup chopped onions
1	green pepper, diced
	Pinch salt
1/4	cup vinegar
1/2	cup water
5	tablespoons sugar
1	tablespoon flour

Cook potatoes in their jackets until tender; set aside. Preheat oven to 350°. Cut bacon and fry until crisp. Remove bacon from pan. Leave grease in pan; sauté onions and green pepper. Add salt and rest of ingredients, except for potatoes. Cook until thick, stirring occasionally. Place sliced and peeled potatoes in a baking dish. Pour sauce over potatoes. Bake 30-45 minutes. CAROL DRASGA

North African Salad

SALAD:

2	medium potatoes, cut into thick slices
2	beets, skinned and sliced
4	carrots, cut into 1/2-inch rounds
1	green bell pepper, sliced
1	red bell pepper, sliced
	Leaf lettuce
4	hard-boiled eggs, peeled and quartered
	Black olives
	Freshly-ground black pepper

DRESSING:

1/3	cup olive oil
21/2	tablespoons vinegar
	Salt and pepper to taste
2	tablespoons chopped fresh parsley

Cook potatoes, beets, carrots and peppers separately, until tender and crisp. Arrange all vegetables on a bed of leaf lettuce. Mix dressing ingredients in a blender until creamy. Pour over salad. Decorate salad plate with hard- boiled egg quarters and black olives. *"Sounds like a strange combination, but it is very flavorful."* (4-6 servings) JERI KELCH

Cucumber Salad

2	cups sugar
1	cup vinegar
2	tablespoons salt
2	tablespoons celery seed
9	cups unpeeled cucumbers, sliced
1	cup sliced onions

Dissolve sugar in vinegar; add salt and celery. Mix well. Pour mixture over cucumbers and onions. Put in refrigerator for 24 hours before using. *"Keeps 9 weeks in the refrigerator."* FRANK MOLER

Asian Black Bean Salad

SALAD:

1	cup cooked black beans
1	pound asparagus
4	lettuce leaves

MARINADE:

1/4	small red onion, diced
1/4	cup minced cilantro
1	tablespoon rice wine vinegar
1	teaspoon soy sauce
1	teaspoon hot sesame oil

In a 1-quart mixing bowl, combine red onions, cilantro, vinegar, soy sauce and sesame oil. Marinate cooked beans in mixture 20-30 minutes. Trim dried, tough ends from asparagus stalks and slice on the diagonal. Blanch asparagus in boiling water 3 minutes. Remove from water and toss with marinated beans. Wash and spin dry lettuce leaves. To serve, place each leaf on a chilled salad plate. Place one fourth of the salad on each lettuce leaf. (4 servings) CANDY ELY

Nicaraguan Tropical Salad

1	cup grated coconut, fresh or dried
2	cups finely-shredded cabbage
1	cup fresh pineapple cubes
1	cup mayonnaise

If coconut is dried, soak in water 15 minutes. Mix all ingredients well and chill. *"Especially good with tortillas."* (6 servings) DOROTHY WARDELL

Cabbage Slaw

1	head cabbage, chopped
8	green onions, chopped
2	3-ounce packages uncooked Ramen noodles
2-3	tablespoons butter or margarine
1/2	cup sesame seeds
1/2	cup slivered almonds

DRESSING:

4	tablespoons sugar
1	cup vegetable oil
1	teaspoon pepper
2	teaspoons salt
6	tablespoons rice vinegar

Toss cabbage, onions and noodles together. (Do not add seasoning package to noodles.) In skillet, melt butter and stir in sesame seeds and almonds. Sauté until lightly browned. Toss with cabbage. Combine sugar, oil, pepper, salt and vinegar in blender. Pour over cabbage and toss; chill. Stir frequently. *"Can be made a day or two ahead."*
(12 servings) JANET SHATUSKY

Freezer Cole Slaw

1	medium head cabbage, shredded
1	teaspoon salt
1	carrot, grated
1	green pepper, chopped

DRESSING:

1	cup vinegar
1/4	cup water
2	cups sugar
1	teaspoon mustard seed
1	teaspoon celery seed

Mix salt with cabbage; let stand 1 hour. Press out excess water; add carrots and peppers. Combine all dressing ingredients and boil 1 minute. Cool to lukewarm. Pour over cabbage. Place in freezer containers and freeze. (Makes about 6-8 pints) SALLY CAYLEY

SALADS

Red Cabbage and Walnut Salad

SALAD:
1   pound curly endive, well-dried and torn into bite-size pieces
3/4   cup minced parsley
1   small wedge red cabbage (4 ounces), sliced
1   cup chopped walnuts (4 ounces)

HERBED VINAIGRETTE:
1   large green onion, cut into 1-inch pieces
1/4   cup minced parsley
1/3   cup red wine vinegar
1   teaspoon Dijon mustard
1   teaspoon salt
1/2   teaspoon dried tarragon
1/8   teaspoon sugar
       Pepper
1   cup vegetable oil

Place endive in large glass salad bowl. Add parsley, cabbage and walnuts. For vinaigrette: In a food processor or blender, mix green onions and parsley together. Add vinegar, mustard, salt, tarragon, sugar and pepper and mix 2 seconds. Add vegetable oil and blend 2 seconds. Just before serving, pour vinaigrette over salad to taste and toss at table.

CHRIS IMAZUMI-O'CONNOR

Croutons in the Bowl

You put croutons in the bowl. Make some salad and put croutons in the bowl. I like salad and in the bowl, croutons. SAHAR, AGE 7

Watercress, Pear and Blue Cheese Salad

SALAD:
1	small head Boston lettuce, torn into bite-size pieces
1 0	ounces watercress leaves
2	Comice pears, cored and cut into 8 pieces each (or 1 can)
1/2	cup crumbled blue cheese (or goat cheese)
1/2	cup walnut halves

DRESSING:
1/2	cup walnut oil
2	tablespoons fresh lemon juice
1-2	teaspoons freshly-ground pepper
1	large shallot, minced
1	teaspoon salt, optional (or to taste)

Divide lettuce and watercress among plates. Arrange pear slices in spiral pattern over greens. Top with blue cheese and walnuts. Combine remaining ingredients in jar and shake well. Pour dressing over salad. (4 servings) CHRIS IMAZUMI-O'CONNOR

Salad with Blue Cheese and Dried Cherries

SALAD:
1/2	head Romaine lettuce, torn into bite-size pieces
1/2	head iceberg lettuce, torn into bite-size pieces
1/4	cup crumbled blue cheese
1/2	cup chopped dried cherries
1	red onion, thinly sliced
1/2	cup chopped walnuts

DRESSING:
2	tablespoons Dijon mustard
1/2	cup olive oil
1/2	cup white wine vinegar or white wine tarragon vinegar
2-3	cloves garlic, minced
	Pepper

Combine salad ingredients in a large serving bowl or individual plates. Whisk dressing ingredients together. Toss with salad just before serving.

KATHY ROBERTS

Triple Green Salad Bowl

SALAD:
1   bunch Romaine lettuce
1   10-ounce package fresh spinach
11/2   pounds green grapes, cut in half

DRESSING:
2/3   cup vegetable oil
1/3   cup cider vinegar
1   teaspoon salt
1   teaspoon sugar
1   teaspoon dry mustard
1/2   teaspoon basil
1/4   teaspoon paprika

WALNUT CROUTONS:
11/2   teaspoons butter
1/4   teaspoon salt
1/3   cup walnuts

The day before: Mix salad dressing ingredients and chill overnight. Combine butter, salt and walnuts and brown in skillet. Wash lettuce and spinach. Break into bite-size pieces, but save several lettuce leaves for lining salad bowl. Line salad bowl with whole Romaine leaves; fill bowl with Romaine and spinach. Arrange grapes and croutons in a pretty pattern. Drizzle dressing over top. (10-12 servings) JERI KELCH

Lilos Salad Dressing

    Salt and ground pepper to taste
1/2   teaspoon sugar
1   teaspoon Dijon mustard
1   clove garlic, minced
1   tablespoon fresh lemon juice
2   tablespoons wine or cider vinegar
2   tablespoons olive oil
2   tablespoons salad oil
1   egg yolk
    Fresh herbs of your choice

Whisk all dressing ingredients together until well blended and pour over your favorite greens. CHRIS IMAZUMI -O'CONNOR

Tangy Spinach Salad

SALAD:

11/2	pounds spinach
1	cup mung bean sprouts
1	medium tomato, cut into small wedges
1	medium carrot, grated or thinly sliced (1/2 cup)
3	fresh mushrooms, thinly sliced
4	spring onions, finely chopped or shaved
1	11-ounce can mandarin orange segments, drained (or 1 cup sliced fresh sliced strawberries, or 1 cup fresh pineapple pieces)
3	tablespoons sliced almonds, lightly roasted

DRESSING:

2	tablespoons balsamic vinegar
3-4	tablespoons barbecue sauce (we like K.C. Masterpiece)
1	tablespoon canola oil
2	tablespoons low-sodium soy sauce

Prepare the spinach (wash, sort, remove stems, dry and tear larger leaves). Combine with remaining salad ingredients. Combine all dressing ingredients in a screw top jar and shake well. Pour dressing over salad, toss well and serve immediately. (Makes 8 servings) Reprinted with permission, MEDSPORT, HIGH FIT - LOW FAT™, REGENTS OF THE UNIVERSITY OF MICHIGAN

Dieter's Delight Dressing

1	can beef broth
2	tablespoons chili sauce or ketchup
2	tablespoons vinegar
1	tablespoon grated onions
2	tablespoons crumbled blue cheese (optional)

Combine all ingredients. Shake well and serve over salad greens. (Makes about 11/4 cups) KATHERINE KERSEY

Korean Spinach Salad

SALAD:
1	bag spinach, torn into pieces
1/2-3/4	pound bean sprouts
1	8-ounce can water chestnuts, sliced
2	hard-boiled eggs, sliced
5	strips bacon, fried and crumbled

DRESSING:
1	cup oil
3/4	cup sugar
1/4	teaspoon onion salt
1/3	cup ketchup
1/4	cup vinegar
2	teaspoons Worcestershire sauce

Toss salad ingredients together. Mix dressing ingredients. Toss together when ready to serve.

COOK'S TIP: Dressing is best if made the day before and refrigerated.

MARTHA JAMES

Creamy Garlic Dressing

1	pint sour cream*
3	tablespoons lemon juice
1	3-ounce package cream cheese, cut in cubes
1/4	teaspoon salt
1	large garlic clove, minced
2	tablespoons minced onions
	Dash cayenne pepper

Put half of sour cream in bowl with other ingredients; blend until smooth. Add remaining sour cream and mix on low speed until smooth. Chill until ready to serve.

*LOW CALORIE SOUR CREAM:
1	pint small curd cottage cheese
1/4	cup water
2	tablespoons lemon juice

Blend in blender until smooth. KATHERINE KERSEY

72

Salad

To make a salad, you take lettuce and cut it up and you put it in the big bowl and you put cut up carrots in the bowl and you put croutons and you put the salad dressing. VERONICA, AGE 6

Bordman's Caesar Salad

1	cup oil
2	cloves garlic, minced
1	small can anchovies
1/4	teaspoon salt
1/4	teaspoon pepper
1/4	teaspoon dry mustard
2	lemons
2	eggs
1	cup grated Parmesan cheese
2	pounds Romaine lettuce
1	box croutons

Into oil, add garlic and only the oil from the can of anchovies. (Save anchovies for garnish.) Add salt, pepper, dry mustard and juice from 13/4 lemons. Stir well. Add 2 coddled eggs (boiled about 1 minute) and stir while adding Parmesan. Combine lightly with the greens and add croutons.

COOK'S TIP: Wash, dry and chill Romaine lettuce early in the day. Prepared dressing can be good for a day, but add croutons just before serving so they are crisp. Anchovies served separately to those who like them. (4-6 servings) ARLENE BORDMAN

Blender Caesar Salad Dressing

1	2-ounce can anchovies, drained
2/3	cup olive oil
33/4	tablespoons lemon juice
1	teaspoon Worcestershire sauce
1	teaspoon Dijon mustard
	Ground pepper to taste
	Pinch salt, optional

Mix all ingredients in blender until smooth. *"Great and no eggs!"*
ELAINE SCHWARTZ

Tortellini Salad

2   pounds cheese tortellini (frozen kind)
8   ounces Mozzarella cheese, cut into triangles
8   ounces cheddar cheese, cubed
      Pepperoni, cut up
      Celery, cut up
      Red onion slices
      Green pepper, optional
1   bottle zesty Italian dressing

Cook tortellini and cool thoroughly. Mix together with other ingredients.

JOANNE BOLAS

Pasta Salad

SALAD:
1   pound shell pasta, cooked al dente
1/2   14-ounce jar roasted red peppers, drained and chopped
1/2   pint green olives, sliced
1/2   cup roasted pine nuts
1/2   cup sliced celery

DRESSING:
2   teaspoons basil
1/4   cup white wine vinegar
1   tablespoon Dijon mustard
1   garlic clove, minced
2   tablespoons minced parsley
      Salt and pepper
1/4   cup oil

Combine all dressing ingredients and whisk until smooth. Pour over pasta salad and serve. LYNN SORRELLS

Mediterranean Salad Sandwich

2	cups shredded lettuce
1/2	mild red onion, sliced
1	21/4-ounce can sliced ripe olives, drained
1/2	small cucumber, thinly sliced
6	radishes, sliced
1	6-ounce jar marinated artichoke hearts, drained (reserve marinade)
1	61/2-ounce can chunk tuna, drained
1-2	cups alfalfa sprouts
	Salt and pepper to taste
4	pita pocket breads

DRESSING:

	Reserved artichoke marinade
2	tablespoons lemon juice
1/4	teaspoon dried basil
1/4	teaspoon oregano

In a salad bowl, combine lettuce, onions, olives, cucumber, radishes, artichoke hearts and tuna. Cover and chill. Combine artichoke marinade, lemon juice, basil, and oregano; let stand at room temperature. Pour dressing over salad mixture and add alfalfa sprouts. Mix gently. Add salt and pepper to taste. Cut 4 pita pocket breads in half and fill each with salad. (8 servings) CHRIS IMAZUMI-O'CONNOR

Summer Salad

SALAD:

2	cups cooked brown rice
1	cup frozen peas, cooked and cooled
1/2	cup sliced celery
1/4	cup chopped green onions
1	cup cooked shrimp (or crab)
1	cup diced cooked chicken (or turkey or ham)

DRESSING:

2/3	cup mayonnaise
2/3	cup sour cream
1	tablespoon lemon juice
	Salt and white pepper to taste

Combine rice, peas, celery and onions. Blend mayonnaise, sour cream and lemon juice together; add salt and pepper. Toss with shrimp and chicken. KATHERINE HAY

Seafood Pasta Salad

SALAD:
1   pound pasta (any variety)
3   cups seafood (any combination of whitefish, shrimp, mussels, sea scallops, lobster or crab)
3/4   cup ripe plum tomatoes, halved and seeded
1/4   cup chopped fresh parsley
3   tablespoons coarsely-chopped basil leaves
1/4   cup chopped pimentos
1   cup chopped fresh dill
1/2   cup chopped shallots
3   tablespoons capers, drained
1/4   cup chopped black olives
1/4   cup grated fresh zucchini, drained

VINAIGRETTE:
1/2   cup fresh lemon juice
1   tablespoon red wine vinegar
1/2   cup olive oil
1/4   cup Dijon mustard

Cook pasta until al dente; drain. Cook seafood until tender; drain and chop. In a large bowl, toss salad ingredients. To prepare the vinaigrette: In a small bowl, whisk together lemon juice, vinegar, olive oil and mustard. Toss vinaigrette with salad (coat lightly). Correct seasoning, if necessary. Refrigerate several hours to allow flavors to blend. Serve well chilled. *"If the salad is refrigerated overnight, it may be moistened with remaining vinaigrette."* (6-8 servings) KAREN BARTSCHT

Artichoke Hearts Grande Mere

1	cup crabmeat
1/4	cup chopped chives
2	tablespoons chopped parsley
1	clove garlic, minced
1	cup mayonnaise
3	tablespoons lemon juice
1/2	teaspoon salt
1/4	teaspoon minced green pepper
1/2	cup sour cream
3	tablespoons minced fresh dill
1 2	canned artichoke hearts, drained
	Garnish: Lemon, lime and cherry tomato

Shred crabmeat in bowl. Combine remaining ingredients (except artichokes) in blender until smooth. Add half of sauce to crab mixture and toss. Trim bottoms of artichokes so they sit evenly on plate. Take out some of center leaves to form cup. Fill each heart with crab mixture. Place 2-3 filled hearts on bed of lettuce and cover with remaining sauce. Garnish with lemon, lime and cherry tomato. Refrigerate at least 30 minutes before serving. (4-6 servings) DIXIE COMSTOCK

Seafood Salad

SALAD:

1	cup chopped celery
1	2-ounce can sliced black olives
3	green onions, chopped
3	hard-cooked eggs, chopped
1	package corkscrew macaroni, cooked
2	cups cooked crab or shrimp

DRESSING:

1	cup mayonnaise
	Dash Worcestershire sauce
1	tablespoon sweet pickle juice
1/4	cup milk
1	teaspoon dry mustard
	Salt and pepper to taste
	Garlic powder to taste
	Dash dill

Mix salad ingredients together. Whisk together dressing ingredients. Combine mixtures. KATHY DOYLE-SCHUELER

Shrimp Aillade

12-14 walnuts, finely chopped
3   cloves garlic, finely chopped
3/4   cup oil
1   tablespoon lemon juice
1/2   teaspoon salt
1   pound cooked shrimp
       Chopped parsley for garnish

Blend all ingredients, except shrimp and parsley. Mix with shrimp and sprinkle with chopped parsley. Chill before serving. ANN SCHRIBER

Salmon and Pear Salad

SALAD:
1   bunch watercress
1   head Boston bibb lettuce
1/4   pound smoked salmon, cut into thin strips
1/4   pound feta cheese, crumbled
3   red and/or green Bartlett pears

DRESSING:
3   tablespoons olive oil
2   tablespoons white wine vinegar or champagne
1   shallot, chopped
2   teaspoons capers
1   teaspoon Dijon mustard

In medium bowl, whisk together dressing ingredients. Remove and discard tough stems from watercress; cut leaves into bite-size pieces. Separate lettuce leaves. Arrange 1-2 large bibb lettuce leaves onto each individual salad plates. Tear or cut remaining bibb lettuce into bite-size pieces. Add watercress, lettuce, salmon and cheese. Pour dressing over salad; toss well to coat. Cut each pear lengthwise in half; core. Cut each half into thin slices. Arrange half on lettuce leaf on salad plate. Spoon some salad mixture on each plate with pears. Pour any remaining salad dressing on pears. (6 servings) KATHERINE KERSEY

Chicken Waldorf Salad

2	cups cooked diced chicken
1	cup diced apples (with skins on for color)
1	cup sliced celery
1/2	cup raisins
1/2	cup chopped walnuts
	Salt to taste
	Pepper to taste
2	tablespoons mayonnaise (or more)
	Garnish: Tomato wedges and cucumber slices

Mix all ingredients well. Serve on a bed of lettuce. Garnish with tomato wedges and cucumber slices. (4 servings) CAROLINE BLANE

Almond Chicken Salad Shanghai

SALAD:

21/2	pounds skinned and boned chicken breasts
2	tablespoons soy sauce
1	teaspoon minced garlic
2	tablespoons vegetable oil
5	cups celery, sliced
2	pounds tomatoes, diced
1/2	cup chopped parsley
1	cup slivered almonds

GINGER DRESSING:

2/3	cup sugar
21/2	teaspoons ground ginger
11/2	teaspoons salt
1/2	cup vinegar
1	cup vegetable oil
3	tablespoons sesame seeds

Make ginger dressing first: Blend sugar, ginger, salt and vinegar together in food processor for 5 seconds. Gradually add oil and blend 30 seconds. Add sesame seeds. Cut chicken into 1-inch pieces. Combine with soy sauce and garlic. Sauté in hot oil 10 minutes, until cooked. Remove chicken and chill. Combine celery, tomato, parsley and 3/4 cup almonds; toss with chicken. Stir in ginger dressing; chill. Spoon onto lettuce leaves. Sprinkle with remaining almonds. (10 servings) BETH PIERCE

SALADS

Greek Chicken Salad

SALAD:
31/2   cups cooked chicken, cut into bite-size pieces
11/2   cups crumbled Monterey Jack cheese
2   medium cucumbers, seeded and chopped
1/4   cup chopped parsley
1/3   cup pitted black olives, sliced
        Pita bread or Boston lettuce
        Garnish: Alfalfa sprouts, optional

DRESSING:
1   cup mayonnaise
1/2   cup plain yogurt
3   cloves garlic, minced
1   tablespoon oregano

In a small bowl, combine mayonnaise, yogurt, garlic and oregano; set aside. In a large bowl, combine chicken, cheese, cucumbers, parsley and olives. Combine the 2 mixtures and toss until coated. Cover and chill at least 1 hour before serving. Serve in pita bread or on a bed of lettuce. Garnish with sprouts. (6-8 servings) MIDGE WAKEFIELD

Chicken Salad

SALAD:
2   packages Ramen noodles (uncooked, broken very small)
1/2   head cabbage, shredded
4   green onions, chopped
4-6   tablespoons sesame seeds, toasted
4   tablespoons minced almonds
1-2   pounds cooked and shredded chicken

DRESSING:
1   cup salad oil
4   tablespoons sugar
1   teaspoon pepper
1   teaspoon salt
6   tablespoons red wine vinegar

Combine salad ingredients. Mix dressing together and combine with salad. Chill overnight. PEGGY JOHNSON

Cold Chicken with Spicy Peanut Sauce

11/2	pounds chicken breasts
1	whole green onion, cut in half
1	quarter-size slice fresh ginger
1	tablespoon dry sherry
1/2	teaspoon salt
1/2	teaspoon sugar
2	cups water
1-3	cups shredded iceberg lettuce

Place chicken in 2-quart pan with onion, ginger, sherry, salt, and sugar. Bring to boil. Cover and turn off heat. Let sit 20 minutes. Remove chicken from broth and let cool. Pull meat from bones and shred. Chill chicken and place over lettuce.

PEANUT SAUCE:

11/2	tablespoons peanut butter
21/2	tablespoons salad oil
2	tablespoons soy sauce
2	tablespoons sugar
2	teaspoons vinegar
1	tablespoon chopped green onions
1/2	teaspoon sesame oil
1/4-1/2	teaspoon red chile oil

Whisk peanut butter and salad oil together. Add rest of ingredients and stir. Pour sauce over chicken and lettuce mixture. (4-6 servings)

KATHY DOYLE-SCHUELER

Hot Chicken or Turkey Salad

3	cups cubed cooked chicken or turkey
1	cup diced celery
1	cup mayonnaise
2	tablespoons lemon juice
1/2	cup chopped pecans
1/2	teaspoon salt
2	teaspoons grated onions
1/2	cup shredded cheese

Preheat oven to 450°. Combine all ingredients and place in buttered baking dish. Sprinkle with cheese. Bake 15 minutes or until bubbly. (4-6 servings) CATHERINE MCDOWELL

Peking Chicken Salad

SALAD:
2-3   cups diced, cooked chicken breasts
1   head lettuce, torn
6   green onions, sliced
1   package sliced almonds, toasted
1/4   cup sesame seeds
1   can chow mein noodles

DRESSING:
3-4   tablespoons sugar
4   tablespoons white vinegar
2 1/2   teaspoons salt*
1   teaspoon Accent seasoning
1/2   teaspoon pepper

Combine dressing ingredients. Toss with salad ingredients. Refrigerate 1/2 hour before serving. Add chow mein noodles just before serving.

*COOK'S TIP: If you make a double batch, don't double amount of salt in the dressing. KRISTI STUTZ

Turkey Noodle Salad

1/2   cup mayonnaise
1/2   cup chutney
1/2   teaspoon curry powder
1   cup chopped celery
1/2   cup currants
1   pound cubed cooked turkey
1   cup frozen peas, thawed
1/2   pound thick noodles, cooked and drained

In a large bowl, stir together all ingredients. Refrigerate about 1 hour to allow flavors to blend. DEBBIE LOWN

SALADS

Pasta, Rice and Potatoes

PASTA, RICE AND POTATOES

Pasta	**87**
Rice	**96**
Potatoes	**100**

Fettuccine with Olives and Toasted Pine Nuts

3/4	cup (2 ounces) freshly-grated Parmesan cheese
3	eggs
1	pound fresh fettuccine
1/2	cup finely-chopped olives, brine-cured (such as Gaeta)
1/2	cup toasted pine nuts
1/4	teaspoon freshly-grated nutmeg
	Salt and freshly-ground pepper

Whisk Parmesan and eggs in large bowl. Cook fettuccine in a large pot of boiling salted water until tender but still firm to bite (al dente). Drain. Toss with Parmesan mixture. Sprinkle with olives, pine nuts, nutmeg, salt and pepper. Toss again. Serve immediately. (6 servings) JANET GILSDORF

Spicy Eggplant and Tomato Pasta

3	tablespoons olive oil
2	garlic cloves, minced
1/2	teaspoon crushed red pepper flakes
1/2	pound eggplant, peel left on, cut into 1/2-1 inch cubes
1	16-ounce can salt-free whole tomatoes, cut into small pieces
1/2	teaspoon dried basil
1/2	teaspoon dried oregano
1	bay leaf
1/4	teaspoon red pepper flakes (optional)
	Fettuccine (to serve 4)
	Salt to taste

In a large skillet, heat olive oil with garlic and pepper flakes. When garlic sizzles, reduce heat. Add eggplant and sauté 2-4 minutes. Add tomatoes and remaining ingredients; cover and simmer until eggplant is tender and sauce is thick, 15-20 minutes. Break up eggplant pieces into sauce. Serve over cooked pasta. (4 servings) JERI KELCH

Spaghetti

Put some spaghetti in a pot. Put some water in too (about one cup). Cook the spaghetti for 3 hours until the noodles are soft. Mash up some tomatoes to make a red sauce. Put on some red cheese. Take it out of the pot. Then we eat it. CAMILLA, AGE 6

Pasta Frittata

1/2	ounce (about 1/2 cup) dried wild mushrooms
11/4	cups cooked pasta
2	teaspoons olive oil
21/2	tablespoons unsalted butter
1	large onion, chopped
1 0	eggs
4	large plum tomatoes, chopped
2	tablespoons heavy cream
1	teaspoon salt
1	teaspoon freshly-ground pepper
1	tablespoon chopped fresh marjoram (or oregano)
4	ounces (about 11/4 cups) Gruyère cheese, grated

Preheat oven to 400°. In a small bowl, soak mushrooms in 1/2 cup boiling water until soft, about 20 minutes. Squeeze dry and chop coarsely. Cook pasta, drain and toss in olive oil. In a skillet, melt 11/2 tablespoons butter, and sauté onions until golden yellow and soft. Beat eggs lightly. Stir in tomatoes, mushrooms, cream, salt, pepper and chopped marjoram. Stir in prepared pasta. When onions are ready, increase heat to high and add remaining 1 tablespoon butter. Heat until butter is almost smoking, then pour in the egg mixture, stirring just to combine onion with the egg. When mixture starts to bubble around edges (about 30 seconds), remove from burner and place skillet in oven. Bake until frittata is just set, or 30 minutes. Using spatula, slide frittata onto a large ovenproof serving dish. Preheat broiler. Sprinkle grated cheese on top of frittata and broil until cheese melts, or 10 seconds. Cut into wedges and serve. Serve warm or at room temperature. (6-8 servings) JANET GILSDORF

Baltimore Spaghetti

1/2	pound bacon
1/2	green pepper, diced
1	can tomato soup
1	soup can of milk
8	ounces Velveeta cheese, cubed
1	pound spaghetti, cooked

Slice bacon in half and fry. Drain on paper towel. Add green peppers to bacon grease and fry until soft (3 or 4 minutes). In a larger pan, add tomato soup and milk. Make soup according to directions for cream of tomato soup. Add cubed cheese, a little at a time, until melted. Stir constantly to avoid burning. Lastly, add bacon and green peppers. Let mixture sit 15 minutes. In a bowl, pour entire cheese mixture over cooked spaghetti. (4-5 servings) *"Very simple and tastes great!"*

MELISSA A. SNAVELY

Easy Layered Pasta Ricotta Pie

1/3	cup finely-chopped onions
4	cloves garlic, minced
1/4	pound vermicelli, broken into thirds, cooked and drained
1	tablespoon olive oil
1	cup grated Romano cheese
3	eggs
1	15-ounce container ricotta cheese
1	10-ounce package frozen chopped spinach, thawed and well drained
1/2	teaspoon salt, optional
1	26-ounce jar spaghetti sauce

Preheat oven to 350°. In a large skillet, cook onions and garlic in oil until tender; remove from heat. Add cooked vermicelli, 1/2 cup Romano cheese and 1 egg and mix well. Press into well-greased 9-inch springform pan or into large Pyrex pie pan. Combine 2 egg yolks, ricotta, spinach, salt and remaining 1/2 cup Romano cheese. Spread over pasta layer. In a small mixing bowl, beat 2 egg whites until stiff but not dry; fold into three-fourths of pasta sauce. Pour over spinach mixture. Bake 50-60 minutes or until set. Let stand 10 minutes. Serve with remaining pasta sauce. (6-8 servings) *"My kids love this. It's also great for a casual dinner party because you can make it ahead."* PENNY PAPADOPOULOS

Spinach Tortellini with Zesty Dressing

DRESSING:

1	16-ounce can plums, undrained
3/4	cup orange marmalade
2	tablespoons vinegar
1/8	teaspoon cayenne pepper
1/2	teaspoon ground ginger
1/2	cup mandarin orange juice
3	tablespoons cornstarch

Remove pits from plums and place plums and juice in a blender. Blend well and pour in medium-sized saucepan. Add orange marmalade, vinegar, pepper and ginger and simmer 1 hour. Combine mandarin orange juice with cornstarch; add to plum mixture and continue cooking until thickened. Refrigerate. *"Flavor is much better if made 1 day ahead."*

SALAD:

1	pound fresh spinach, torn into small pieces
1	cup red cabbage
1	small onion
1	16-ounce can mandarin oranges
1	9-ounce package cheese tortellini
3	tablespoons grated Romano cheese
1	cup cashew halves

Place spinach in a large bowl. Cut cabbage into pieces no larger than 1/2 inch, but don't shred. Cut onion in thin rings. Drain mandarin oranges, reserving 1/2 cup. Cut orange sections in half and drain very well. Cook tortellini according to package directions; cool thoroughly. Refrigerate all ingredients until ready to serve.

To serve, combine salad ingredients in large serving bowl; toss well. Add Romano cheese and toss again. Warm dressing and pour over spinach mixture; toss well. Top with cashews. (10 servings) TANYA BLACKMER

Salsa Rosa with Pasta

4	tablespoons butter
1	bay leaf
1	small onion, finely chopped
1	carrot, finely chopped
1	stalk celery, finely chopped
2	tablespoons fresh parsley
3/4	pound very lean sausage
1/2	pound mushrooms, sliced
3/4	cup white wine
1	14-ounce can peeled, cooked tomatoes
1 1/2	cups heavy cream
	Cooked pasta

Over very low heat, melt butter in a saucepan and add bay leaf, onions, carrots, celery and parsley. Add sausage to the pan after vegetables have cooked, about 10-15 minutes. Add mushrooms and simmer 10 minutes. Add wine and tomatoes. Reduce liquid by simmering about 1 hour. Just before serving, add cream and heat through. Serve over hot cooked pasta.

PAMELA IANNOTI

Spinach Stuffed Shells

1	box (16-18) jumbo pasta shells
1/2	cup chopped onions
1	clove garlic, minced
1	tablespoon margarine
1 6	ounces ricotta cheese
1/2	cup grated Parmesan cheese
1	egg, slightly beaten
1	teaspoon salt
1/4	teaspoon pepper
4	ounces shredded Mozzarella cheese
1	9-ounce box frozen chopped spinach, thawed
1	32-ounce jar spaghetti sauce

Preheat oven to 350°. Cook pasta shells according to directions; drain and cool. Sauté onions and garlic in margarine. Mix together on low speed: ricotta, Parmesan, egg, onions, garlic, salt and pepper. Stir in Mozzarella and very drained (squeezed) spinach. Fill pasta shells with cheese mixture. Lay shells in baking dish, cover with spaghetti sauce. Bake 30 minutes. (4 servings) PHYLLIS MANN

91

Spinach Lasagna

TOMATO SAUCE:
1/2	cup chopped onions
1	clove garlic, minced
1	tablespoon olive oil
1/2	teaspoon dried basil
1 0	ounces tomato puree
3/4	teaspoon salt
1/8	teaspoon black pepper
1/2	teaspoon sugar

FARINA MIXTURE:
1	cup milk
1/2	teaspoon salt
21/2	tablespoons Cream of Wheat (don't use "Instant")
2	tablespoons grated Parmesan cheese
1	egg

SPINACH FILLING:
2	tablespoons margarine
1/2	cup chopped onions
1	package frozen chopped spinach (thaw and drain)
2	cups ricotta or cottage cheese
1	egg
9	lasagna noodles
8	ounces shredded Mozzarella cheese

To make tomato sauce: In a medium saucepan, sauté onions and garlic in olive oil. Add basil, tomato, salt, pepper and sugar. Heat to boiling; simmer 5-7 minutes; remove from heat. To make farina mixture: In a small pan, heat milk to boiling; add salt and Cream of Wheat. Remove from heat; stir in Parmesan and egg. To make spinach filling: In a large frying pan, melt margarine and sauté onions and spinach 3-5 minutes, until spinach is dry and onions are soft. Remove from heat and add ricotta and egg. Cook lasagna noodles according to package directions.

Preheat oven to 350°. In a 9-inch square baking dish, spread approximately one-third tomato sauce to cover the bottom. Arrange 3 noodles; trim if necessary. Layer half of the spinach filling and one-third of the Mozzarella. Arrange second noodle layer. Spread farina evenly. Spread rest of spinach, one-third tomato sauce, one-third Mozzarella. Arrange third noodle layer. Top with remaining tomato sauce and Mozzarella. Cover with foil and bake 35 minutes or until hot and bubbly. Remove from oven and let rest 10 minutes before serving. *"This dish can be prepared, baked and frozen. To reheat, thaw, cover, heat at 350°, 20-25 minutes."* DIANE AR

Lasagna

Boil the noodles in water. Take them out and put them into the strainer. And then you make the sauce. And then you put the sauce onto the noodles. And then you put them on the plate and then they're done.

BRIDGET, AGE 7

Cheesy Chicken Lasagna

8	ounces lasagne noodles
3	cups cooked chicken pieces

MUSHROOM SAUCE:

1/2	cup chopped onions
1/2	cup chopped green pepper
3	tablespoons butter
1/3	cup milk
1	can cream of mushroom soup
8	ounces fresh mushrooms, sliced
1/4	cup chopped pimentos
1/2	teaspoon basil

CHEESE MIXTURE:

2-3	cups shredded cheeses (mixture of cheddar, Swiss and Monterey Jack)
11/2	cups cottage cheese
1/2	cup grated Parmesan cheese

Cook and drain noodles, rinse in cold water. Preheat oven to 350°. Make the mushroom sauce: sauté onions and green pepper in butter; add rest of sauce ingredients. Combine cheeses in a separate bowl. In a buttered 9 x 13-inch glass dish, layer noodles, chicken, sauce, and cheeses. Repeat layers. Bake 45-55 minutes. Let stand 10 minutes, cut and serve. (8-10 servings) JOAN GREGORKA

Pasta and Turkey Meatballs

3/4	cup chopped onions
3	cloves garlic, minced
3	tablespoons olive oil
1	16-ounce can tomatoes
1	6-ounce can tomato paste
1	cup water
1	tablespoon sugar
1	teaspoon pepper
1-2	bay leaves
1/2	cup sweet vermouth
2	tablespoons crushed oregano
2	tablespoons Italian herbs
	Salt to taste
	Hot cooked spaghetti
	Grated Romano or Parmesan cheese

MEATBALLS:

1/2	cup bread crumbs
1	pound ground turkey meat
3	fluid ounces Second Nature egg product
1/2	cup grated Romano cheese
2	tablespoons chopped parsley
1	clove garlic, minced
1	teaspoon crushed oregano
	Salt and pepper to taste

Cook onions and garlic in hot oil until tender. Stir in next 10 ingredients. Simmer, uncovered, 30 minutes. Cover and cook 1-2 hours; remove bay leaf. Combine meatball ingredients and form into small to medium balls (about 10-12), brown slowly in 2 tablespoons hot olive oil. Add to sauce, cook 30 minutes. Serve over hot spaghetti. Pass bowl of grated Romano or Parmesan cheese. (6 servings) BETTY KONNAK

Sweet Noodle Kugel

1	pound box flat noodles (medium size)
6	eggs
1	pound cream cheese, room temperature
2	cups milk
1	20-ounce can crushed pineapple (use juice)
11/2	cups sugar
4	ounces apple jelly
4	tablespoons butter or margarine, melted

TOPPING:

1/2	cup dark brown sugar
2	teaspoons cinnamon
3	cups crushed cornflakes
4	tablespoons butter or margarine, melted

Preheat oven to 350°. Cook noodles. In a mixing bowl, beat eggs and cream cheese. Add all other ingredients. Place in a 9 x 13-inch baking dish. Mix all topping ingredients together. Spread on top of noodle mixture. Bake 45 minutes to 1 hour. (10-12 servings) *"This can be frozen before baking, but thaw first."* SHARON GREENFIELD

Peach Noodle Kugel

1	1-pound package wide egg noodles (or yolkless noodles)
4	eggs
1	8-ounce container large curd cottage cheese
1	pint sour cream
1	can peaches in syrup, sliced
11/2	cups sugar
1	teaspoon salt
1/2	cup butter, melted

Preheat oven to 350°. Cook noodles as directed on package. Pour all ingredients (including peach juice) into bowl; mix together. Pour into greased 9 x 13-inch baking dish. Bake, uncovered, 11/2 hours until golden brown. Cut into squares. (16-20 servings) *"Even delicious cold the next day. Can be assembled, then frozen, to be baked when needed. No defrosting necessary, just bake about 15-20 minutes longer, uncovered."*
ELAINE SCHWARTZ

Rice and Rye Pilaf

1/2	cup rye or whole wheat berries (available at health food stores)
5	tablespoons butter
1	medium onion, chopped
2	cups long-grain converted rice
3	cups chicken broth
1/2	teaspoon salt (optional)

Bring 1/2 cup water to simmer in medium saucepan over low heat. Add rye or whole wheat berries. Cover and cook until all water is absorbed, about 45 minutes. Set aside. This can be prepared up to two days in advance and refrigerated with a cover. One hour before serving, melt butter in large skillet over medium high heat. Add onions and sauté until transparent. Mix in rice, stirring until sizzling. Add broth, cooked rye and salt and bring to boil. Reduce heat, cover and simmer 20 minutes. Remove from heat. Transfer to chafing dish and keep warm until ready to serve. (10-15 servings) CHRIS IMAZUMI-O'CONNOR

Rice Pilaf

1/4	cup margarine
1	small onion, diced
1/4	cup yellow raisins
1	cup long-grain rice, raw
1/4	cup slivered almonds
2	cups hot chicken broth

Preheat oven to 375-400°. Grease 1/2-quart baking dish. Melt butter in frying pan; sauté onions and raisins until golden. Add rice and mix well; add almonds and place in casserole. Add boiling chicken broth and bake, covered, 30 minutes or until all liquid is absorbed.

COOK'S TIP: The secret is to make sure oven is hot enough so that broth is boiling in casserole. Once boiling is achieved, oven temperature can be reduced to 375°. (4-6 servings) KENNETH R. SILK

Rice, Cheese and Corn Bake

1 1/2	cups chopped celery
3	tablespoons chopped onions
1/4	cup butter
3 1/2	cups (20-ounce bag) frozen corn
1	cup white rice, cooked
1 2	ounces cheddar cheese, shredded
1 1/2	cups milk
1	teaspoon salt
1/8	teaspoon paprika

Preheat oven to 300°. Sauté celery and onions in butter about 5 minutes. Mix with remaining ingredients and place in a buttered 2-quart baking dish. Cover and bake 1 hour. (6-8 servings) *"This is easy to make well ahead and slowly reheat."* NANCY WHITE

Rice with Zucchini and Spinach in Cheese Sauce

2 1/2	pounds zucchini
1	cup chopped onions
2	cloves garlic, minced
4	tablespoons oil
2	tablespoons flour
	Milk
1 1/2	cups cooked rice
2	pounds fresh spinach (or 10 ounces frozen spinach)
2/3	cup grated Parmesan cheese
	Salt and pepper to taste

Preheat oven to 425°. Grate, salt and drain zucchini. Reserve juices. Saute onion and garlic in oil and cook until tender. Add zucchini. Stir in flour. Add enough milk to zucchini juices to measure 1 1/2 cups. Stir into zucchini mixture. Cook and stir until thickened. Add cooked rice, spinach, all but 2 tablespoons cheese, salt and pepper. Turn into baking dish. Sprinkle with remaining cheese. Bake about 30 minutes or until bubbly and lightly browned. ELLA M. ALLEN

PASTA, RICE AND POTATOES

Cheese Soufflé

1	cup cold cooked rice
3	eggs, separated
1/4	pound cheddar cheese, shredded
2	tablespoons soft margarine
1/2	cup milk
	Pinch salt

Preheat oven to 300°. Beat egg whites until stiff. Combine yolks, rice, cheese, margarine and milk. Fold in egg whites. Put in greased baking dish. Bake 45 minutes. Can be doubled easily. (4 servings) *"Different and delicious."* CATHERINE MCDOWELL

Mexican Bean and Rice Casserole

1	box Spanish rice (or 1 cup regular rice with one package of taco seasonings)
1	green pepper, diced
1	onion, diced
1	package frozen corn
1	cup shredded mild cheese
1	can chili beans, Texas beans or kidney beans
	Bread crumbs or wheat germ, for topping

Preheat oven to 350°. Cook the rice. Stir-fry green peppers and onions. Mix together rice, green pepper and onions with remaining ingredients. Spoon into baking dish and sprinkle bread crumbs on top. Bake 30 minutes, uncovered. *"You may substitute peas or broccoli."*
CINDY PINKHAM

Wild Rice Summer Breakfast

1	cup wild rice, uncooked
21/2	cups water
1/2	teaspoon salt
	Fresh blueberries, raspberries or strawberries
	Skim milk (or plain yogurt or light cream)
	Sugar to taste

The night before, cook wild rice in salted water until flaky. Cool and refrigerate overnight. Serve rice in cereal bowls topped with fresh berries, milk and sugar. (4-6 servings) JANET GILSDORF

98

Wild Rice and Apples

11/2 cups wild rice, washed thoroughly
3 cups chicken broth
11/2 cups dry white wine
3 Delicious apples, peeled and sliced thinly*
1/3 cup butter or margarine
2 tablespoons brandy, optional (good for serving this dish with a flourish)

Preheat oven to 400°. Put rice, broth and wine in a buttered 11/2-2 quart baking dish. Cover and bake one hour until rice is tender. Sauté apples in butter until soft but not mushy. Add apples to rice mixture. Fork stir the rice. Add brandy and ignite, if using, and serve.

*COOK'S TIP: You may substitute grapes, toasted almonds, mushrooms, or cooked peas for the apples. BRIDGET MCGILLICUDDY

Pistachio Rice Pudding (Kheer)

4 cups half-and-half cream
1/2 cup long grain rice
1/2 teaspoon powdered cardamom
3 tablespoons sugar
1/2 cup chopped pistachios (don't use red-dyed variety)
1/4 cup golden raisins
2 teaspoons rosewater

Combine all ingredients except rosewater in a heavy saucepan. Cook over low heat until rice is soft and mixture is thick, 45 minutes to 1 hour. Stir frequently to prevent burning. Remove from heat and add rosewater. Transfer to serving bowl and refrigerate at least 3-4 hours. *"May be made several days ahead."* JANET GILSDORF

Sweet Potatoes with Apricots

21/2   pounds sweet potatoes, peeled and cut into 1/2-inch slices
1/4   cup packed dried apricots, chopped
2   tablespoons butter
        Salt and pepper to taste

Steam sweet potatoes and apricots together, about 20 minutes. Puree in a food processor with butter, salt and pepper until smooth. *"Serve like mashed potatoes with butter."* NANCY LIVERMORE

Rosemary-Scented Potato Pie

1 0   Idaho baking potatoes, unpeeled
4   cloves garlic, minced
4   shallots, chopped
3   tablespoons chopped parsley
1   tablespoon minced fresh rosemary
4   tablespoons freshly-grated Parmesan cheese
1   cup shredded low-fat Mozzarella cheese
1   can chicken broth
        Salt to taste
        Coarsely-ground pepper to taste

Preheat oven to 350°. Slice potatoes into 1/8-inch slices in food processor. Coat 12-inch round baking dish with oil. Slightly overlap potato slices in a spiral to cover bottom of dish. Combine garlic, shallots, parsley, rosemary and cheeses in a small mixing bowl. Season with salt and pepper. Sprinkle about a third of the mixture over potatoes lining baking dish. Continue to layer potatoes and mixture. Cover with chicken broth and bake 45 minutes or until potatoes are firm. Cut into 12 wedges and serve. (12 servings) *"The unpeeled potatoes add color and vitamins."*

JANET GILSDORF

Potato Bake au Gratin

1	2-pound bag frozen hash brown potatoes, thawed
1/2	cup margarine or butter, melted
1	can cream of chicken soup, undiluted
1	pint sour cream
11/2	cups shredded cheddar cheese
2	cups crushed cornflakes

Preheat oven to 350°. Mix all ingredients together, except crushed cornflakes. Place in 3-quart baking dish. Top with cornflakes. Bake 1 hour and 15 minutes. (12-18 servings) DENISE BROOKS

Potato-Spinach Casserole

1 2	large potatoes, peeled
11/2	cups sour cream
2	teaspoons sugar
	Pepper to taste
3/4	cup (11/2 sticks) margarine
3 - 4	teaspoons salt
4	tablespoons chopped chives
2	9-ounce packages frozen chopped spinach (cooked and squeezed dry)
3	teaspoons dill
2	cups shredded cheddar cheese

Cook and mash potatoes. Preheat oven to 350°. Add sour cream, sugar, salt, pepper and margarine. Add chives, cooked spinach and dill. Place potato-spinach mixture into greased 9 x 12-inch baking dish. Top with shredded cheese. Bake 30 minutes or until hot. (10-12 servings) *"This can be made the day before serving."* MARIEL PECK

PASTA, RICE AND POTATOES

Baked Potato Slims

4	medium potatoes, cut into 1/2-inch strips
1/4	cup water
2	tablespoons vegetable oil
1/2	teaspoon Tabasco sauce
1/4	cup grated Romano or Parmesan cheese
1	envelope Shake 'n Bake seasoned coating mix for chicken

Preheat oven to 400°. Using a plastic bag, combine potatoes, water, oil and Tabasco. Close bag and shake potatoes until evenly coated. Shake off excess liquid. In another bag, combine cheese with coating mix. Add potato strips, a handful at a time and coat evenly. Bake potatoes in a single layer on a cookie sheet lined with foil, 30-35 minutes. *"You may leave the skins on or off."* ANN BETZ

Fast and Easy Potato Skins

1/2	cup mayonnaise
2	tablespoons grated Parmesan cheese
2	teaspoons grated onions
1	box Keebler potato skin snacks

Mix mayonnaise, cheese and onions together. Spread potato skin snacks with mixture. Place on ungreased cookie sheet. Broil until browned and bubbly. (Be careful, it burns easily.) Serve immediately or will loose crispness. (Enough for 18-20 snacks) ROBERTA LAPIDES

Onion-Roasted Potatoes

1	envelope Lipton onion soup mix
2	pounds potatoes, cut into large chunks
1/3	cup olive or vegetable oil
	Chopped parsley, optional

Preheat oven to 450°. In a large plastic bag, add all ingredients. Close bag and shake until potatoes are evenly coated. Empty potatoes into shallow baking or roasting pan. Bake, stirring occasionally, 40 minutes or until potatoes are tender and golden brown. Garnish with chopped parsley. (8 servings) ANN BETZ

Breads

BREADS

Amish Friendship Starter

1 cup sugar, 1 cup milk, 1 cup flour

Combine ingredients in a large, glass or plastic container. Cover lightly. If the bowl has a lid, leave it ajar. Or, place a piece of cheesecloth over the container and secure it with a rubberband. Store at room temperature. Stir every day for 17 days. On day 18, do nothing. On days 19, 20, and 21, stir. On day 22, stir and add 1 cup flour, 1 cup sugar and 1 cup milk. Stir again. On days 23, 24, 25 and 26, stir. On day 27, add 1 cup flour, 1 cup sugar and 1 cup milk; stir. You should have about 4 cups of starter. Give 1 cup each to two friends and keep the remaining 2 cups for yourself. Use one in the Amish Friendship Bread recipe and use the other to keep the starter going. When you give away the starter, include these instructions.

COOK'S TIPS: Don't look for yeast, because this recipe doesn't contain any. Don't refrigerate the mixture. The lactic acid acts as a natural preservative, and harmful bacteria will not grow. Also, don't stir the mixture with a metal spoon. Use a wooden or plastic spoon.

Amish Friendship Bread

Day 1: The day you receive your starter - do nothing. Day 2, stir. Day 3, stir. Day 4, stir. Day 5, stir and add 1 cup flour, 1 cup sugar, 1 cup milk. Day 6, stir. Day 7, stir. Day 8, stir. Day 9, stir. Day 10, add: 1 cup flour, 1 cup sugar, 1 cup milk. Stir, then pour into 3 one-cup containers and give to 2 friends with these instructions. Keep one cup for yourself as a new starter, and begin at Day 1 again. (Or if you are tired of stirring, give all 3 cups away!)

To the remaining 2 cups batter, add:

2/3	**cup oil**
3	**eggs**
2	**cups flour**
1	**cup sugar**
1/2	**teaspoon vanilla**
1 1/4	**teaspoons baking powder**
1/2	**teaspoon cinnamon**
1/2	**teaspoon salt**
1/2	**teaspoon baking soda**
1/2-1	**cup apples, nuts, dates, raisins, bananas or pumpkin**

Preheat oven to 350°. Grease and sugar 2 loaf pans. Bake bread 50-60 minutes for large loaves, 40-50 minutes for small loaves. Cool 10 minutes and remove from pans. (Yields 2 loaves) LIZ BARKER

English Muffin Cheese Pizza

Take English muffin, cut in half. Spread tomato sauce on 1 slice of muffin with spoon. Put 1 slice of Mozzarella cheese on top. Put in oven for about 10 minutes until cheese melts. Then you eat it. MICHAEL, AGE 8

Killer Bread

1	cup mayonnaise
1	cup freshly-grated Parmesan cheese (about 3 ounces)
1 1/2	teaspoons minced garlic
	Butter
1	pound round sourdough bread, halved horizontally
2	tablespoons finely-chopped basil (or 2 teaspoons dried)

Preheat broiler. Mix mayonnaise, Parmesan and garlic in large bowl to blend. Butter bread halves and place on baking sheet. Broil until crisp and brown. Spread Parmesan mixture over cut sides of bread. Broil until top is puffed and golden brown. Sprinkle with chopped basil. Cut bread into wedges and serve warm. JANET GILSDORF

Swiss Cheese Bread (Gougere)

1	cup milk
1/4	cup butter
1/2	teaspoon salt
	Dash pepper
1	cup flour, unsifted
4	eggs
1	cup shredded Swiss cheese

Preheat oven to 375°. Heat milk and butter in heavy saucepan and add salt and pepper. Bring to a full boil; add flour all at once, stirring over medium heat, about 2 minutes, or until mixture leaves sides of pan and forms a ball. Remove pan from heat; by hand, beat in eggs, one at a time until mixture is smooth and well blended. Beat in 1/2 cup of cheese. Divide dough into 8 equal portions with a spoon and place mounds of dough in a circle on a baking sheet, with each mound touching the next one. Sprinkle remaining 1/2 cup cheese over all. Bake about 55 minutes or until puffs are lightly browned and crisp. (Makes 8 puffs) JANET GILSDORF

Dill Bread

```
2        cups grated Mozzarella
11/3     cups mayonnaise
1/2      teaspoon onion powder
1/2      teaspoon garlic powder
1/2      teaspoon dill
6        hoagie buns, split and cut in two
```

Preheat oven to 350°. Mix first five ingredients together. Spread on hoagie buns. Bake 25 minutes. (Makes 24 pieces) *"Extremely easy and always a popular addition to the menu."* MARY BRANDAU

Irish Dill Soda Bread

```
21/3     cups flour
2        cups whole wheat flour
1        teaspoon baking soda
3/4      teaspoon baking powder
2        tablespoons sugar
1/2      teaspoon dry dill
2        tablespoons margarine
12/3     cups buttermilk
1/3      cup raisins
```

Preheat oven to 375°. Blend everything except 1/3 cup flour, buttermilk and raisins in food processor. Slowly drizzle in buttermilk while running processor until mixture is too sticky to run. Turn into bowl and knead with 1/3 cup additional flour. Knead in raisins and make into round shape. Butter round 8-inch pan. Place dough in pan and flatten (1-2 inches high). Bake 40 minutes. Freezes well. CAROLINE BLANE

Herbed Buttermilk Biscuits

2	cups flour, unsifted
21/2	teaspoons baking powder
1/4	teaspoon salt
1/2	teaspoon soda
1	tablespoon sugar
2	tablespoons minced parsley (or green onion)
1/3	cup butter
3/4	cup buttermilk

Preheat oven to 400°. In a food processor, stir together flour, baking powder, salt, soda, sugar and parsley. Cut butter into chunks and process into flour mixture until the texture of cornmeal. Pour in buttermilk and process a couple turns until milk is barely mixed in. Turn dough onto floured board and shape into a ball. Flatten ball until circle of dough is 3/4-inch thick. Cut biscuits with biscuit cutter and place on ungreased baking sheet. Bake 15 minutes or until golden brown. Serve directly from oven with butter and honey. (Makes about 12 biscuits) JANET GILSDORF

Corn Bread

11/2	cups cornmeal
1/2	cup flour
21/2	teaspoons baking powder
1/2	teaspoon salt
3	tablespoons brown sugar
1	tablespoon maple syrup
1	egg
1/4	cup butter, melted
1/2	cup milk
1/2	cup buttermilk

Preheat oven to 375°. Combine all dry ingredients. Separately, combine remaining ingredients and mix with dry. (Don't overmix.) Bake in a buttered 9-inch pie plate about 30 minutes. Test earlier for doneness.
SUSAN HURWITZ

Hush Puppies

2   cups white cornmeal (water-ground is preferred)
1   teaspoon baking powder
3   tablespoons sugar
1   tablespoon salt
31/2 cups boiling water
1/4   cup butter

Combine cornmeal, baking powder, sugar and salt. Add slowly to boiling water, stirring briskly. As soon as mixture is smooth, remove from heat. Stir in butter. Cool. Form into finger-shaped rolls and fry in 2 inches hot fat (375°) until golden brown. (Makes 3 dozen) *"From a trip to Dixie - the real thing! A good sidedish to serve with dinner."* DOROTHY WARDELL

Tortillas

3/4   cup cornstarch
1   cup milk
1/3   cup cornmeal
2   tablespoons butter, melted
2   eggs
1/2   teaspoon salt

Mix cornstarch and milk to make a smooth paste. Add cornmeal and mix. Add butter and eggs; beat well. Pour into a greased skillet. Cook until thin and brown on both sides. Serve with butter and salt. (Makes 6) *"Hard to stop eating!"* DOROTHY WARDELL

Liberian Bread

6   cups flour
1   teaspoon salt
8   teaspoons baking powder
1   cup sugar
1   cup cooking oil
3   cups milk

Preheat oven to 350°. Mix all dry ingredients in a large bowl. Mix in oil and milk. Pour into greased and floured 9 x 13-inch pan. Bake 45 minutes. Eat with butter and honey. (12 servings) *"We made this at school and it was delicious!"* LOUISA JENISTA (of Mrs. Van Alstine's 2nd grade class at Mack School, Ann Arbor)

Yuletide Cranberry Loaf

2	cups flour
1/2	teaspoon salt
11/2	teaspoons baking powder
1/2	teaspoon baking soda
1	cup sugar
1/4	cup margarine, melted
1/2	cup orange juice
1	egg, well beaten
1	tablespoon grated orange rind
11/2	cups fresh cranberries, halved
3/4	cup chopped nuts

Preheat oven to 350°. Combine dry ingredients. Combine juice, egg and margarine; stir just to moisten. Mix dry ingredients with juice-egg mixture. Stir in berries and nuts. Spoon into greased and floured loaf pan. Bake 1 hour. (Makes 1 loaf) MARGIE VAN METER

Mom's Mango Bread

2	cups flour
2	teaspoons baking soda
1/2	teaspoon salt
1	teaspoon cinnamon
11/2	cups sugar
1/2	cup shredded coconut
1/2	cup chopped nuts
2	cups chopped mangoes
3/4	cup vegetable oil
3	eggs, beaten
2	teaspoons vanilla

Preheat oven to 350°. Sift together flour, soda, salt and cinnamon. Stir in sugar, coconut and nuts. Add remaining ingredients and mix well. Pour into 3 greased and floured 71/2 x 31/2-inch pans. Bake 1 hour and 15 minutes or until done. (Makes 3 small loaves) *Mango season in Hawaii is like zucchini season in Michigan. This recipe is one of the ways my mother copes with the superabundance.* MARIAN OSHIRO

Parmesan Honor Rolls

1	packet dried yeast
1/4	cup warm water
1	cup soft margarine
3	cups sifted flour
2	eggs, slightly beaten
1	cup lukewarm, scalded milk*
1/4	cup sugar
1	teaspoon salt
11/2-2	cups sifted flour
1/3	cup butter, melted
3	tablespoons grated Parmesan cheese

Dissolve yeast in warm water. Cut margarine into flour until particles are the size of large peas. Add eggs, scalded milk, sugar, salt and yeast and mix well. Gradually add remaining flour to form a stiff dough. (You will probably have to abandon the mixer and use a large spoon at this point.) Cover and chill 2-3 hours or overnight.

To shape rolls: Divide dough into 5 parts. Roll out 1 part on floured surface to a 9-inch circle. Brush each with 1-2 tablespoons melted butter and sprinkle with Parmesan cheese. Cut into 8 pie-shaped wedges. Starting at wide end, roll each wedge to the point. Place point-side down on a greased baking sheet. Let rise in a warm place (see tip below) until light (1 hour). Preheat oven to 375°. Bake 15-18 minutes. You can freeze rolls unbaked. Freeze them on the cookie sheet and then put into a baggie. When you are ready to bake them, put on a greased cookie sheet and let them rise (takes longer).

*COOK'S TIP: To scald, bring milk just to a simmer, not a boil; a film will form on top. A warm place for the dough to rise could be your oven. If you have a gas oven, the pilot light creates enough warmth. For an electric oven, put a large saucepan of boiling water in the oven along with the rolls. *"These are my favorite dinner rolls and they don't require kneading, which is a big plus. You don't have to serve with butter because they're already buttered."* MARJORIE BEST

Ma Ferri's Soft German Pretzels

1	package dry yeast
2	tablespoons warm water
1	teaspoon sugar
1	cup lukewarm water
1	egg, beaten
2	tablespoons sugar
1/4	cup margarine, melted
1/2	teaspoon salt
4	cups flour
1	quart water
2	tablespoons granulated lye
1/2	cup kosher salt

Dissolve yeast in 2 tablespoons warm water and sugar. When fluffy, add 1 cup lukewarm water, egg, sugar, margarine, salt and flour. Turn out on floured board and knead until smooth. Let rise 1/2 hour. Cut off small portions; roll in rope-like fashion with hands to 1/2-inch thickness and about 15 inches long. (If sticky, flour hands and/or surface.) Form into pretzel shape. Place right side down on cloth and let rise about 20 minutes. Have ready 1 quart water in a granite, glass or iron saucepan. Add granulated lye and heat to simmering. Preheat oven to 475°. Drop pretzels one at a time into solution. Let remain 2-3 seconds only. With slotted stainless steel spatula, skim out and turn right side up onto baking sheet that has been covered with aluminum foil. Sprinkle with kosher salt. Bake 7-8 minutes. (Makes about 20 pretzels) *"Best if eaten right out of the oven!"*

MIDGE WAKEFIELD

113

Cheddar Cheese Bread

2   cups lukewarm water
11/2 ounces dried yeast
2   ounces (1/4 cup) honey
11/2 cups heated milk
6   cups (approximately) unbleached white flour
4   cups shredded cheddar cheese
3/4   tablespoon salt
1   egg, beaten

Mix water and yeast in food processor and let proof 3-5 minutes. Add honey and milk that has been scalded and cooled. Add half the flour, cheese and salt; mix. Add remaining flour until dough is "right". May need more or less, depending on the humidity. Mix until well blended. Place dough in an oiled bowl and cover with a damp cloth. Let rise until double in bulk. Punch down and divide dough into three equal pieces. Preheat oven to 350°. Place each loaf into a well-oiled loaf pan, cover with a damp cloth and let rise again. Brush tops of loaves with beaten egg. Bake for 1 hour. (Makes 3 loaves) JANET GILSDORF

Helen's French Bread

3/4   cup warm water (as hot as one can comfortably hold one's finger in)
1   tablespoon yeast
1   teaspoon sugar
1/2   teaspoon salt
11/2 cups flour (or as much as needed)
      Olive oil (about 2 tablespoons)

Put yeast in water with sugar and let bubble. Add salt to flour and stir into yeast mixture to form dough. Place dough onto floured board and knead until smooth and not sticky, adding more flour as needed. Oil a large bowl; place dough in bowl, turning it so it is covered with oil; let rise until doubled. Preheat oven to 400°. Gently punch down dough and roll into a long sausage shape. Place in French bread pan or on a cookie sheet. (If a cookie sheet is used, sprinkle it with cornmeal.) Let rise until almost doubled. Bake 15-20 minutes or until slightly golden on top. (Makes 1 loaf) "*Very Easy.*"

COOK'S TIP: Recipe is easily multiplied, but do not add more than 2 tablespoons sugar and 11/2 teaspoons salt. HELEN WELFORD

Apple Streusel Muffins

TOPPING:
1/2   cup chopped walnuts
1/4   cup flour
3   tablespoons sugar
2   tablespoons butter, room temperature
1/4   teaspoon ground cinnamon

Preheat oven to 375°. Grease muffin cups or use foil baking cups. Put streusel topping ingredients into a medium-size bowl. Mix with a fork, then crumble with fingers until mixture looks like chopped walnuts.

BATTER:
11/2   cups flour
1/2   cup sugar
2   teaspoons baking powder
1   teaspoon ground cinnamon
1/4   teaspoon ground allspice
1/4   teaspoon baking soda
1/4   teaspoon salt
2   large eggs
1   cup sour cream
1/4   cup (1/2 stick) butter, melted
1   cup diced, unpeeled apple (preferably Granny Smith)

To make muffin batter, mix flour, sugar, baking powder, cinnamon, allspice, baking soda and salt in a large bowl. Break eggs into another bowl. Add sour cream and melted butter and whisk until well blended. Stir in diced apple. Pour egg mixture over flour mixture and fold in just until dry ingredients are moistened. Scoop batter into muffin cups. Top each muffin with about 2 teaspoons streusel topping. Bake 20-25 minutes or until browned. (A toothpick inserted into the center should come out clean.) Remove from pans and let cool 1 hour before serving.

ROXANNE SCHIELKE

Beer Muffins

4   cups Bisquick or Jiffy Mix
5   tablespoons sugar
1   12-ounce can or bottle beer, chilled

Preheat oven to 350°. In large bowl, combine Bisquick and sugar; mix well. Gradually add beer and stir until well blended. Divide batter equally into well-greased muffin tins. Bake 40-45 minutes or until large, puffy and lightly browned on top. (Makes 12 muffins) SALLY CAYLEY

Whole Grain Blueberry Apple Muffins

11/2	cups flour
1/2	cup oat bran
1/2	cup wheat bran (or Allbran)
1/2	cup whole wheat flour
1	tablespoon baking powder
2	teaspoons cinnamon
1/2	cup brown sugar
1	cup chunky applesauce
1	cup apple cider (or juice)
2	tablespoons canola oil
2	egg whites
1	cup blueberries (fresh or frozen)

Preheat oven to 400°. Combine dry ingredients. Combine all liquid ingredients and add them to the dry; mix well. Fold in blueberries. Pour batter into papered muffin cups.

TOPPING:

2	tablespoons oatmeal
1	tablespoon brown sugar

Mix topping ingredients together and sprinkle on top of muffins. Bake for approximately 20 minutes or until done. (Makes 12 muffins) Reprinted with permission, MEDSPORT, HIGH FIT - LOW FAT™ THE REGENTS OF THE UNIVERSITY OF MICHIGAN

Strawberry-Pecan Muffins

3/4	cup whole wheat flour
3/4	cup all-purpose flour
1/2	teaspoon baking powder
1/2	teaspoon baking soda
1/2	teaspoon cinnamon
1/2	cup chopped pecans
1/2	brown sugar
1	egg
1	cup buttermilk
1/4	cup corn oil
1	teaspoon vanilla
11/4	cups coarsely-chopped strawberries

Preheat oven to 375°. Combine all dry ingredients. In another bowl, combine egg, buttermilk, oil and vanilla. Add flour mixture to wet mixture and mix gently until all is moistened. Gently fold in strawberries. Pour into muffin tins and bake 20-25 minutes. (Makes 1 dozen) SUSAN HURWITZ

Tradewind Muffins

1	20-ounce can crushed pineapple (drain and reserve syrup)
1/2	cup sliced almonds
2	cups flour
1	teaspoon soda
1	teaspoon salt
1	3-ounce package cream cheese, room temperature
1	cup sugar
2	teaspoons vanilla
1	large egg, beaten
1/2	cup sour cream

GLAZE:

1	tablespoon soft margarine
1	cup sifted powdered sugar
2	tablespoons syrup from pineapple

Preheat oven to 350°. Heavily grease muffin pans and sprinkle with almonds. Sift together flour, soda and salt. In separate bowl, beat cream cheese, sugar, and vanilla together until smooth. Blend in egg. Add flour mixture alternately with sour cream. Fold in drained pineapple. Spoon into prepared muffin pans. Bake 18 minutes or until muffins are brown and test done. Remove from oven and let stand in pans 5-10 minutes. Turn out onto wire rack. Combine glaze ingredients and blend until smooth. Spread glaze over warm muffins. (Makes 30 muffins)

JOAN DOOP

Applesauce-Raisin Muffins

2	cups crushed Cheerios cereal
1 1/4	cups flour
1/3	cup packed brown sugar
1	teaspoon cinnamon
1	teaspoon baking powder
3/4	teaspoon baking soda
1	cup applesauce
1/3	cup skim milk
1/3	cup raisins
3	tablespoons vegetable oil
1	egg white

Preheat oven to 400°. Grease bottoms only of 12 muffin cups. Put Cheerios in a Ziplock bag; seal. Hand the kids toy hammers and let them crush cereal (makes about 1 cup crushed). Mix dry ingredients in a large bowl. Stir in remaining ingredients just until moistened. Pour into muffin cups. Bake 18-22 minutes. (Makes 1 dozen) *"Great fun for kids!"*

Michigan Dried Cherry and Oatmeal Scones

13/4	cups flour
1/3	cup sugar
11/2	teaspoons baking powder
3/4	teaspoon baking soda
1/2	teaspoon salt
3/4	cup unsalted butter, chilled and cut into pieces
11/3	cups rolled oats
1/2	cup Michigan dried cherries
10	tablespoons chilled buttermilk

Preheat oven to 375°. Combine first 5 ingredients in food processor. Add butter and cut in until mixture resembles fine meal. Transfer to large bowl. Mix in oats and cherries. Add buttermilk and mix just until dough comes together, adding more buttermilk if necessary. Turn dough onto floured surface. Pat into round shape (approximately 1-inch thick). Cut into 6-8 wedges and transfer wedges to a cookie sheet (keeping wedges separated). Bake until brown, about 30 minutes, and serve immediately.
(Makes 6-8 scones) JANET GILSDORF

Breakfast Scones

2	cups flour
1/2	cup sugar
2	teaspoons cream of tartar
1	teaspoon baking soda
1/2-3/4	teaspoon salt
1/2	cup margarine
1/2	cup raisins or chopped dates
3	eggs, slightly beaten

Preheat oven to 400°. Sift flour with sugar, cream of tartar, baking soda and salt. Cut margarine into flour mixture until it resembles fine bread crumbs. Add raisins and 2 eggs; mix with fork until mixture forms a ball. Roll or pat to 1/2-2/3 inches thick on lightly-floured board. Cut with biscuit cutter and place on greased baking sheet. Brush tops with remaining egg. Bake 15 minutes.

COOK'S TIP: These are good hot or cold. Use margarine instead of butter, less salt and Eggbeaters instead of real egg to lower the sodium content and calories. GAIL OHANIAN

Raisin Scones

2	cups flour
1	tablespoon baking powder
1/2	teaspoon baking soda
1/2	cup (1 stick) margarine
2	tablespoons sour cream
1/2	cup milk
1/2	cup raisins

Preheat oven to 400°. Mix flour, baking powder, soda and margarine in food processor until margarine is in tiny lumps and fairly well distributed (about 30 seconds). Add sour cream. Turn processor on and drizzle in milk. Turn into floured bowl or surface and fold in raisins. Pat into round 1-inch thick disc shape. Place in buttered pan. Bake 25-30 minutes. (Makes 4 scones) CAROLINE BLANE

Blueberry Coffee Cake

1	cup butter
2	cups plus 2 teaspoons sugar
3	eggs
1	cup sour cream
2	teaspoons vanilla
2	cups flour
1	teaspoon baking powder
1/2	teaspoon salt
1	teaspoon cinnamon
1	cup chopped pecans (optional)
11/2	cups blueberries

Preheat oven to 350°. Cream butter and 2 cups sugar; beat until fluffy. Add eggs and beat well. Fold in sour cream and vanilla. Add flour, baking powder and salt. In separate bowl, combine rest of sugar, cinnamon and nuts. Place one-third of batter in well-greased and floured Bundt pan. Layer with sugar and cinnamon mixture, then berries. Continue to alternate layers until batter and sugar/cinnamon mixture has been used. If a Bundt pan is used, the top layer should be the batter. Bake 1 hour and 15 minutes. MARTHA JAMES

119

Cranberry Kuchen

1	egg, beaten
1/2	cup sugar
1/2	cup milk
2	tablespoons shortening, melted
1	cup flour
2	teaspoons salt
2	teaspoons baking powder
1/2	pound (2 cups) cranberries (or 1 can whole berry sauce)
3/4	cup flour
1/2	cup sugar
3	tablespoons butter

Preheat oven to 375°. Combine egg, sugar, milk and shortening. Add flour, salt and baking powder. Beat until blended. Pour into greased 8-inch baking dish. Chop berries coarsely and sprinkle over batter, adding all the juice. Mix the last 3 ingredients until crumbly and sprinkle over. Bake about 35 minutes or until golden brown. May be served cool or reheated. (4-6 servings) *"I double or triple this recipe, and eat half of it myself!"* DOROTHY WARDELL

Raspberry Kuchen

CRUST:

1	cup flour
1/4	teaspoon salt
2	tablespoons sugar
1/2	cup butter
1	tablespoon vinegar

FILLING:

2/3	cup sugar
2	tablespoons flour
1/4	teaspoon cinnamon
4	cups fresh or frozen raspberries (reserve 1 cup for topping)
	Powdered sugar

Preheat oven to 400°. Combine flour, salt and sugar. Work in butter with fingers. Mix in vinegar. Press into springform pan; set aside. Combine sugar, flour and cinnamon. Add 3 cups berries and pour mixture onto crust. Bake 1 hour. When done, spread 1 cup uncooked berries on top. Dust with powdered sugar. (8-10 servings) *"May substitute blueberries."*
EILEEN MOLLEN

Swedish Kringle

CRUST:
1	cup flour
1/2	cup butter
2	tablespoons water

KRINGLE:
1	cup water
1/2	cup butter
1	cup flour
3	eggs
1/2	tablespoon almond extract

Preheat oven to 350°. Mix crust ingredients together until smooth and pat into 8 x 8-inch greased pan. To make Kringle: Put water and butter in saucepan; heat to boiling. As you remove from heat, add flour and stir until smooth. Stir in eggs, one at a time, beating well after each one. Add almond extract. Spread this mixture on top of crust. Bake 55-60 minutes; cool.

FROSTING:
1	cup powdered sugar
1	teaspoon butter
1/2	teaspoon almond extract
	Milk

Blend powdered sugar, butter and extract. Add enough milk to make a spreadable consistency. Frost cooled cake. *"Recipe can be doubled to cover a jelly roll pan."* NANCY FROST COLLINS

Shaker Plum Coffee Cake

3/4	cup sugar
1/4	cup shortening
1	egg
1/2	cup milk
11/2	cups flour
2	teaspoons baking powder
1/2	teaspoon salt
6	plums, pitted and sliced

TOPPING:

1/2	cup packed brown sugar
3	tablespoons flour
1	teaspoon cinnamon
3	tablespoons butter or margarine, melted
1/2	cup chopped nuts

Preheat oven to 375°. In a large bowl, cream sugar, shortening and egg until fluffy. Stir in milk. Sift flour with baking powder and salt. Beat into creamed mixture. Spread batter into greased 9-inch square pan. Top with rows of plum slices. Combine brown sugar, flour, cinnamon, butter and nuts; mix with fingers until crumbly. Sprinkle crumbs over plums. Bake 35 minutes or until done. Cut into squares; serve warm.

KATHERINE KERSEY

Cream Cheese Coffee Cake

2	packages refrigerated crescent rolls
2	8-ounce packages cream cheese, room temperature
1	egg yolk
1	cup sugar
1	teaspoon vanilla
1/4	cup sugar
1/2	cup chopped nuts
1	teaspoon cinnamon

Preheat oven to 350°. Lay one package crescent rolls in bottom of buttered 9 x 13-inch baking dish. Combine cream cheese, egg yolk, 1 cup sugar and vanilla; spread on rolls. Top with second package of rolls. Sprinkle 1/4 cup sugar, nuts and cinnamon mixture on top. Bake 30-35 minutes.

TOPPING:

11/2	cups powdered sugar
4	tablespoons milk

Whisk powdered sugar and milk together until smooth. Pour over top of cake. NANCY FROST COLLINS

Lemon Coffee Cake

3	cups flour
2	cups sugar
1/4	cup poppy seeds
1	cup buttermilk*
4	eggs
1/2	teaspoon baking soda
1/2	teaspoon baking powder
1/2	teaspoon salt
4	teaspoons grated lemon peel
1/2	teaspoon vanilla

GLAZE:

1	cup powdered sugar
1-2	tablespoons lemon juice

Preheat oven to 325°. In large mixer bowl, combine all ingredients. Beat at low speed scraping bowl often until all ingredients are moistened. Beat at high speed, scraping bowl often, until smooth, 1-2 minutes. Pour into greased and floured 12-cup Bundt pan or 10-inch tube pan. Bake 55-65 minutes until done. Cool 10 minutes; remove from pan. Cool completely. In small bowl, blend together powdered sugar and lemon juice until smooth. Drizzle over cake.

*COOK'S TIP: 1 tablespoon vinegar plus enough milk to equal 1 cup can be substituted for 1 cup buttermilk. KATHERINE KERSEY

Sour Cream Coffee Cake

1	cup butter or margarine
2	cups sugar
1	teaspoon vanilla
2	eggs, beaten
1	cup sour cream (or plain yogurt)
2	cups flour
1	teaspoon baking powder
1/2	teaspoon salt

TOPPING:

1/2	cup brown sugar
1	teaspoon cinnamon
1/2	cup chopped nuts

Preheat oven to 350°. Cream together butter, sugar and vanilla. Add eggs. and sour cream. Add dry ingredients; mix. Pour into greased Bundt pan. Sprinkle topping over batter. Bake 1 hour. MARTHA JAMES AND LISA STOCK

Best-Ever Banana Bread

2	ripe medium bananas, mashed
2	eggs
13/4	cups flour
11/2	cups sugar
1	cup chopped walnuts
1/2	cup vegetable oil
1/4	cup plus 1 tablespoon buttermilk
1	teaspoon baking soda
1	teaspoon vanilla
1/2	teaspoon salt

Preheat oven to 325°. Grease and flour 9 x 5-inch loaf pan. Combine all ingredients in large bowl and mix well. Transfer to prepared pan. Bake until top is golden brown and splits slightly (about 1 hour and 20 minutes). Do not double recipe. (Makes 1 loaf) CHRIS IMAZUMI-O'CONNOR

Blueberry Bread with Cream Cheese Filling

FILLING:

1	8-ounce package cream cheese, room temperature
1/3	cup sugar
1	tablespoon flour
1	egg

Preheat oven to 350°. In a small bowl, combine cream cheese, sugar and flour. Beat in one egg. Set aside.

BREAD:

1	egg, slightly beaten
1/2	cup orange juice
1/4	cup water
1	13-ounce blueberry muffin mix
1	teaspoon grated orange rind
1	cup chopped nuts (optional)

In another bowl, beat the other egg and add orange juice and water. Add bread mix and stir until moistened. Add nuts and orange peel. Pour 2/3 of batter into greased loaf pan. Pour cream cheese mixture over batter. Spoon rest of batter over top. Bake 45-60 minutes or until a toothpick comes out clean. Cool 10 minutes. Remove from pan and continue cooling on cake rack. Wrap in foil and keep refrigerated. LIZ BARKER

Pumpkin Bread

3	cups flour
1	teaspoon baking soda
1	teaspoon salt
3	teaspoons cinnamon
2	cups sugar
2	cups canned pumpkin
4	eggs, beaten
11/2	cups oil (or melted shortening)
1/2	cup chopped nuts

Preheat oven to 350°. Sift flour, soda, salt, cinnamon and sugar together. Place in large mixing bowl, making a well in the center. In this, add the rest of the ingredients. Stir just until moistened. Pour batter into 2 greased loaf pans and bake 1 hour. (Makes 2 loaves) *"Moist - keeps well. My mother's recipe . . . with me for 25 years, at least!"* SUSAN FLANDERS

Rhubarb Bread

1/3	cup butter, softened
11/4	cups firmly-packed brown sugar
2	eggs
1/4	cup milk
1	teaspoon vanilla
2	cups flour
1/2	teaspoon baking soda
1/2	teaspoon salt
2	teaspoons baking powder
11/2	cups chopped rhubarb
1/2	cup chopped pecans

Preheat oven to 325°. Grease and flour two 71/2 x 31/2-inch loaf pans. In a large bowl, cream butter and sugar. Add eggs, milk and vanilla. Combine flour, baking soda, baking powder and salt. Stir into the mixture. Fold in rhubarb and pecans. Spoon batter into pans. Bake 45-50 minutes. (Makes 2 loaves) SHARON SMITH

Strawberry Bread

3	eggs, beaten
2	cups sugar
1	cup oil
1	tablespoon vanilla
2	cups flour
1	cup oatmeal
1	tablespoon cinnamon
1	teaspoon baking soda
1	teaspoon salt
1/2	teaspoon baking powder
2	cups crushed strawberries
1	cup chopped nuts (if desired)
	Whipped cream (optional)
	Garnish: Whole strawberries

Preheat oven to 350°. Combine eggs, sugar, oil and vanilla. Beat well until light yellow. In a separate bowl, combine remaining ingredients and add to egg mixture. Spread batter in a 9 x 5-inch loaf pan. Spray vegetable oil on pans. Do not fill too full. Bake 1 hour (bread should be "reddish"). It is good "aged" 24 hours and chilled. Can be topped with whipped cream and whole berries. *"Great for teas and luncheons. Good made as muffins also."* MELISSA SNAVELY

Wonderful Zucchini Bread

3	eggs, lightly beaten
21/2	cups sugar
1	cup oil
3	cups flour
3	teaspoons cinnamon
1	teaspoon salt
1	teaspoon baking soda
1	teaspoon baking powder
3	teaspoons vanilla
2	cups grated zucchini
1	cup raisins (optional)
1/2	cup chopped nuts (optional)

Preheat oven to 350°. Mix together eggs, sugar and oil. Combine dry ingredients and add to wet mixture. Fold in grated zucchini, vanilla, nuts and raisins. Pour into 2 greased loaf pans. Bake 1 hour (or until toothpick inserted in center comes out clean). (Makes 2 loaves) AILEEN CLARK

Poppy Seed Bread

3	cups flour
11/2	teaspoons salt
11/2	teaspoons baking powder
21/2	cups sugar
11/2	tablespoons poppy seeds
3	eggs
11/2	cups milk
11/2	cups oil
11/2	teaspoons vanilla
11/2	teaspoons almond flavor
11/2	teaspoons butter flavor

Preheat oven to 350°. Combine all dry ingredients. Mix in eggs, milk, oil and flavorings. Beat 2 minutes. Pour into loaf pans (81/2 x 41/2 inches). Bake 55 minutes. Leave in pans about 10 minutes before removing. Place on a square of tin foil.

GLAZE:

1/2	teaspoon almond flavor
1/2	teaspoon butter flavor
1/2	teaspoon vanilla flavor
1/4	cup orange juice
3/4	cup sugar

Combine all glaze ingredients and mix well. Drizzle on top of bread and down the sides. Wrap tightly in foil and freeze while warm.
(Makes 3 loaves) NANCY GOLDSTEIN

Ginger Bread

1/2	cup sugar
1/2	cup butter
1	egg, well beaten
1	cup molasses
2	cups flour
1/2	cup raisins (optional)
1	heaping tablespoon ginger
1	teaspoon baking soda
1	cup boiling water

Preheat oven to 400°. Mix sugar, butter, egg and molasses together in a bowl. In another bowl, mix all dry ingredients. Combine ingredients from both bowls and add boiling water. Grease a loaf pan. Pour batter into pan and bake 1 hour. *"This treasured family recipe passed on by successive wives is attributed to Decima Shubrick Heyward, daughter of Colonel Thomas Heyward of the Continental Army."* LYNN HARRIS

Spicy Green Tomato Bread

2	cups unbleached flour
1	teaspoon baking powder
1	teaspoon baking soda
1/2	teaspoon salt
1/4	teaspoon cloves
1/4	teaspoon allspice
1/4	teaspoon nutmeg
1	teaspoon cinnamon
2	eggs
1	cup brown sugar
1/2	cup oil
1	teaspoon vanilla
1 1/2	cups shredded and drained green tomatoes
1/2	cup coarsely-chopped walnuts
1/2	cup dark raisins

Preheat oven to 350°. Grease and flour a 9 x 5-inch loaf pan. Sift flour, baking powder, baking soda, salt, cloves, allspice, nutmeg and cinnamon together in a bowl. In a separate bowl, beat eggs. Beat brown sugar, oil and vanilla into eggs. Stir green tomatoes and dry ingredients into this mixture. Add walnuts and raisins. Turn into prepared pan. Bake 65 minutes (or until toothpick comes out clean). Cool in pan 5 minutes. Turn out onto wire rack. (Makes 1 loaf) KATHLEEN E. READY

French Toast

Take egg and milk and then you put the egg in and you stir it up. Then you need a pan to put butter in. Take a piece of bread with a fork and put in the egg and then in the pan to cook. Cook for 15 minutes. Then take it out and eat it. COLLEEN, AGE 7

Freezer French Toast

4	eggs
1	cup milk
2	tablespoons sugar
1	teaspoon vanilla
1/4	teaspoon nutmeg
8	slices day-old French bread, cut 3/4-inch thick

Preheat oven to 500°. In a bowl, mix eggs, milk, sugar, vanilla and nutmeg. Place bread slices on a rimmed baking sheet. Pour egg mixture over bread; let stand a few minutes. Turn slices over and let stand until all mixture is absorbed. Freeze, uncovered, until firm; then package airtight and return to freezer. To serve, place desired number of frozen (without thawing) slices on a greased baking sheet. Brush each slice with melted butter. Bake 8 minutes. Turn slices over, brush with melted butter; bake another 10 minutes until nicely browned. Serve topped with powdered sugar, honey or syrup. (4, 2-slice servings) CHRIS IMAZUMI-O'CONNOR

Cottage Cheese Pancakes

1 1/2	cups large curd cottage cheese
1/2	cup dairy sour cream
1/2	teaspoon salt
3	eggs, separated
1	cup sifted all-purpose flour
	Butter or buttered-flavor Crisco

Combine cottage cheese, sour cream, salt and egg yolks in a medium-size bowl. Stir in flour until well mixed. Beat egg whites in a small bowl with an electric mixer until stiff peaks form; fold gently into cottage cheese mixture. Melt butter in a large skillet. Drop cottage cheese mixture by scant 1/3 cupfuls into hot butter (adding more butter if needed). Flatten with pancake turner to make an even thickness. Cook until golden brown on both sides. (Makes 12 four-inch pancakes) *"This is good served with sour cream and fresh strawberries."* JOAN DOOP

Stuffed French Toast

1	8-ounce package cream cheese, room temperature
1	teaspoon vanilla
1/2	cup pecans, chopped
1	16-ounce loaf French bread
4	eggs (or Eggbeaters)
1	cup heavy cream (or low-fat condensed milk)
1/2	teaspoon vanilla
1/2	teaspoon nutmeg
1	12-ounce jar apricot preserves mixed with 1/2 cup orange juice, optional sauce

Mix cream cheese, 1 teaspoon vanilla and pecans until fluffy. Slice bread into 11/4-inch slices and cut a pocket into top of each slice. Fill pocket with 1 tablespoon cream cheese mixture. Gently squeeze pocket together. This can be done ahead and refrigerated overnight or longer. Mix eggs, cream, 1/2 teaspoon vanilla and nutmeg. Dip filled bread into mixture and cook on lightly-greased pan or griddle. If desired, serve with warmed preserves and juice mixture. CHARLOTTE BETZ

Pancakes

First you get a bowl and then you get the flour. Then you put in milk. Then you put in eggs. Then you put in sugar and then you put in melted butter. Then you mix it up. Grease the pan. When ready, put the pancake mix in the pan. Set it on 5°. Let the pancake stay on for 10 minutes. Then it is ready to eat. KRISTINA, AGE 7

131

BREADS

Poultry

POULTRY

Chicken	**135**
Turkey	**160**

Artichoke Chicken

4	chicken breast halves, skinned and boned
1	teaspoon cooking oil
	Juice from 1-2 limes
4	tablespoons butter or margarine
1 1/2	tablespoons fresh dill
1	10-ounce can artichoke hearts, water-packed
	Cooked rice

Cut chicken into bite-size pieces. Sauté chicken in oil, browning all sides. Add juice from limes and cook until done. Add butter and dill, then add artichokes. Heat through and serve over rice. (4 servings) EILEEN MOLLEN

Chicken Bordeaux

1	package chicken parts
6	tablespoons flour
1	teaspoon salt
	Pepper to taste
1/4	cup oil
1/2	cup stewed tomatoes
2	teaspoon sugar
1/2	cup white Bordeaux wine
2	cups sliced fresh mushrooms

Dust chicken parts with a mixture of flour, salt and pepper. Brown dusted chicken in oil. Make a paste from left-over flour mixture, tomatoes and sugar. Add paste to chicken. Add wine and fresh mushrooms and simmer 1 hour. KATHY DUNN FINGER

Chicken Catch-a-Man

1 1/2	pounds of chicken breast, skinned and boned
1	bunch fresh broccoli
1 2	ounces Mozzarella cheese, shredded
2	cans cream of chicken soup
2	cups prepared stuffing (Pepperidge Farm works great)

Boil chicken 1 hour or until done. Preheat oven to 350°. Cook broccoli. Cut chicken and broccoli into bite-size pieces. In a 9 x 13-inch pan, layer chicken on bottom, then broccoli, and then cheese. Repeat layers. Spread both cans of undiluted soup over this mixture. Cover with stuffing. Bake 30 minutes or until bubbly. *"This was a single friend's recipe. It was the only dish she knew how to make and served it to all her dates. It worked! She's been happily married for 8 years!"* SUSAN ENGLAND

Chicken Caruso and Rice

2	whole chicken breasts (11/2 pounds), skinned, boned, cut into strips
	Garlic salt and pepper
3	tablespoons butter or margarine
1	151/2-ounce jar spaghetti sauce (2 cups)
1	teaspoon Italian seasoning
2	cups sliced celery
3	cups hot cooked rice
	Grated Parmesan cheese (optional)

Season chicken with garlic salt and pepper. Sauté in butter about 2 minutes. Stir in spaghetti sauce and Italian seasoning; cover and simmer 10 minutes. Add celery; continue cooking until celery is tender crisp. Serve over beds of fluffy rice. Sprinkle with Parmesan cheese, if desired. (Makes 6 servings) ELLA M. ALLEN

Opulent Chicken

4	whole chicken breasts, deboned (or chicken parts)
	Paprika
	Salt and pepper to taste
1/2	cup butter
1	15-ounce can artichoke hearts
1/2	pound fresh mushrooms, sliced (or canned)
	Pinch tarragon
3	tablespoons flour
1/3	cup sherry
11/2	cups chicken broth
	Cooked rice

Preheat oven to 375°. Cut chicken breasts into pieces; sprinkle with paprika, salt and pepper. Sauté in butter until golden brown. Place chicken in large baking dish and add artichokes. Put mushrooms in the remaining butter left in pan. Season with tarragon and sauté 5 minutes. Whisk in flour gently and add sherry and chicken broth; simmer 5 minutes. Pour sauce over chicken and artichokes. Cover; bake 45 minutes or until tender. Serve over rice. (Makes 4 servings)

DOROTHY HENESSEY AND GRACE BOXER

Tarragon Chicken

4	chicken breasts, skinned and boned
2-3	tablespoons butter or margarine
1	garlic clove, minced
1/2	cup diced onions
2	tablespoons flour
2	tablespoons tomato paste
1 1/2	cups chicken broth
1 1/2	teaspoons tarragon
	Salt and pepper to taste
1	cup sour cream (or plain yogurt)
	Cooked rice or noodles

Sauté chicken breasts in butter until brown. Remove chicken from pan. Sauté garlic and onions in remaining butter. Add flour and tomato paste to form a roux. Add chicken broth and spices. Return chicken to pan of sauce and cook approximately 45 minutes. Remove chicken and add sour cream. Heat through but do not boil. Spoon some of the sauce over the chicken and serve the rest in a bowl. Serve with rice or noodles.

CINDY MEYERS

Crunchy Chicken Imperial

1	pint sour cream
4	tablespoons lemon juice
4	teaspoons Worcestershire sauce
2	teaspoons celery salt
1	teaspoon garlic salt
1/4	teaspoon pepper
6	boneless chicken breasts, cut in half
1	package Pepperidge Farm stuffing mix
1 1/4	cups (2 1/2 sticks) butter or margarine

Combine all ingredients except the chicken, stuffing mix and butter. Dip chicken in mixture and then coat with stuffing mix. Fold in half and place seam side down in buttered baking dish. Refrigerate overnight.

Preheat oven to 350°. Melt butter and pour over chicken. Bake, uncovered, 45 minutes to 1 hour. (10-12 servings) DENISE BROOKS

Chicken with Rosemary and Garlic

1/3	cup olive oil
1	onion, thinly sliced
5	garlic cloves, sliced
2	21/2-pound chickens, cut into pieces
	Salt and pepper
5	tablespoons flour
3/4	cup dry white wine
1	tablespoon tomato paste
1/4	cup chicken stock
1	tablespoon rosemary
	Additional chicken stock

Heat oil in a large Dutch oven over medium heat. Add onions and garlic and sauté until softened, about 5 minutes. Transfer to bowl using slotted spoon. Season chicken with salt and pepper. Dredge in flour; shake off excess. Add half of chicken to Dutch oven and brown well. Transfer to plate. Repeat browning with remaining chicken. Transfer to plate. Increase heat to medium high. Add wine and tomato paste to Dutch oven and bring to boil, scraping up browned bits. Return chicken pieces and onions to pan. Reduce heat to low. Cover and cook 30 minutes, turning chicken occasionally. Add 1/4 cup stock and rosemary. Cover and continue cooking until chicken is tender, turning occasionally, about 20 minutes. Transfer chicken to platter. Pour pan juices into measuring cup. Add enough stock to measure 11/2 cups liquid. Return liquid to pan and bring to boil. Pour juices over chicken. (6 servings)

CHRIS IMAZUMI-O'CONNOR

Roasted Chicken with Tarragon

2	medium onions, sliced thin
2-3	cups carrots, sliced thin
	Olive oil
2	tablespoons tarragon
	Salt and pepper
1	roasting chicken
2	cans chicken broth

Preheat oven to 350°. Sauté onions and carrots in olive oil. Add tarragon, salt and pepper. Stuff chicken with carrot mixture and place in large roasting pan. Pour chicken broth over chicken. Sprinkle with tarragon and salt. Bake, covered, 11/2 hours. Uncover and bake another 1/2 hour to brown. (6-8 servings) CATHERINE MCDOWELL

138

Sautéed Chicken Breasts with Grapes

4	chicken breast halves, skinned and boned (about 1 pound)
1-2	tablespoons peanut oil
1/4	teaspoon salt
	Black pepper
1/2	cup Madeira wine (or cream sherry)
1/4	cup finely-chopped green onions
1/2	teaspoon crushed mustard seeds
1/4	teaspoon thyme
1/4	pound (about 3/4 cup) seedless green grapes, cut in half
2	tablespoons sour cream
2	teaspoons plain low-fat yogurt
1	teaspoon cornstarch, mixed with 1 tablespoon lime juice
1	tablespoon chopped parsley

In a skillet, heat peanut oil and cook chicken breasts until lightly browned on one side, about 4 minutes. Sprinkle with salt and pepper. Cook 3 minutes on second side; place on a platter and set aside. Pour wine in the skillet and simmer until reduced by half, about 3 minutes. Add green onions, mustard seeds and thyme and simmer 2-3 minutes more. Return chicken to pan; reduce heat, add grapes. In a bowl, stir sour cream and yogurt into cornstarch-lime juice mixture and pour into the pan. Simmer mixture until chicken is cooked through. Garnish with parsley and serve immediately. (4 servings) *"Excellent company fare."* ANN BETZ

Chicken Sauté with Raspberry Vinegar

6	chicken breast halves, skinned and boned
	Salt and pepper
1	tablespoon oil
3	tablespoons butter
1	tablespoon minced shallots or onions
3-5	tablespoons raspberry vinegar
2-3	tablespoons water

Sprinkle each side of breasts with salt and pepper. Heat oil and butter in sauté pan. Sauté chicken breasts a few minutes on each side until opaque. Set aside and keep warm. Sprinkle shallots in pan, sauté for a few seconds. Add raspberry vinegar and 2-3 tablespoons water. Stir well to loosen all cooking residue. Cook for one minute, return breasts to pan and continue to cook until done (another 10-15 minutes), turning once. Serve immediately with sauce. (3 or 4 servings) CHRIS IMAZUMI-O'CONNOR

Chicken with Beer

6	slices bacon, cut into 1/2 inch pieces
1	broiler-fryer chicken (21/2 - 3 pounds), cut up
2	cups thinly-sliced onions (2 large)
1/2	cup sliced carrots
1	garlic clove, minced
1	12-ounce can beer
1	tablespoon cider vinegar
1	teaspoon salt
1	teaspoon sugar
1/2	teaspoon thyme
1/4	teaspoon rosemary
1/8	teaspoon pepper
2	tablespoons flour
3	tablespoons water

In a large skillet, cook bacon until crisp. Remove with slotted spoon and drain on paper towels. Add chicken to bacon drippings, and cook until well-browned on all sides, about 5-10 minutes. Remove chicken and set aside. In remaining drippings, add onions, carrots and garlic; sauté, stirring frequently, about 5 minutes or until onions are translucent. Discard excess fat. Stir in beer, vinegar and seasonings and cook over high heat, stirring constantly, until sauce bubbles. Return chicken to skillet. Reduce heat; cover and simmer 30-35 minutes until chicken is tender. Skim off excess fat. Mix flour and water until smooth; stir into skillet. Cook until sauce thickens. Return bacon to skillet and stir. (4 servings)

DORIE SOUTHWELL

Breaded Chicken

You take the chicken out of the freezer and cut off the yukky stuff. Get two eggs and crack them and put them in a bowl. Take the chicken and roll it in the eggs and roll it in the breading. Put it on a pan and cook it for about 5 minutes. Then eat. JUSTINE, AGE 8

Country-Style Chicken Kiev

2/3	cup butter (or margarine), melted
1/2	cup dry bread crumbs
2	tablespoons grated Parmesan cheese
1	teaspoon basil
1	teaspoon oregano
1/2	teaspoon garlic salt
2	chicken breasts, halved, skinned and boned (about 11/2 pounds)
1/4	cup dry white wine
1/4	cup chopped green onions
1/4	cup chopped parsley
1/4	teaspoon salt

Preheat oven to 375° Melt butter. In a small bowl, combine crumbs, cheese and spices. Dip chicken in butter, then roll in crumb mixture. Place in greased 9-inch glass baking dish and bake 50-60 minutes, or until golden brown and tender. Meanwhile, add wine, onions and parsley to remaining butter. When chicken is golden brown, pour sauce around and over. Return to oven 3-5 minutes more, just until sauce is hot. (4 servings) *"This is really good."*

COOK'S TIP: For variation, this same recipe can be turned into Chicken Cordon Bleu. Pound uncooked chicken breasts thin and follow above recipe. Before baking chicken, place 1 thinly-sliced piece of ham and 1 slice of Swiss cheese between 2 pieces of chicken. Pour wine-butter sauce on top. LORRIS AND ANN BETZ

Savory Chicken

21/2-3	pounds chicken pieces
1/4	cup mayonnaise
1	package dry onion soup mix
1/2	cup bottled Russian dressing
1	cup apricot-pineapple preserves
	Cooked pasta

Preheat oven to 350°. Arrange chicken pieces in a 12 x 8-inch baking dish with the thickest pieces on the outside. Combine remaining ingredients and spread evenly over the chicken. Bake 45 minutes to 1 hour, uncovered. *"This sounds a bit unusual, but it is really delicious. Can be served on a base of noodles, using plenty of the sauce on each serving."* ISABEL KERNS

141

Chicken Stew with Cognac and Mustard

2	tablespoons butter
2	tablespoons vegetable oil
2	large chickens, cut into serving pieces and patted dry
3	tablespoons cognac
4	medium onions, quartered
2	cloves garlic, minced
2	tablespoons flour
1	teaspoon rosemary
1	teaspoon oregano
1/2	teaspoon tarragon
1/2	teaspoon sage
2	cups dry white wine or chicken broth
1	cup heavy cream
2	tablespoons Dijon mustard
	Salt and pepper
1/4	cup minced fresh parsley for garnish
	Thin pasta

Preheat oven to 350°. Heat butter and oil in a heavy Dutch oven or baking dish. Add chicken and brown on all sides. Pour cognac in corner of pan and ignite, spooning cognac over chicken until flames subside. Remove meat using slotted spoon. Add onions and garlic and sauté until limp and golden, about 10 minutes (add more oil and butter if necessary). Stir in flour and cook until flour just begins to brown, 1-2 minutes. Add rosemary, oregano, tarragon, sage and wine and blend well. Return chicken to pot. Bring to boil. Transfer to oven. Cover and cook until meat is very tender, 1-11/2 hours, stirring occasionally. Transfer chicken to platter and keep warm. Skim fat from sauce. Bring sauce to boil, stir in cream, scraping any browned bits. Boil gently until sauce is reduced to desired consistency. Stir in mustard. (Do not boil.) Blend well. Season with salt and pepper. Spoon sauce over chicken. Sprinkle parsley on top and serve. (8 servings) *You may also substitute rabbit for chicken. Serve with thin egg noodles.* CHRIS IMAZUMI-O'CONNOR

Lemon Chicken

4	chicken breast halves, skinned, boned and flattened
1	egg yolk, slightly beaten
1/2	cup seasoned bread crumbs (Progresso the best)
1/4	cup olive oil
1	tablespoon lemon juice
1	tablespoon minced garlic
1	cup chicken broth
1/4	cup white wine (optional)
	Parmesan cheese, grated

Preheat oven to 350°. Dip chicken in egg yolk; dust with bread crumbs. Fry breasts in olive oil, lemon juice and garlic. Arrange in a 9 x 13-inch dish and cover with chicken broth and wine. Sprinkle with Parmesan. Bake 25 minutes. KATHY DUNN FINGER

Stir-Fried Chicken in Pita

4	large chicken breast halves, skinned and boned
1/4	cup soy sauce
1	tablespoon cornstarch
2	tablespoons cooking or dry sherry
1	teaspoon sugar
1/4	teaspoon ground ginger
1/4	teaspoon crushed red pepper
1	small head green cabbage
4	medium green onions
2	medium carrots
4	tablespoons salad oil
4	6-inch pita bread halves
8	small lettuce leaves

Preheat oven to 350°. Slice chicken into 1/8-inch slices. Cut each slice into matchstick thin strips. In medium bowl, combine next 6 ingredients. Add chicken and turn until well-coated; set aside. Discard tough green outer leaves from cabbage; remove core; thinly slice cabbage to make about 5 cups. Cut each green onion into 3-inch pieces. Cut carrots into matchstick thin strips. In large skillet or wok over medium heat, in 2 tablespoons hot salad oil, cook cabbage, onions, and carrots, stirring quickly and frequently until tender (about 5 minutes). With slotted spoon, remove vegetables to bowl. In same skillet over medium heat, in 2 tablespoons more hot salad oil, cook chicken mixture, stirring quickly and frequently until chicken is tender (about 2-3 minutes). Return vegetables to skillet; heat through. Warm pita halves about 3 minutes. Place lettuce leaf in each pita and fill with stir-fry mixture. (4 servings) LAURIE HENDRICK

143

Chicken with Apricots, Sweet Potatoes and Prunes

8	chicken breast halves, skinned and boned
3/4	cup dried prunes
3/4	cup dried apricots
2	cups cubed sweet potatoes
1/4	cup olive oil
1/4	cup vinegar
1	cup dry vermouth
2	tablespoons brown sugar
4	teaspoons oregano

Place chicken breasts, prunes, apricots and sweet potatoes in medium-large bowl. Combine olive oil, vinegar, vermouth, brown sugar and oregano and pour over chicken, fruit and sweet potatoes. Cover and marinate in refrigerator several hours or overnight.

Preheat oven to 375°. Arrange chicken, fruit and potatoes in shallow baking dish. Pour marinade over mixture and bake, covered, for 45 minutes to 1 hour or until chicken is cooked through and sweet potatoes are soft. (8 servings) *This dish is colorful and a pleasure to eat. What's more, it is quick and easy and can be prepared ahead of time.* ANN HANTON

Rolled Chicken Breasts

6	chicken breast halves, skinned and deboned
6	thin slices boiled ham
6	slices Mozzarella cheese
1	small can sliced mushrooms
1	cup sour cream
1	can cream of mushroom or chicken soup
1/2	soup can sherry wine
	Paprika

Preheat oven to 350°. Using a mallet, pound breasts lightly to 5 x 5 inches. Place a ham slice and a slice of cheese on each cutlet. Roll up jelly-roll style, pressing to seal well and skewer with toothpick. Arrange in a shallow baking dish. Sprinkle with mushrooms. Mix sour cream, condensed soup and sherry together; pour over chicken. Dust with paprika. Bake 1 1/2 hours. MARIAN JOHNSON

Tanduri Chicken

1	tablespoon coriander
1	teaspoon red chili powder
1	teaspoon salt
1	teaspoon ground ginger
1	teaspoon turmeric
1	teaspoon cumin
1/2	cup lemon juice
11/2	cups plain yogurt
2	pounds chicken breasts
	Vegetable oil for brushing on chicken

Mix the spices, lemon juice and yogurt together. Make cuts in the chicken removing the skin as much as possible and stuff the cuts with the lemon-yogurt mixture. Spread remaining mixture evenly over the chicken. Marinate for 24 hours in the refrigerator.

Preheat oven to 450°. Remove most of the yogurt paste from the chicken, brush with vegetable oil and place in the hot oven. Roast for 5 minutes, then turn heat down to 375°. Roast for another 40 minutes basting periodically with marinate to prevent burning. Submitted by HEMALATA C. DANDEKAR, reprinted with permission from *Beyond Curry: Quick and Easy Indian Cooking Featuring Cuisine from Maharashtra State.*

Chicken George

4	chicken breast halves, skinned and boned
	Dried parsley flakes to cover all
1	teaspoon thyme
1/2	teaspoon each, salt and pepper
	Paprika to cover all
1	4-ounce can drained mushrooms (or fresh), sliced
1	can cream of mushroom soup
1/2-3/4	cup white wine

Preheat oven to 350°. Put chicken in ungreased shallow baking dish. Cover with seasoning, adding paprika last. Add mushrooms. Combine soup and wine. Pour over all. Bake about 1 hour. (4 servings)

MRS. DANIEL LINDSEY

145

Wedding Casserole

2	whole chicken breasts
5	tablespoons butter or margarine
1	cup bread crumbs
4	ounces fresh mushrooms, sliced
1	cup mayonnaise
2	tablespoons lemon juice
1	can cream of chicken soup
1/2	teaspoon curry powder
1	6-ounce can sliced water chestnuts, drained
1	tablespoon chopped pimentos
1	tablespoon slivered almonds, toasted
	Cooked rice

Preheat oven to 350°. Cook chicken; debone and cut into bite-size pieces. Melt 3 tablespoons butter and toast bread crumbs in sauté pan. Remove bread crumbs and set aside. Melt 2 tablespoons butter and sauté mushrooms. Combine mayonnaise, lemon juice, chicken soup and curry powder. Add chicken, water chestnuts, pimento, almonds and mushrooms. Place in baking dish and cover with crumbs. Bake 20 minutes (until it bubbles). Serve over rice. (4 servings) *"Always a great hit. Freezes well, too!"* INGRID DEININGER

Sour Cream and Chive Chicken Breasts

1	pint sour cream
2	tablespoons chopped chives
1/2	teaspoon tarragon
2	tablespoons vinegar
1/2	teaspoon salt
2	teaspoons sugar
2	tablespoons butter or margarine
4	chicken breast halves
	Flour

Preheat oven to 400°. Mix all ingredients together except the butter, chicken and flour. Melt butter and pour in baking dish. Dust chicken with flour. Dip in sour cream mixture and place in baking dish. Bake 45 minutes. (4 servings) ANDREA WOO

Chicken Casserole

2/3	cup minced onions
1	cup sliced celery
3	tablespoons butter
4	cups cooked, diced chicken
4	hard-boiled eggs, chopped
2	cups cooked rice
1	teaspoon salt
2	teaspoons lemon juice
1	cup mayonnaise
2	cans cream of mushroom soup
	Shredded cheese or buttered bread crumbs (optional)

Preheat oven to 350°. Sauté onions and celery in butter. Mix with remaining ingredients. Put in large baking dish. Top with cheese or bread crumbs, if desired. Bake 45 minutes. (8-10 servings)

CATHERINE MCDOWELL

Easy Chicken Tetrazzini

3-4	tablespoons margarine
1	clove garlic, minced
3/4	pound mushrooms, sliced
1	can cream of chicken soup
1/4	cup half-and-half cream
1/2	cup dry white wine
2-3	cups cubed cooked chicken
1/2	cup grated Parmesan cheese
	Salt and pepper to taste
6-8	ounces spaghetti

Melt margarine and sauté garlic and mushrooms. Using a wire whisk, mix in chicken soup, cream and wine. Add chicken, Parmesan cheese, salt and pepper. Heat to bubbling and reduce to a simmer. Cook pasta. For individual servings, ladle sauce on top of pasta. ANN BETZ

Chicken Broccoli Crescent Bake

1   3-ounce package cream cheese, room temperature
1   can cream of chicken soup
2   cups diced cooked chicken
1   9-ounce package frozen chopped broccoli, cooked and
    drained
1/2 onion, chopped fine
    Salt and pepper
    Mushrooms (optional)
2   8-ounce cans crescent rolls
1   cup shredded cheddar cheese (or cheese of choice)
1   egg, beaten (optional)*

Preheat oven to 350°. Mix all of the above ingredients well except the cheese and crescent rolls. Spread dough from one can of crescent rolls out flat on a baking sheet. Spoon the chicken mixture on top and sprinkle with shredded cheddar cheese. Place second crescent roll rectangle on top of the chicken and seal the edges well. Bake 25-30 minutes. Let stand a few minutes before serving. (8 servings) KATHY DOYLE-SCHUELER

*COOK'S TIP: If you brush the top with 1 beaten egg, it browns even better.

Creamy Crunchy Chicken Bake

1   8-ounce jar Cheez Whiz
11/2 cups hot cooked rice
2   cups cooked chicken pieces
1   10-ounce package frozen peas, cooked
1   2.8-ounce can onion rings

Preheat oven to 350°. Combine cheese and rice. Add chicken, peas and half of the onions. Bake 15 minutes. Top with the remaining onions and bake 5 more minutes. MELISSA SNAVELY

Chicken Casserole

1	box Uncle Ben's long grain and wild rice
3	whole chicken breasts, cut in pieces
3	tablespoons peanut oil
1	10-ounce box frozen French-cut green beans
1	small onion, chopped
1	small can of mushrooms
1	can sliced water chestnuts
1	can cream of celery soup
1	cup mayonnaise
1	small jar pimentos

Preheat oven to 350°. Cook rice according to packing directions. Sauté chicken in oil until cooked through; remove chicken from pan. Cook and drain green beans. Combine ingredients in a 9 x 13-inch baking dish. Bake 30-40 minutes or until heated through. (4-6 servings)

MRS. GEORGE CAVENDER

Chicken Kelly

6	chicken breasts, skinned and boned (cut into pieces)
4	eggs
2	cups seasoned bread crumbs
	Oil
2	tablespoons margarine
11/2	pounds Muenster cheese, sliced
	Fresh mushrooms, sliced
1	can chicken broth
	Cooked rice or noodles

Marinate chicken in eggs for 2 hours or overnight. Preheat oven to 350°. Shake chicken in bread crumbs. Brown in oil and drain. Melt margarine in a 9 x 13-inch baking dish. Add chicken and mushrooms. Cover with sliced cheese. Pour chicken broth over mixture. Bake, covered, 25 minutes and uncovered, 20 minutes. Serve over rice or noodles. (8 servings) LAURIE LOGAN

149

Chicken à la Martha

6   chicken breasts, skinned and boned
1   can cream of chicken soup
1   can cream of mushroom soup
1   can cream of celery soup
8   ounces shredded sharp cheddar cheese
1/4   cup grated onions
1/4   cup sherry

Preheat oven to 350°. Combine all ingredients in an oven-proof baking dish and bake 3 hours. (6 servings) DOROTHY COONS

Barbecued Chicken and Dumplings for a Crowd

1-2   chickens
1   8-ounce container allspice
1   4-ounce container Lawry's seasoned salt
4-8   ounces garlic salt or powder
1   32-ounce bottle ketchup
1   8-ounce bottle Open Pit barbecue sauce
1   8-ounce jar mustard
1   8-ounce bag sugar
1   cup water

In a large Dutch oven, place chicken, enough water to cover chicken, allspice, seasoned salt and garlic salt. Parboil chickens for 1-11/2 hours until cooked through and tender. (Reserve chicken broth for dumplings.) Preheat oven to 350°. Place chicken into a 9 x 13-inch baking dish. Mix ketchup, barbecue sauce, mustard and sugar together; add 1 cup of water. Pour over chicken and bake about 1-11/2 hours.

DROP DUMPLINGS:
   Pinch salt
1/4   cup pepper
1   2-ounce container allspice
6   eggs
1   20-ounce bag self-rising flour
   Chicken broth from parboiled chicken

Mix salt, pepper, allspice, eggs, flour and enough water to make a consistent batter and drop by spoonfuls into boiling chicken broth. Leave in for 5-10 minutes or until done. *(This recipe was served to all of the families who were staying at the Ronald McDonald House with the Ruggs.)* KEITH RUGG

Oven Barbecue Chicken

1	package chicken pieces
1	cup ketchup
1/3	cup wine vinegar
1/2	cup water
1/3	cup brown sugar
1/2	teaspoon Worcestershire sauce
1/2	teaspoon dry mustard

Preheat oven to 450°. Arrange chicken, skin side up, in a baking dish. Mix all other ingredients together and pour sauce on top of chicken. Bake 30 minutes. Reduce heat to 325° and bake 1 more hour, turning every 15 minutes. (6 servings) *"Delicious sauce!"* CATHERINE MCDOWELL

Barbecued Chicken in Bourbon Marinade

1	package chicken parts

MARINADE:

1/4	cup soy sauce
1/4	cup bourbon
2	tablespoons hot Dijon mustard
2	tablespoons brown sugar
1	green onion, chopped
4	drops Worcestershire sauce

Combine all marinade ingredients. Marinate chicken parts for 6-8 hours in refrigerator. Cook on barbecue grill over medium heat, 25-35 minutes, basting often with marinade. (4 servings) CAROLINE BLANE

Sweet and Sour Chicken

6-8	whole chicken breasts, split
1	jar apricot preserves
1	bottle Russian salad dressing
1	envelope onion soup mix

Preheat oven to 350°. Place chicken in a large shallow baking dish. Combine remaining ingredients. Pour over chicken, coating all . Bake 1 hour and 15 minutes. *"Sauce is good spooned over rice."* BARB SLATTERY

POULTRY

Spicy Orange Chicken

2	tablespoons corn oil
1	pound skinned and boned chicken breasts, cubed
1/4	cup slivered orange peel
1	clove garlic, minced
1/2	teaspoon ground ginger
2	tablespoons cornstarch
1	cup chicken broth
1/4	cup soy sauce
1/4	cup dry sherry
1/4	cup orange marmalade
1/2	teaspoon crushed red pepper
	Cooked rice

In a wok or large skillet, heat corn oil over medium heat. Add chicken a third at a time. Stir-fry 3 minutes or until browned. Return all chicken to wok. Add orange peel, garlic and ginger. Stir-fry 1 minute. Combine remaining ingredients. Mix with chicken. Stirring constantly, bring to boil over medium heat and boil 1 minute. Serve over rice. (4 servings) *"You may substitute 1 pound beef flank or round steak, thinly sliced, and beef broth."* LORRIS BETZ

Joan's Chicken Teriyaki

21/2-3 pounds chicken parts or boneless breasts

MARINADE:

1	cup soy sauce
2	cloves garlic, minced
	Juice of 2 lemons
2	tablespoons honey
2	tablespoons cooking oil
2	teaspoons grated onions

Combine all marinade ingredients. Marinate chicken 3-4 hours in refrigerator, turning occasionally. Grill or broil chicken until juices no longer flow when pierced with a fork. (6 servings) SUSAN ENGLAND

Chinese Chicken

5	tablespoons peanut oil
1	pound chicken strips
2	cloves garlic, minced
1/2	cup chopped onions
1/2	cup chopped carrots
1/2	cup chopped celery
2	tablespoons soy sauce
1	tablespoon sugar
	Sliced water chestnuts (optional)
	Snow peas (optional)

Heat 3 tablespoons peanut oil in wok or frying pan. Add sliced chicken and garlic. Cook until no longer pink (about 10 minutes). Remove from pan and add remaining oil and sauté onions, carrots and celery for 2 minutes. Add soy sauce, sugar and chicken to vegetables and cook 5-10 minutes longer. If desired, add water chestnuts and/or snow peas and cook 5 minutes. (4-6 servings) CATHERINE MCDOWELL

Chicken with Walnuts

1/4	cup oil
1/2	cup walnut pieces
4	chicken breasts, skinned, boned and diced
2	tablespoons soy sauce
1/2	tablespoon cornstarch
1	teaspoon salt
1/2	teaspoon sugar
6	large fresh sliced mushrooms (optional)
	Cooked rice

Heat oil and fry nuts until golden brown. Remove from pan and put on paper towel to drain. Sauté chicken pieces 2 minutes. Mix soy sauce, cornstarch, salt and sugar together. Pour over chicken and stir. Add mushrooms, if desired, and stir 5 minutes. Remove from heat. Add walnuts and serve with rice. (4 generous servings) DEB REISER

Hoisin-Grilled Chicken Wraps

4	chicken breast halves, skinned and boned (cut into 1-inch pieces)
10	flour tortillas
	Duck Sauce
3	green onions and tops, finely cut

HOISIN MARINADE:

1/4	cup brown sugar
1/4	cup soy sauce
1/4	cup rice wine vinegar
1/4	cup hoisin sauce
2	cloves garlic, minced
1	tablespoon sesame oil
1	tablespoon cooking oil
1	teaspoon red pepper flakes

DUCK SAUCE:

3	tablespoons sweet bean sauce
3	tablespoons hoisin sauce
1	teaspoon sugar
1	tablespoon sesame oil

Prepare marinade. Marinate chicken in a glass dish at least 30 minutes. Thread meat onto skewers. Cook over a barbecue grill, basting often with marinade and turning frequently to prevent burning, until done (no more than about 5 minutes total cooking time). Remove chicken from skewers and fold into warmed flour tortillas which you have thinly spread duck sauce and sprinkled green onions. (4-6 servings) ANN BETZ

Multipurpose Herb Mix

1/3	cup nonfat dried milk powder
1	tablespoon salt
1	tablespoon paprika
2	teaspoons dry mustard
2	teaspoons dry dill
1/4	teaspoon pepper
2	teaspoons crushed oregano
11/2	teaspoons thyme
1	teaspoon onion powder
1/2	teaspoon garlic powder

Place all ingredients in a covered jar and shake well. JEAN WEAVER

154

Stir-Fry Chicken, Broccoli and Red Pepper

1	pound chicken breasts, skinned and boned
	Vegetable oil spray
1	tablespoon olive oil
2	large red or green bell peppers, cut into wide strips
1	large onion, cut into thick slices
2	large cloves garlic, minced
1	teaspoon basil
1/2	teaspoon thyme
1/2	teaspoon ground pepper
1/4	teaspoon rosemary
6	cups broccoli flowerettes
1/2	teaspoon salt
4	tablespoons grated Parmesan cheese

Pound chicken breasts between sheets of waxed paper to thickness of 1/4 inch. Cut chicken crosswise into wide strips. Cover large skillet with vegetable spray. Add olive oil and heat on high 1 minute. Add red peppers, onions, garlic and seasonings to skillet. Stir-fry 2 minutes. Rinse broccoli with cold water, drain (do not shake off excess water) and add to skillet. Stir-fry 3 minutes. Reduce heat to medium low, cover and steam 2 minutes. Stir in chicken and salt. Cover and steam until chicken is almost cooked, approximately 1 minute. Uncover; increase heat and stir-fry until liquid is reduced slightly, approximately 1 minute. Top with Parmesan cheese. (4 servings) CHRIS IMAZUMI-O'CONNOR

Stir-Fry Chicken with Oyster Sauce

2	pounds boned chicken breasts
2	tablespoons cornstarch
4	tablespoons soy sauce
3	tablespoons water
1	teaspoon sugar
3	tablespoons oil
1	green pepper, sliced
2	onions, sliced
3	stalks celery, sliced 1/4 inch, diagonally
4	tablespoons oyster sauce
	Cooked rice

Slice chicken into 1/8-inch thick strips. Combine cornstarch, soy sauce, water and sugar. Add chicken and toss until well coated. Heat oil in wok. Add green pepper, onions and celery. Stir-fry over high heat until onions are tender yet crisp. Add chicken mixture; stir-fry until chicken is cooked. Stir in oyster sauce; cook 1 minute longer. Serve over rice. MOLLY WALSH

Sour Cream Chicken Enchiladas

1	package flour tortillas (8)
1	pint sour cream
1	cup milk
3	cups shredded, cooked chicken
1/2	pound shredded Monterey Jack cheese
1	cup chopped green onions
1/2	cup coarsely-chopped fresh cilantro

Preheat oven to 325°. Warm covered tortillas in microwave (about 45 seconds) to soften. In a bowl, whisk together sour cream and milk. Dip tortillas, one at a time, in sour cream mixture. Divide chicken and cheese into 8 equal portions. Place a portion of chicken and cheese on each tortilla and top with about 1 tablespoon green onions and a teaspoon of cilantro. Roll tortillas and place in a baking dish. Pour remaining sour cream mixture over tortillas; garnish top with left-over green onions and cilantro. Bake about 20 minutes. (4 servings) JANET GILSDORF

Easy Chicken with Taco Sauce

1	package chicken pieces, skinned
1	package Ortega taco seasoning
1	cup warm water

Preheat oven to 350°. Place chicken in a 9 x 12-inch baking dish. Mix taco seasoning with water. Spread over chicken. Bake 1-11/2 hours. *"This tastes like you are dining in Mexico!"* THERESA KELSCH

Chicken Flautas

5	chicken breast fillets
1	package taco seasoning
11/4	cups water
1	16-ounce carton nonfat plain yogurt
1	package flour tortillas (8-10)
1	8-ounce package shredded Mozzarella cheese

Preheat oven to 350°. Boil chicken breasts until cooked. Cut into bite-size pieces. Place chicken in skillet and add taco seasoning. Add water and cook until heated through. Spread 1-2 tablespoons of yogurt on each tortilla. Spoon 2 tablespoons of chicken mixture on top of each. Sprinkle 1-2 tablespoons Mozzarella cheese on top and roll up. Place rolled tortillas in greased 9 x 13-inch baking dish. (May spoon any left-over yogurt on top of tortillas and sprinkle with left-over Mozzarella cheese.) Cover pan with foil and bake 25 minutes. (5 servings) RITA LAREAU

Chicken Fajitas

11/2   pounds chicken breasts, cut in small pieces

MARINADE:
1   clove garlic, minced
1/2   teaspoon chili powder
1/2   teaspoon crushed red pepper
2   tablespoons vegetable oil
2   tablespoons lemon juice
11/2   teaspoons ground cumin
11/2   teaspoons seasoned salt

FAJITAS:
3-4   tablespoons oil
1/2   cup chopped onions
1/2   cup chopped green onions
1   cup sliced red, green or yellow bell pepper (or combination)
8   flour tortillas, warmed
1   avocado, peeled and sliced
        Sour cream (as desired)
        Salsa (as desired)

Combine marinade ingredients and marinate chicken at least 2 hours in refrigerator. Quickly sauté fajitas vegetables in oil and remove from pan. Remove chicken from marinade with slotted spoon. Sauté chicken about 5 minutes and toss with vegetables. Spoon into tortillas. Serve with avocado, salsa and sour cream. (8 servings) *Serve with Spanish rice and refried beans for a complete dinner.* MARTY MCCLATCHEY

Layered Chicken Casserole

1	tablespoon plus 1 teaspoon margarine
1 0	ounces chicken pieces
1/4	cup diced onions
3	diced jalapeño chiles
1/4	cup milk
1/4	cup tomato sauce
	Pinch of salt, pepper, oregano, garlic powder
6	ounces shredded cheddar or Monterey Jack cheese
6	corn tortillas, cut into sixths
4	sliced black olives

Preheat oven to 350°. Melt margarine in a skillet and cook chicken. Add onions and jalapeño chiles. Cook a few minutes. Cover and set aside. In a saucepan, heat milk, tomato sauce and seasonings. Bring to a slow boil. Add chicken mixture, blend thoroughly and cover. Simmer a few minutes. Brush margarine on bottom of a baking dish and line with tortilla triangles. Add a portion of chicken, sprinkle with cheese and add another layer. Repeat until all ingredients are used. Bake 20 minutes. Garnish with olives and return to oven for 5 minutes. Serve warm. (4 servings) *"This recipe was created by me for Weight Watchers, Inc."* JANINE MOURGUET

Chicken Roll-Ups

1	package frozen phyllo pastry sheets (thawed)
1/2	pound unsweetened butter, melted
1	pound chicken breasts, skinned and boned (thinly sliced or pounded)
1	cup shredded Monterey Jack and Mozzarella cheese (4 ounces each)
1	tablespoon chopped fresh tarragon or fresh basil

Preheat oven to 350°. Brush 2 sheets of phyllo with melted butter. Sprinkle one-half of chicken breast with a small amount of cheese and spice. Roll up in jelly roll or egg roll fashion. Place roll-ups in a 9 x 12-inch baking dish. Drizzle with left-over butter. Bake 35-40 minutes. (6-8 servings) *"This can be made ahead and refrigerated."* THERESA KELSCH

Acupulco Chicken

1	envelope taco seasoning mix
1	pint sour cream
1	package soft tortillas (8-10)
2-3	cups cooked chicken pieces
1	can cream of mushroom soup
1	can cream of celery soup
2	soup cans water
8	ounces shredded cheddar cheese

Preheat oven to 350°. Mix taco seasoning with sour cream and spread mixture on each tortilla. Place 2 tablespoons of chicken on top and fold like an envelope. Place face down in an 11 x 13-inch baking dish. Mix soups and water, pour over tortillas and spread cheese on top. Bake until melted. LEOTA KINAITIS

Cajun Curry Chicken

1	tablespoon plus 1 teaspoon margarine
11/2	cups chopped onions
1	4-ounce can green chiles, chopped
1	green pepper, chopped
1/2	red pepper, chopped
11/2	teaspoons plus 1 tablespoon Cajun seasoning
1	tablespoon curry powder
8	ounces chicken pieces
1	cup water
1	package chicken broth mix
1	tablespoon plus 1 teaspoon flour
1	small apple, chopped
2	tablespoons raisins
1	cup cooked rice

In a large skillet, heat margarine and sauté onions, peppers, 11/2 teaspoons Cajun seasoning and curry powder for 5 minutes. Work 1 tablespoon of Cajun seasoning into chicken. Add chicken and sauté 15 minutes. Whisk together water, broth mix and flour. Add to pan and stir. Mix in apple and raisins. Heat until thick and smooth, about 5 minutes. Divide recipe and serve over 1/2 cup of rice. (2 servings) *"This recipe was created by me for Weight Watchers, Inc."* JANINE M. MOURGUET

Chicken Imperiale

4	large chicken breasts, halved, skinned and boned
4	tablespoons butter or margarine
1/4	cup flour
3/4	cup milk
3/4	cup chicken broth
1/3	cup dry white wine
1/4	cup chopped onions
1	71/2-ounce can crabmeat, drained, flaked and cartilage removed
1	3-ounce can chopped mushrooms, drained
1/2	cup (10 crackers) coarsely-crumbled saltine crackers
2	tablespoons snipped parsley
1/2	teaspoon salt and dash pepper
1	cup (4 ounces) shredded Swiss cheese
1/2	teaspoon paprika

Preheat oven to 350°. Place 1 chicken piece, boned side up, between 2 pieces of waxed paper. Working from the center out, pound chicken lightly with meat mallet to make cutlets about 1/8-inch thick (8 x 5 inches); set aside. In saucepan, melt 3 tablespoons butter; blend in flour. Add milk, chicken broth and wine; cook and stir until mixture thickens and bubbles. Set aside. In skillet, sauté onions in remaining butter (do not brown). Stir in crab, mushrooms, cracker crumbs, parsley, salt and pepper. Stir in 2 tablespoons of sauce. Top each chicken piece with 1/4 cup crab mixture. Fold sides in; roll up. Place seam side down in a 12 x 7-inch baking dish. Pour remaining sauce over all. Bake, covered, 1 hour or until chicken is tender. Uncover; sprinkle with cheese and paprika. Bake 2 minutes longer or until cheese melts. (8 servings)

BRIDGET MCGILLICUDDY

Turkey Burgers

11/4	pounds ground turkey
1	egg or 2 egg whites
1	shredded carrot
1/2	cup Quaker oats
1	cup crushed bran flakes
4	hamburger buns

Mix the first 4 ingredients together. Shape into 4 equal patties. Coat with bran flakes. Place in a glass rectangular dish and cover with wax paper. Microwave on high 7 minutes giving the dish a half turn after 4 minutes. Place the turkey burgers on 4 hamburger buns and garnish as you wish. (4-6 servings) SUZANNE PEHRSON

Stuffed Turkey Burgers

1	pound ground turkey
3/4	cup Italian bread crumbs
1/4	clove garlic, minced
11/2	cups cooked broccoli (fresh or frozen)
1/2	cup shredded cheese (cheddar or Monterey Jack)

Preheat oven to 400°. Mix turkey, 1/4 cup bread crumbs and garlic together and form into 4 patties. In a square baking dish, sprinkle some bread crumbs. Place 2 patties in dish. Put broccoli and cheese in center of patties. Place remaining 2 patties on top and pinch the 2 patties together to cover the fillings. Sprinkle remaining bread crumbs on top of each patty. Cover with foil and bake 22 minutes or until done. Uncover and bake an additional 5 minutes. (2 servings) PATRIC BORDNICK

Spicy Turkey Chili

1	pound lean ground turkey
1	onion, chopped
1	package chili seasonings
1	pound frozen whole kernel corn
2	14-ounce cans red kidney beans
2	141/2-ounce cans stewed tomatoes (no salt added)
2	tablespoons tomato paste
1	cup tomato purée
1/2	teaspoon salt (optional)
	Dash hot sauce

In a large heavy saucepan, sauté turkey over low heat, stirring constantly until it gives off moisture. Add onions and chili seasonings and increase heat, continue to sauté until slightly brown. Add remaining ingredients; bring to a boil, reduce heat. Simmer 30-40 minutes. (Makes 8 servings) *"Excellent over baked potatoes."* Reprinted with permission, MEDSPORT, HIGH FIT - LOW FAT™, REGENTS OF UNIVERSITY OF MICHIGAN

POULTRY

Meats

MEATS

Beef	165
Pork	190

Sloppy Joes (Wimpies)

1	pound ground beef
1	onion, chopped
1/2	green pepper, chopped
2	stalks celery, chopped
2	tablespoons vinegar
1/2	cup ketchup
1/4	cup water
1	teaspoon Worcestershire sauce
1	teaspoon salt
1	teaspoon sugar
1/4	teaspoon chili powder
1/8	teaspoon pepper
	Hamburger buns

Brown ground beef in a skillet. Add onions and cook until transparent. Drain fat from pan. Add rest of ingredients and simmer 45 minutes. Serve on hamburger buns. (6 servings) CATHERINE MCDOWELL

Stuffed Meatloaf

1	pound ground round or chuck
1	slightly-beaten egg (or 1/4 cup Egg Beaters)
1	tablespoon dried onion flakes
1	teaspoon Mrs. Dash spice mix
1/4	cup Quaker oats
1	teaspoon Worcestershire sauce
	Salt and pepper to taste
1	package frozen spinach, thawed and squeezed dry
1/2	cup shredded Provolone cheese
2	tablespoons grated Parmesan cheese
1	small can beef gravy (optional)

Preheat oven to 350°. Mix ground beef, egg, onion flakes, spice mix, oats, Worcestershire sauce, salt and pepper lightly, but thoroughly. Place half of meat mixture in a loaf-sized baking dish. Mix together spinach and cheeses. Spoon spinach mixture over beef layer and place remaining beef mixture on top. Bake 40-50 minutes or until meat is cooked. Warm beef gravy and serve on the side. *"A variation on an old favorite. Must serve with mashed potatoes!"* ANN BETZ

Microwave 6-Layer Meatloaf Ring

MEATLOAF:
11/2   pounds ground beef
2   eggs, slightly beaten
1/2   medium onion, chopped
1/4   cup dry bread crumbs
1   tablespoon Worcestershire sauce
1   teaspoon seasoned salt

FILLING:
3/4   cup water
2   tablespoons butter
1/4   teaspoon thyme
2   cups seasoned stuffing mix

TOPPING:
1   cup sliced mushrooms, drained
1/2   medium onion, sliced and separated into rings

Combine loaf ingredients and mix well. Divide into thirds. Measure water into a 1-quart measuring bowl. Add butter and thyme and microwave on high 1-2 minutes until boiling. Stir in stuffing mix. Assemble loaf: In a microwave ring or Bundt pan, place half of mushrooms in the bottom, then onion rings, then 1/3 of loaf mixture. Mix remaining mushrooms into stuffing. Spoon half of stuffing over meat. Top with the second 1/3 meat mixture. Press edges to seal. Repeat with remaining stuffing and meat. Seal edges. Microwave on high 5 minutes. Reduce power to 50%. Microwave 10-13 minutes, rotating dish 1/2 turn halfway through cooking time, until meat is firm and has lost its pink color. Turn out onto a platter to serve. (4-6 servings) SUE MATTANO

No Salt Seasoning Blend

1   tablespoon garlic powder
1   tablespoon dry mustard
1   tablespoon paprika
1   teaspoon basil
1/2   teaspoon thyme
1/2   teaspoon white pepper

Combine all ingredients and put into shaker container. (Makes 11/2 ounces) NANCY DHUE

166

Sherry Barbecued Loaves

1	cup fresh bread crumbs
1	egg, slightly beaten
1	pound ground beef
4	tablespoons minced onions
1	teaspoon salt
1/4	teaspoon pepper
1/2	cup tomato sauce
4	tablespoons minced parsley
1	teaspoon fine herbs
1/2	cup chopped mushrooms

Preheat oven to 350°. Combine all ingredients, mixing lightly but thoroughly. Shape into two loaves and place each in shallow baking dish. Bake 40 minutes.

SHERRY SAUCE:

1	tablespoon cornstarch
2	tablespoons brown sugar
1/4	cup sherry
1	tablespoon vinegar
1	teaspoon prepared mustard
1	tablespoon beef stock base
3/4	cup hot water
1/2	cup tomato sauce

While meat loaves are baking, mix cornstarch with brown sugar in a saucepan. Stir in remaining ingredients. Cook over low heat, stirring until thickened. Pour over meat. Bake 30 minutes longer. (4-5 servings)

KAREN BARKS

Basic Italian Meatballs

1	pound ground beef
1/4	cup dry bread crumbs
2	eggs, slightly beaten
1/4	cup grated Romano cheese
1/4	cup grated Parmesan cheese
2	tablespoons chopped parsley
1	clove garlic, minced
11/2	teaspoons salt
1/4	teaspoon pepper
1/4	teaspoon oregano
1/2	teaspoon fennel seed

Preheat oven to 350°. Place meat in a large bowl. Add all ingredients and mix lightly with your hands. Oil your hands and form mixture into balls. Put onto a shallow baking pan and bake 25-30 minutes or until meatballs are browned and cooked through. (Makes about 8 large meatballs)

ANN BETZ

Black Bean Chili

2/3-1	bag dried black beans, soaked (or 4 cans black beans)
3	pounds ground beef
2	tablespoons minced garlic
1/4	cup vegetable oil
3	tablespoons flour dissolved in 4 tablespoons water
4	tablespoons chili powder (or as desired)
1	tablespoon red pepper (if desired)
1	teaspoon oregano
1	teaspoon cumin
2	cups water or 2 cups burgundy wine
2	cans beef broth
1	14-ounce can niblet corn
	Hot rice
	Sour cream
	Shredded cheddar cheese

Soak dried beans in water a few hours and drain. In a Dutch oven or stock pot, brown beef and garlic in oil. Add flour and water mixture and spices; mix well. Add water (or wine), beef broth, black beans and corn. Simmer 4-6 hours or longer. Serve chili over cooked rice with a generous dollop of sour cream and sprinkle with cheddar cheese. (Makes 15-20 servings)

NANCY FROST COLLINS

(Meatless) Meatballs

First you put egg in. Then you put another egg in. Now you squish it and then you roll it. Now you put another egg in. Then stir it for 3 minutes. Put the meatballs on the stove to cook for 5 minutes. Then we eat it.

MICHAEL, AGE 21/2

Tom's Toxic Chili

1	onion, coarsely chopped
1	green pepper, chopped
3	tablespoons olive oil
1 1/2	pounds meat (cook's choice, diced or ground)
2	16-ounce cans stewed tomatoes
2	6-ounce cans tomato paste
1	can tomato soup
2	16-ounce cans kidney beans (1 dark red and 1 light red)
1-2	jalapeño chiles, chopped
1-2	Finger Hot peppers, chopped
1-2	Hungarian medium-hot peppers, chopped
1/4	teaspoon oregano
1/4	teaspoon cinnamon
1/4	teaspoon nutmeg
1/4	teaspoon dry mustard
1	tablespoon ground cumin
1-4	tablespoons chili powder (or to taste)
1/2	teaspoon minced garlic
	Dash crushed red pepper

Sauté onions and green pepper in small amount of olive oil until onion is transparent. Transfer to a crockpot. Brown meat, drain off excess fat and transfer to crockpot. Add remaining ingredients and stir well. Cook 6-8 hours on low. (Makes approximately 5 quarts) TOM BOERSMA

Male Chauvinist Chili

6	slices bacon
1 0	ounces sweet Italian sausage, cut into 1-inch slices
1	pound lean ground beef
1	large Spanish onion, cut into large pieces
1	bell pepper, cut into large pieces
2	cloves garlic, minced
1/2	jalapeño chile pepper, diced (optional)
1	cup red wine
1/2	cup Worcestershire sauce
1	teaspoon hot dry mustard
1	teaspoon celery seeds
11/2	teaspoons chili powder
11/2	teaspoons freshly-ground black pepper
1/2	teaspoon salt
6	cups Italian tomatoes (pear-shaped)
1	15-ounce can pinto beans
1	15-ounce can garbanzo beans
1	15-ounce can kidney beans

Brown bacon in a large Dutch oven. Drain, crumble and set aside. Brown sausage and ground beef; drain meat and set aside. Cook onions, bell pepper, garlic and chile pepper over low heat, 2-3 minutes. Stir in wine and Worcestershire sauce; simmer, uncovered, 10 minutes. Stir in mustard, celery seed, chili powder, salt and pepper; simmer 10 minutes. Mash tomatoes; add with liquid and meats to onion mixture. Heat to boiling. Reduce heat, cover and simmer 1/2 hour stirring occasionally. Stir beans (with liquid) into chili; heat to boiling. Reduce heat; cover and simmer 1 hour, stirring occasionally. (10 servings)

COOK'S TIP: This is best made a day ahead and reheated as flavors will meld to their spicy best. CASEY O'GARA-WILHELM

Stuffed Hamburger Rolls

8	unsliced French bread sandwich rolls
1	pound ground beef
1/4	cup chopped onions
2	garlic cloves, minced
1	egg, slightly beaten
3	tablespoons snipped parsley (or more)
1-2	tablespoons prepared mustard (or more)
2	tablespoons water
3/4	teaspoon salt
1/2	teaspoon oregano
	Dash pepper
2	tablespoons margarine

Preheat oven to 375°. Cut one end off of each sandwich roll. Hollow out with a serrated knife. Crumble the bread into a bowl. (You don't want fine crumbs, but you don't want hunks of bread, either.) Put the hollowed-out rolls in a plastic bag so they won't get stale. Brown ground beef and add onions and 1 clove garlic. Cook until tender. Drain off excess fat. Add egg, parsley, mustard, water, salt, oregano and pepper. Then add the crumbled bread. Mix everything together well. Stuff the hollow rolls with the meat mixture. Melt margarine and sauté the other clove of garlic. Brush this over rolls. Bake about 20 minutes. *"Don't leave out the parsley and mustard - I think this combination really makes it."*

COOK'S TIP: If you freeze these, you will have to adjust the heating time. They're not bad cold, either! MARJORIE BEST

Hamburgers

The ingredients: First you flatten it round. Then you put pepper and onion on it. Then you put it in the oven. JOE, AGE 6

Spicy Beef and Raisin Sandwich

1/4   cup slivered almonds
1   pound lean ground beef
1   small onion, chopped
1/2   cup chili sauce
1/2   cup water
1/4   cup raisins
1/4   teaspoon cinnamon
1/8   teaspoon ground cumin
        Salt and pepper to taste
2   tablespoons sliced green onions
1-11/2 cups shredded Monterey Jack cheese
2   cups shredded iceberg lettuce
2-3   tomatoes, cut in thin wedges
3   pita breads, cut in half

Place almonds in a frying pan over medium heat and stir until golden, then set aside. Crumble ground beef into pan and cook until browned. Add onions and cook until limp. Drain fat. Mix in chili sauce, water, raisins cinnamon, cumin and salt and pepper. Cook, uncovered, stirring often for 5 minutes or until liquid has evaporated. Stir in almonds. Turn into a bowl and top with green onions. Spoon hot meat mixture into pocket bread and top with cheese, lettuce and tomato. (6 servings)

CHRIS IMAZUMI-O'CONNOR

Jumbo Pizza Loaf

1   medium-size loaf of French bread
1   pound lean ground beef
1/3   cup grated Parmesan cheese
1/4   cup finely-chopped onions
1   can ripe olives, chopped
1   teaspoon salt
1   teaspoon oregano
1   6-ounce can tomato paste
        Dash pepper
11/2   cups shredded cheddar cheese

Cut loaf of bread in half lengthwise. Combine rest of ingredients except cheese. Spread mixture over each cut surface of bread. Be sure to cover the bread entirely, all the way to the edges. Broil about 5 inches from the heat about 12 minutes or until meat looks cooked. (I usually turn the broiler off and bake about 10-15 minutes to get the bread warm and finish cooking hamburger.) Watch carefully when you're broiling. Top with cheese and broil until melted. Cut in chunks. (5-6 servings)

MARJORIE BEST

172

Yorkshire Pudding and Beef

3	tablespoons butter or margarine
1	pound ground beef
3	tablespoons bottled steak sauce
1/4	cup chopped onions
1	tablespoon chopped parsley
1	teaspoon salt
1/8	teaspoon nutmeg
2	eggs
1	cup milk
1	cup flour
1/4	teaspoon salt

Preheat oven to 400°. Melt butter in a 6-cup baking dish. Combine meat, steak sauce, onions, parsley, salt and nutmeg until blended. In a second bowl, beat eggs with a wire whisk until foamy. Stir in milk. Beat in flour and salt until smooth. Pour half the batter into heated casserole. Drop in meat mixture over batter. Pour remaining batter over meat mixture. Bake 35 minutes or until batter is crisp and brown at the edges. FRANK MOLER

Taglarini

1	cup chopped onions
3/4	cup chopped green pepper
2	cloves garlic, minced
2-3	tablespoons olive oil
11/2	pounds ground beef
2	cups canned tomatoes, drained
1/2	can (3 ounces) tomato paste
2	teaspoons salt
1	teaspoon oregano
1/2	teaspoon pepper
1/4	teaspoon allspice
11/2	cups shredded cheddar cheese
1	small can chopped or sliced ripe olives
	Cooked spaghetti

Sauté onions, green pepper and garlic in olive oil. Add ground beef and brown; drain excess fat. Drain the canned tomatoes and purée slightly in blender. Add to beef mixture along with tomato paste. Season with salt, oregano, pepper and allspice. Simmer on low heat 20 minutes. Stir in cheese and olives. Serve over hot spaghetti or mix with cooked spaghetti in a baking dish and reheat to serve. *"This is a good candidate for a potluck or for a crowd."* MARJORIE BEST

173

Yupper Cornish Pasties

1	cup shortening or lard
11/4	cups boiling water
1	teaspoon salt
41/2-5	cups flour
11/4	pounds ground beef
4	medium potatoes, diced
1	large onion, finely chopped
1	cup finely-chopped rutabega
1	cup sliced carrots
11/2	teaspoons salt
1/2	teaspoon pepper

In a large bowl, combine shortening and water; stir until melted. Add salt and enough flour to form a stiff dough. Make a ball; wrap in plastic wrap and refrigerate at least one hour. Preheat oven to 350°. In a separate large bowl, combine meat and vegetables with salt and pepper. Divide chilled dough into 8 pieces. On lightly-floured surface, roll one dough piece into a 9-inch circle. Place on large cookie sheet. Spoon approximately 1 cup of meat mixture, pinching in center to seal. Fold edge over to form a double-thick, 1/2-inch seam. Crimp seam with fingers. Repeat to make 8 pasties. Bake 1-11/4 hours. *"May be frozen."* IRENE ANN PALUCH

Enchilada Squares

1	pound ground beef
1/4	cup chopped onions
1	clove garlic, minced
4	eggs
2/3	cup evaporated milk
1	8-ounce can tomato sauce
1	package enchilada sauce mix
1	2-ounce can sliced ripe olives
1	cup corn chips
1	cup shredded sharp cheddar cheese

Preheat oven to 350°. Brown ground beef, onions and garlic in skillet until beef is cooked and onions and garlic tender. Drain off fat and spread beef mixture in bottom of baking dish. Beat eggs, milk, tomato sauce and enchilada sauce mix together and pour over beef layer. Sprinkle olives and corn chips on top. Bake, uncovered, 20-25 minutes or until firm in center. Sprinkle with cheese and bake 3-5 minutes longer until cheese is melted. *"This has all the flavor and texture of enchiladas with half the work."*
MARJORIE BEST

Beef Jerky

First put these spices: Soy sauce, Tabasco sauce, red pepper, garlic, Worcestershire sauce, black pepper and liquid smoke. Add venison or beef. Mix it together. Put it in the refrigerator all day. Cook it for 12 hours. Then take it out and let it sit for all night. Then you eat it.

MARK, AGE 8

Meat and Cheese Tortilla Lasagna

1/2	pound Monterey Jack cheese, shredded
1 0	ounces Mozzarella cheese, shredded
1	tablespoon oil
1	onion, chopped
1	teaspoon minced garlic
1	cup chopped green pepper
2	4-ounce cans whole green chile peppers
11/2	pounds ground chuck
1	28-ounce can crushed tomatoes
1	141/2-ounce can Italian-style tomatoes
1	6-ounce can tomato paste
2	tablespoons chili powder
1	tablespoon oregano
1	teaspoon salt
1	teaspoon ground cumin
1/2	teaspoon cayenne pepper
1	package (12 large) corn tortillas

Preheat oven to 350°. Lightly oil inside of a 9 x 13-inch glass baking dish. Mix shredded cheeses together in a small bowl, reserve. Heat oil and cook garlic, onions, green pepper and chiles for 5 minutes. Remove to bowl, reserve. Add beef to pan, cook until brown. Add all tomatoes, tomato paste, chili powder, oregano, salt, cumin and cayenne pepper. Cook; add vegetables and simmer 15 minutes, stirring often. Cover bottom of baking dish with 6 tortillas, overlapping some cheese. Add half of meat mixture, then cheese, then more tortillas, meat and top with cheese. Bake until melted and lasagna is heated through, about 30 minutes. Let stand 10 minutes before cutting into squares. (8 servings) NANCY SCHLEICHER

Beef Stroganoff I

3	pounds beef stew meat
3	medium onions, chopped
2-3	tablespoons vegetable oil
1	package dry onion soup mix
1	can mushroom soup
1	cup dry red wine
2	stalks celery, sliced
2	carrots, chopped
1/2	pound mushrooms, sliced
1/2	cup sour cream
	Cooked rice or noodles

Preheat oven to 325°. Brown stew meat and sauté onions in oil. Drain excess fat and place in a baking dish. Combine dry onion soup mix, soup, wine, celery, carrots and mushrooms in a bowl. Pour mixture over meat. Bake 3 hours. Add sour cream just before serving. Serve over rice or noodles. (6-8 servings)

Beef Stroganoff II

11/2	pounds beef fillet (sirloin or porterhouse steak)
	Salt and freshly-ground pepper to taste
3	tablespoons butter
1	tablespoon flour
1	cup beef broth
1	teaspoon Dijon mustard
1	pound fresh mushrooms, sliced
1	medium onion, sliced
3	tablespoons sour cream, room temperature
11/2	pounds fresh pasta (fettuccine)

Remove all fat from meat. Cut into narrow strips about 2 inches long and 1/2 inch thick. Season with salt and pepper; refrigerate 2 hours. In a saucepan, melt 11/2 tablespoons butter. Add flour and stir with a wire whisk until well-blended. Meanwhile, bring beef broth to a boil. All at once, add butter-flour mixture, stirring vigorously with the whisk until sauce is thickened and smooth. Stir in mustard. Simmer mushrooms for 5 minutes, then drain. Boil pasta in a large kettle 5-7 minutes; drain and keep warm. In a separate pan, heat remaining butter. Add meat and sliced onion and brown quickly on both sides. Remove meat to a large platter. Add sour cream to mustard sauce and heat for 3-4 minutes; add mushrooms. Pour sauce over meat and serve with warm pasta. (6 servings) GAIL LOZELLE

Marinated London Broil I

3-31/2 pounds London broil

MARINADE:
1/2   cup sherry
1/2   cup soy sauce
1/4   cup salad oil
1/4   cup lemon juice
2   tablespoons brown sugar
1/2   teaspoon grated ginger
1   clove garlic, minced
1/2   teaspoon hot sauce (optional)

SAUCE:
4   teaspoons cornstarch
1/2   pound mushrooms, sliced
1/4   cup sliced green onions

Combine marinade ingredients. Add meat and refrigerate overnight. The next day, remove steak, reserving marinade, and grill about 7 minutes per side. Carve meat into thin slices. For sauce, stir marinade into cornstarch in sauté pan. Add mushrooms and green onions and stir over low heat until thickened. Serve sauce with meat. CHRIS IMAZUMI-O'CONNOR

Marinated London Broil II

21/2-3 pound London Broil (21/2 to 3-inches thick)
2   teaspoons unseasoned meat tenderizer

MARINADE:
2   tablespoons instant minced onions
2   teaspoons marjoram
2   teaspoons thyme
1   large bay leaf
1/4   cup red wine vinegar
3/4   cup red wine
1/2   cup olive oil
3   tablespoons lemon juice
1/4   cup coarsely-cracked black pepper

Sprinkle meat evenly with tenderizer on both sides. Pierce meat deeply, all over, with fork. Combine rest of marinade ingredients. Pour over meat in shallow baking dish. Refrigerate at least 4 hours, turning meat once. Barbecue as desired. MIA BROULLIRE

Beef Marinade

1 envelope Italian salad dressing mix
1/2 cup water
1/2 cup ketchup
1 teaspoon prepared mustard
1/4 teaspoon Worcestershire sauce

Combine ingredients. Pierce meat in several spots and place in zipper bag with marinade. Refrigerate several hours.

Wake-Up Sandwiches

1/2 8-ounce carton whipped cream cheese
2 tablespoons milk
1 3-ounce package thinly-sliced corned beef, chopped
1/2 cup (2 ounces) shredded Swiss cheese
2 hard-cooked eggs, chopped
3 English muffins, split and toasted
1 hard-cooked egg, sliced
Chopped parsley

Combine cream cheese and milk, stirring until smooth. Stir in corned beef, cheese and chopped eggs. Spread corned beef mixture on English muffin halves. Serve cold or broil 2-3 minutes, until thoroughly heated. Garnish each half with an egg slice and parsley. (6 servings) *"Good for a brunch."*
DEBBIE ZIES

Corned Beef Casserole

1 12-ounce can corned beef, crumbled
1/4 pound American cheese, shredded
1 can cream of chicken soup
1 cup milk
1/2 cup chopped onions
1 8-ounce package egg noodles, cooked and drained
Buttered bread crumbs

Preheat oven to 350°. Mix all ingredients together except bread crumbs and place in a 2-quart baking dish. Top with buttered bread crumbs. Bake until heated through, about 40 minutes. (8 servings) MAGGIE BROWNRIDGE

Herbed Veal Roast Stuffed with Sweet Peppers

41/2	pounds veal shoulder, boned and butterflied
1/4	cup Worcestershire sauce
1	tablespoon fresh thyme or 1 teaspoon dried
1	teaspoon crushed red pepper
1/2	teaspoon coarsely-cracked black pepper
2	large yellow bell peppers
2	large red bell peppers
1/2	cup fresh bread crumbs
2	tablespoons olive oil

In a large baking dish, lay veal out flat and brush with half of the Worcestershire sauce. Sprinkle with half of the thyme, hot pepper and black pepper. Turn the meat over and repeat with the remaining seasonings. Wrap and let marinate in refrigerator 2-3 hours or overnight. Roast the peppers directly over a gas flame or under the broiler as close to the heat as possible, turning until charred. Place peppers in a bag and let steam for 10 minutes. Peel and discard the cores, seeds and ribs. Cut peppers into 11/2-inch strips. When ready to cook the veal, remove from the dish and place on a work surface, skin side down. Evenly distribute peppers and bread crumbs. Carefully roll up the veal to form a neat package. Tie roast securely with kitchen string. Preheat oven to 450°. In a large heavy ovenproof skillet, heat olive oil until it just begins to smoke; add veal and place in oven. Roast the meat, turning every 10 minutes, until evenly browned all over, about 40 minutes. Reduce oven temperature to 350°. Continue cooking for about 40-50 minutes until baking thermometer inserted in the center of the roast reads 150°. Let roast cool completely on a rack. *(The meat can be prepared to this point and refrigerated overnight.)* When ready to serve, remove strings and thinly slice meat. Serve at room temperature. PRUE ROSENTHAL

Roast Veal with Spinach Stuffing

STUFFING:

1/2	pound fresh spinach, stems removed
1/2	pound ground beef (or ground pork)
11/2	cups chopped onions (3 medium)
2	teaspoons minced garlic
1/4	pound mushrooms, chopped (about 13/4 cups)
2	sprigs fresh thyme, chopped (or 1 teaspoon dried)
1	bay leaf, chopped
1	cup fresh bread crumbs
2	eggs, beaten slightly

To make stuffing, clean and rinse spinach. Place in a saucepan and cook over high heat 30 seconds until just wilted. Drain and squeeze dry when cool enough to handle. Chop and set aside. Place beef in a saucepan and add onions and garlic. Cook, stirring, about 3 minutes. Add mushrooms, thyme and bay leaf. Cook 10 minutes. Add spinach and stir. Remove from heat. Add bread crumbs. Add eggs, stir and let cool.

ROAST:

5	pound shoulder of veal, boned, with a pocket
	Salt and pepper to taste
2	tablespoons vegetable oil
1	cup chopped onions (2 medium)
1	cup diced celery, 1/2-inch pieces
2	carrots, diced (1/2-inch pieces)
1	teaspoon garlic, minced
1	bay leaf
2	sprigs fresh thyme
11/2	cups chicken broth

Preheat oven to 400°. Stuff veal with spinach mixture. Overlap edges of meat to enclose the whole mixture. Tie securely with string. *(Can be prepared to this point up to a day ahead. Cover and refrigerate until ready to cook.)* When ready to cook, sprinkle veal with salt and pepper. Place in roasting pan. Brush with oil, scatter onions, celery, carrots, garlic, bay leaf and thyme over meat. Roast 11/2 hours, basting occasionally with chicken broth and stirring vegetables. Cover with foil and roast 30 minutes longer, basting occasionally. Remove roast from oven and cut away string. Slice and serve with cooking juices. (10 servings) *"This roast can be cooked the morning of the dinner and served later at room temperature or reheated, covered, in a 375° oven for 30 minutes."* PRUE ROSENTHAL

Osso Buco

4	veal or lamb shanks
1/2	cup flour
2	teaspoons salt
1/4	teaspoon pepper
1/3	cup vegetable oil
1	onion, chopped
3	cloves garlic, minced
1	stalk celery, chopped fine
2	carrots, diced
1	bay leaf
1	tablespoon Italian seasoning
1/2	cup dry red wine
2	tablespoons tomato paste
4	potatoes, quartered
1	tablespoon grated lemon rind
2	tablespoons chopped parsley
	Cooked rice

Preheat oven to 200°. Dust meat in flour, salt and pepper. Brown evenly in vegetable oil. Add onion, 1 clove minced garlic, celery and carrots to remaining oil and cook 6-7 minutes. Add bay leaf, Italian seasoning and wine; boil rapidly to reduce volume. Put meat back into pan. Add tomato paste and potatoes. Bring to boil. Cover and bake 6-7 hours. 10 minutes before serving, add lemon rind, parsley and remaining 2 cloves minced garlic. Serve over rice. (4-6 servings) LOU SPEARS

Mustard Short Ribs

2	pounds lean beef short ribs
2	medium onions, sliced
6	tablespoons prepared mustard
3	tablespoons lemon juice
3	teaspoons sugar
3	teaspoons salt, optional
1	clove garlic, minced
1 1/2	teaspoons pepper

Place ribs in crockpot with onions on top. Mix remaining ingredients and pour over meat. Set on "low" setting and cook all day. (2 servings)
MARY ANN WILSON

181

Butterflied Lamb

1   leg of lamb

MARINADE:
1/2   cup red wine (burgundy is nice)
1/4   cup olive oil
1/8   cup sesame seed oil
1/4   cup cider vinegar
1   tablespoon sugar
1   large clove garlic, minced
3   bay leaves
1   teaspoon salt
1   teaspoon pepper
4   green onions, sliced
1   tablespoon parsley, optional
       Dash thyme, optional
       Dash nutmeg, optional
       Hot sauce, optional

Butterfly leg of lamb. Remove as much fat as possible. Combine marinade ingredients. Place meat and marinade in leak-proof plastic bag. Squeeze extra air from bag so that meat is covered by marinade. Seal bag. Marinate in refrigerator 24-72 hours. Charcoal broil for approximately 10 minutes per side for thick pieces. Serve rare to medium-rare for best flavor and texture. (6-8 servings) *"Believe me, this is wonderful!"* SARA HICKEY

Great Pot Roast

1   4-pound pot roast
1   can cream of mushroom soup
1   package onion soup mix
1   large onion, chopped
3   cloves garlic, minced
2   cups red wine
2   cups water
1   bay leaf
1   teaspoon thyme
1   teaspoon basil

Preheat oven to 350°. Put all ingredients in a large baking dish. Bake for 31/2 hours. *"Simple, but great!"* SUSAN HURWITZ

Beef Brisket

5   pounds beef brisket

MARINADE:
1   can beef broth
1   small bottle soy sauce
1/4   cup lemon juice
       Garlic to taste
1   tablespoon liquid smoke*

Combine all marinade ingredients. Pour over meat and marinate overnight in refrigerator. Preheat oven to 300°. Place meat and liquid in baking dish. Cover and bake 5 hours, basting occasionally. Let cool and slice on diagonal. *"This is great for appetizers or to have around for sandwiches."*

VARIATION: 1/2 cup barbecue sauce can be poured over the brisket the last hour of baking. Remove cover and increase oven temperature to 350° if sauce is used.

*Available at most large grocery stores. ANN SCHRIBER

Barbecued Beef

3   tablespoons oil
3-4   pounds boneless beef chuck roast
21/2   cups water
2   cups finely-chopped onions
11/2   cups finely-chopped celery
3/4   cup finely-chopped green pepper
3   cloves garlic, minced
1   6-ounce can tomato paste
3   tablespoons Worcestershire sauce
3   tablespoons cider vinegar
2   teaspoons Tabasco sauce
2   teaspoons salt
2   tablespoons barbecue sauce
       Hamburger buns

In a large pan, heat oil; brown beef on all sides. Add remaining ingredients. Cover; simmer 3-4 hours, stirring occasionally until beef can be easily shredded. (May need to cook, uncovered, for a period of time if there is too much liquid.) Serve on hot buttered buns. (6-8 servings)

ANN BETZ

183

Flamed Pepper Steak
(Steak au Poivre Flambé)

4	8-ounce steaks (club, tenderloin or top sirloin), 1-inch thick
2	tablespoons crushed pepper
1/2	cup beef broth
1	tablespoon cornstarch
1	tablespoon Dijon mustard
5	tablespoons margarine or butter
1/2	teaspoon salt
1/4	cup finely-chopped green onions
2	tablespoons brandy
1/2	cup dry red wine
1	teaspoon Worcestershire sauce
2	teaspoons finely-chopped fresh parsley

Dry steaks with paper towels. Press steaks into pepper and, with back of a spoon, work pepper into steaks. Allow to sit at room temperature 1 hour. In a bowl, blend beef broth, cornstarch and mustard. In a large heavy skillet, over high heat, melt 3 tablespoons margarine. When butter begins to brown, sear steaks 1 minute on each side. Reduce heat and continue cooking 2 minutes more on each side for rare, 3 minutes for medium rare or 4 minutes for medium. Transfer steaks to a heated platter; sprinkle with salt and keep warm. Pour off fat from skillet. In same skillet, over low heat, melt 1 tablespoon margarine. Sauté onions, stirring constantly, 1 minute; remove from heat. In a small saucepan, over low heat, warm brandy; ignite and pour into skillet. Stir until flames die. Add wine and, over high heat, bring to a boil (stirring constantly and scraping brown bits on bottom and sides of pan). Reduce liquid by half, about 3 minutes. Reduce to low heat and add remaining tablespoon margarine, Worcestershire sauce and lemon juice. Cook, stirring 1 minute. Pour sauce over steaks and sprinkle with parsley. (4 servings) LORRIS BETZ

Korean Barbecue

1 pound thinly-sliced sirloin tip (sliced across the grain)

MARINADE:
1 tablespoon sugar
1 tablespoon vegetable oil
1 tablespoon sesame oil
1/4 cup soy sauce
1 green onion, thinly sliced   (tops included)
1 clove garlic, minced
1 tablespoon toasted sesame seeds
1/8 teaspoon black pepper

Mix all marinade ingredients in a 11/2-quart glass bowl. Add meat slices, one at a time, to coat evenly. Let stand 1 hour (or overnight in the refrigerator), turning meat occasionally. Grill over hot coals about 3-4 inches above flame, about 30 seconds on each side. *"This is a great appetizer or main dish, but it keeps the cook very busy."* DIANE AR

Sukiyaki

1/4 cup beef suet, cut up
2 onions, sliced thin
1 cup chopped celery
2 cups canned sliced mushrooms
1 pound spinach, cut in 1-inch strips
6 green onions, sliced
2 cups canned bean sprouts, drained
2 pounds round steak, sliced thin
1/2 cup beef broth
1/4 cup soy sauce
1 teaspoon sugar
Black pepper
Cooked rice

Heat large iron skillet and rub with suet. Fry suet 5 minutes or until skillet is well-greased. Discard suet. Sauté onions 5 minutes. Add celery, mushrooms, spinach, green onions and sprouts. Cook over high heat for 5 minutes, stirring often. Push vegetables to one side; add beef and fry 3 minutes. Stir together. Add beef broth, soy sauce, sugar and pepper. Cook 5 minutes, stirring often. Serve on rice. *"This dish is pronounced 'ski yah key'."* DOROTHY WARDELL

Steak With Mustard Butter

21/2-3 pound Porterhouse steak

MUSTARD BUTTER:
1   cup butter, melted
3   tablespoons Dijon mustard
1/4   cup minced shallots

In a small saucepan, mix all butter ingredients together; set aside. Place steaks on lightly-greased grill 4-6 inches from coals. Cook, turning several times, until browned and done to your liking (for thick cut, 20-30 minutes for medium-rare). Accompany steak with Mustard Butter. (Makes 4-6 servings) ANN BETZ

Steak Kew

1/2   pound fillet mignon or other steak*
1   clove garlic, minced
2   slices ginger, shredded
1   tablespoon chopped green onions
1   tablespoon oyster sauce
1   tablespoon light soy sauce
1/2   teaspoon sugar
2   teaspoons cornstarch
1/4   pound snow peas
3   tablespoons peanut oil
8-10 Chinese mushrooms
1/2   teaspoon salt

Cut steak into 1-inch cubes. Mix with garlic, ginger, green onions, oyster sauce, soy sauce, sugar and cornstarch. Rinse mushrooms; cover with warm water and soak 15 minutes or until soft. Drain and quarter. Remove and discard tips of snow peas; wash and drain. Add snow peas to 1 quart boiling water; stir well. When water boils again, remove from heat; drain and run cold water over snow peas. Heat oil in wok. Add mushrooms and stir-fry 1/2 to 1 minute. Add soy sauce mixture; stir-fry 1-2 minutes. Add snow peas and mix well. Stir in salt. Pour onto serving dish and serve hot.

*COOK'S TIP: If less expensive cut is used, sprinkle meat with 1/4 teaspoon meat tenderizer and let stand 5 minutes. GRACE JORDISON BOXER

Mexican Stir-Fry

2-3 tablespoons vegetable oil
1 teaspoon cumin
1 teaspoon garlic salt (or 1/2 teaspoon garlic powder)
1 teaspoon oregano
1/4 teaspoon black pepper
1 medium onion, sliced thin
1 pound steak (flank, round, sirloin), sliced thin
2 red or green sweet bell peppers, cut into strips
Flour tortillas
Garnishes: Sour cream, guacamole, salsa, tomatoes

Heat oil (preferably in a wok). Quickly add spices, then onions and stir-fry briefly. Add meat and stir-fry a few more minutes. Lastly, add bell pepper strips and stir-fry until meat is cooked through and bell pepper is just starting to soften. Serve wrapped in soft flour tortillas with any or all of the garnishes. (4-6 servings) JANE MESSINK

Mexican Flank Steak

11/2-2 pounds flank steak

MARINADE:
1/2 teaspoon turmeric
1 teaspoon cumin
1/2 teaspoon thyme
1 teaspoon ginger
1/4 teaspoon ground cloves
1/4 teaspoon cinnamon
2 tablespoons soy sauce
1 teaspoon paprika
2 teaspoons oil
1 teaspoon minced garlic

Mix all ingredients for marinade. Place steak in mixture and marinate up to 2 hours. Broil meat in oven 5 minutes. Turn oven off and leave in oven 5 more minutes. (Or, you may grill meat 10-15 minutes to desired doneness.) (3-4 servings) *Given to us by a friend and native Mexican, Christina Wilcox.* FRANKE SIMON

Breaded Steak

2-3   pounds round steak
1/4   cup vegetable oil

BREAD CRUMB MIXTURE:
3   cups bread crumbs
1   tablespoon grated Romano cheese
1   tablespoon grated Parmesan cheese
    Garlic powder, to taste
    Salt and pepper, to taste

Trim round steak, cut into serving pieces and pound with meat mallet to tenderize. Dip meat into vegetable oil and then into bread crumb mixture. Cook under the broiler until lightly browned. (6-8 servings)

SUSAN ENGLAND

Mandarin Beef Stir-Fry

2   tablespoons cornstarch
11/4   cups water
1/3   cup soy sauce
1/3   cup light or dark corn syrup
1/4-1/2   teaspoon crushed dry red pepper flakes (more will make spicier)
1   pound flank steak
2   tablespoons peanut oil
2   cloves garlic, minced
2   cups (1/2 pound) broccoli flowerets and stems
2   onions, cut into thin wedges
2   carrots, cut into strips
1/2   pound mushrooms, halved or quartered
    Green pepper, cut into strips (optional)
    Cooked rice

In a small saucepan, mix cornstarch and water until well blended. Add soy sauce, corn syrup and red pepper. Cook on low bringing to light boil. Remove from heat. Cover and set aside. Slice steak across the grain into thin strips. In a large skillet or wok, heat oil and add beef and garlic. Stir-fry until meat is brown on all sides; remove to platter. Add broccoli, onions and carrots to skillet and cook about 2 minutes; remove vegetables. Add more oil to skillet if necessary. Add mushrooms and green pepper and cook about 2 minutes. Put all ingredients back into skillet; add sauce and let boil one minute. Serve over rice. (4 servings) *"You may substitute chicken for the beef and use chicken broth instead of water. Can also substitute chili sauce or cocktail sauce for the red pepper flakes."*

LARISSA GHISO

Thai Basal Beef

2	pounds sirloin
4	tablespoons vegetable oil
2	cloves garlic, minced
4	tablespoons brown sugar
2	tablespoons water
	Nam Pla to taste (see recipe below)
2	sliced hot red or green chiles
4	tablespoons fresh basil leaves (or 1/2 tablespoon dried)

NAM PLA:

1	teaspoon curried fish powder (or anchovy paste)
4	teaspoons soy sauce
4	teaspoons water

Cut sirloin into thin strips (so sauce will permeate meat). Set aside. Heat vegetable oil in heavy skillet. Sauté garlic in oil. While garlic cooks, combine sugar and water; set aside. Add meat to skillet cooking on all sides. When meat is almost done, add sugar water and nam pla. Simmer slowly until meat is cooked through. Add chiles and increase heat. Allow sauce to caramelize and coat the meat (few minutes). Add basil; stir and serve at once. *"Nam pla is a fish sauce used instead of salt in Thai cooking. Add as much as you want to get the taste you like. This dish goes well with brown or white rice."* FRED KARSCH

Madeira Sauce

2-3	garlic cloves, peeled
3-4	large shallots, peeled
2	tablespoons margarine
1	cup Madeira wine
1	cup beef broth
2	tablespoons cornstarch
1/4	cup Beaujolais wine
2	drops Kitchen Bouquet

In a food processor with metal blade, mince garlic and shallots. Melt margarine in a skillet and sauté garlic and shallots gently over medium heat 5 minutes or until soft. Add Madeira and 3/4 cup of broth and simmer until mixture is reduced to 1 cup. Dissolve cornstarch in remaining broth and whisk into Madeira mixture. Cook sauce, stirring occasionally, about 5 minutes or until thick enough to coat a spoon lightly. Stir in Beaujolais and Kitchen Bouquet. Adjust seasoning and strain sauce into a bowl. (Makes 1 1/4 cups) *"This sauce is excellent served over steaks; also good on venison."* BETTY KONNAK

189

Special Ham with Candy Corn

1	12-pound ham
2-3	cans sliced pineapple
1	container cloves
1	pound bag brown sugar
1-2	cans crushed pineapple
3-4	16-ounce cans creamed corn
2	cans cherry ham glaze

Preheat oven to 350°. Place ham in a deep roasting pan. Arrange sliced pineapple on ham; secure with toothpicks and cover pineapple with cloves. Mix brown sugar with crushed pineapple and spoon around ham in bottom of baking dish. Pour half the creamed corn also in bottom of dish. Cut a deep hole in ham in middle of every pineapple ring so pineapple juice will penetrate ham and keep it moist. After about 11/2 hours baking time, spread half of the cherry ham glaze over top; after 2 hours spread half of second jar of glaze and the other half in corn. Stir well. (30 servings) *This wonderful dinner was made for the families who were staying at the Ronald McDonald House at the same time as the Rugg family.* KEITH RUGG

Upside-Down Ham Loaf

11/2	pounds ground smoked ham
1/2	pound ground fresh pork
2	eggs, slightly beaten
1	cup milk
1/2	teaspoon salt
1/8	teaspoon pepper
1	cup cracker crumbs
3/4	cup brown sugar
1/4	cup vinegar
1	teaspoon dry mustard
6	slices pineapple
1 0	maraschino cherries

Preheat oven to 375°. Mix together meats, eggs, milk, salt, pepper and cracker crumbs. Grease a large bread pan generously and pour brown sugar that has been mixed with vinegar and mustard, over the bottom. On this, press six slices of pineapple with a cherry in the center and between each slice. Over this, spread meat, packing in place. Bake 1 hour. KATHERINE KERSEY

Third World Dinner

2   pounds dried black beans
2   cloves garlic, minced
1   large yellow onion, chopped
11/2 teaspoons whole cumin seeds
1/4   pound ham, cut into small pieces (optional)
1   teaspoon salt
1/4   teaspoon pepper
      Cooked brown rice
      Chopped sweet white onions (Vidalia the best)

Soak beans overnight in water; drain. Cover with fresh water and boil 1 hour. Add garlic, yellow onions, cumin, ham, salt and pepper. Cover; cook slowly 4 hours or until beans thicken. Layer rice, equal amount of beans and thin layer of chopped sweet onions in each bowl.

SONDRA GUNN

Ham and Broccoli Pie

2   unbaked pie crusts
3   tablespoons minute tapioca, uncooked
1   16-ounce package frozen broccoli pieces, thawed
1   pound baked ham, sliced thin
2   cups shredded Colby-Jack cheese

Preheat oven to 400°. Sprinkle tapioca over bottom crust. Drain broccoli and squeeze to remove excess liquid; set aside. Cut ham into 1-inch squares. Fill pie by alternating broccoli, cheese and ham. Place top crust on pie and bake 35 minutes. (6-8 servings) JOANNE BOLAS

Baked Ham Sandwich

1/4   pound butter
1   tablespoon poppy seeds
11/2 tablespoons prepared mustard
1/2   tablespoon Worcestershire sauce
1   small onion, grated
      Hamburger buns or Kaiser rolls
1   pound ham, slivered
1/4   pound Swiss cheese, sliced

Preheat oven to 350°. Combine butter, poppy seeds, mustard, Worcestershire and onion. Spread mixture on both sides of roll. Place ham and cheese in the middle. Wrap in foil. Bake 20 minutes. *"You may wrap hot sandwiches in newspaper and pack in cooler or basket for a picnic."* CAPRICE WARREN

PORK

Pork Chops with Rice

6	medium pork chops, 3/4 inch thick
11/3	cups cooked rice
1	cup orange juice
1	can chicken with rice soup
	Salt and pepper to taste

Preheat oven to 350°. Brown pork chops in a skillet. Place rice in a 12 x 7-inch baking dish. Pour orange juice over rice and place meat on top. Pour undiluted soup over top. Cover and bake 45 minutes; uncovered, 10 minutes. MARY DOYLE

Pork in Sour Cream

1-2	pounds pork tenderloin
	Salt and pepper to taste
	Flour
	Oil
1	cup white wine or broth
1	cup sour cream
1-2	teaspoons Dijon mustard
1/4	teaspoon basil (optional)

Cut tenderloin into 11/2-inch slices. Sprinkle with salt and pepper. Pound pork pieces with a mallet until about 3/4-inch thick medallions. Dust with flour and cook about 5 minutes per side in oil at medium-high heat. Remove and keep warm. Add wine to pan and scrape up brown pieces and simmer about 1 minute. Add sour cream and heat about 2 minutes until thickened. Add mustard and basil. Add pork to coat and heat through. (3-4 servings) NANCY LIVERMORE

Aimee's Breakfast Casserole

8	frozen hash brown patties
11/2	pounds sausage, browned
8	eggs
2	cups milk
2	cups shredded cheddar cheese
	Salt and pepper to taste

Preheat oven 350°. Grease 9 x 13-inch baking dish. Cover bottom with hash browns. Cover hash browns with browned sausage. In a bowl, beat together eggs, milk, cheese, salt and pepper. Pour mixture over sausage. Refrigerate overnight. Bake 45 minutes to 1 hour. (8 servings)
GRACE BACON

Hawaiian-Style Pork Chops

5-6   thick pork chops
3   tablespoons brown sugar
1   tablespoon cornstarch
1   tablespoon soy sauce
1/2   teaspoon salt
1/4   cup vinegar
1/2   cup ketchup
1   20-ounce can crushed pineapple or chunks

Preheat oven to 350°. Brown chops lightly on both sides. Combine remaining ingredients and cook until thickened, stirring constantly. Arrange a layer of chops in roasting pan; cover with some pineapple mixture. Add another layer of chops and then rest of sauce. Cover and bake 1 hour or until chops are tender. LARISSA GHISO

Medallions of Pork

11/2-2 pounds pork tenderloin
2   teaspoons dry mustard
1   teaspoon salt
1/4   teaspoon freshly-ground pepper
2   tablespoons butter
2-3   cloves garlic, minced
1/4   cup dry vermouth
1/2   cup white wine
1   cup orange juice
3-4   tablespoons parsley
1   tablespoon flour
2   tablespoons water
        Orange zest, optional
        Orange slices, optional

Trim fat from tenderloin and cut into 1/2-inch slices. Combine dry mustard, salt and pepper and rub into meat. Melt butter in a large skillet over medium heat and add pork slices and garlic. Brown meat for 3-5 minutes on each side. Add vermouth, wine, orange juice and parsley; reduce heat. Cover and simmer 8-10 minutes or until meat is tender. Remove medallions to a warm plate and cover. Make a paste of flour and water. With a whisk, stir the paste into pan juices and simmer to thicken. Return medallions to pan gravy for a minute and then arrange on a serving platter and cover with gravy. May sprinkle with orange zest and arrange slices of orange around platter. Serve with rice. (6 servings) "Fantastic!" ANN BETZ

Hot and Sour Pork or Chicken

1-2	pounds pork tenderloin
2-3	tablespoons vegetable oil
4	green onions, sliced
1	large or 2 medium yellow onions, sliced
3	tablespoons lime juice*
11/2	tablespoons brown sugar
1/4	teaspoon salt
3	tablespoons dark soy sauce
3	red or green chiles, sliced in rounds without removing seeds*
	Cooked white rice

Cut pork into thin slices. Heat oil in a wok or frying pan until hot. Add green and yellow onions and stir-fry 1 minute, until fragrant. Stir in pork, lime juice, sugar and salt. Continue stir-frying, sprinkling with a little water from time to time. When pork has completely changed color (about 5 minutes), add soy sauce and chiles. Stir-fry another minute and remove. Serve with lots of white rice. (3 servings) *"The use of lime juice and chiles identifies this dish as a favorite of Chinese in Southeast Asia. Depending on the type of chiles used, this dish can be fiery-hot. For a less spicy dish, you reduce the number of chiles or seed them."*

*COOK'S TIP: Vinegar may be substituted for lime juice, for a slightly different flavor. For a hotter, spicier dish, stir-fry chiles with green and yellow onions before adding meat.

VARIATION: Chicken thigh meat, cut into bite-size pieces, can be substituted for pork, but will take longer to cook. After frying onions, add chicken only and stir-fry for 10 minutes before adding other ingredients (lime juice, sugar, salt and soy sauce). Simmer for another 5-7 minutes until chicken is tender and sauce is thick. You may have to add more water during cooking. LINDA LIM

194

Tasty Barbecue Sauce

1/4	cup brown sugar
1	tablespoon paprika
1	teaspoon salt
2	teaspoons mustard
1/2	teaspoon chili powder
1/2	teaspoon cayenne pepper
1/4	cup Worcestershire sauce
1/2	cup cider vinegar
2	cups V-8 tomato juice
1/2	cup ketchup

Mix all ingredients in microwave container and cover. Microwave 5 minutes (full power) and stir. Continue to microwave with cover ajar for 5-minute intervals, stirring, until sauce reduces and thickens. *"Great on chicken or ribs."* LEON PASTALAN

Sweet and Sour Sauce

3/4	cup sugar
1/4	cup soy sauce
1/3	cup wine vinegar
3	tablespoons cornstarch

Mix all ingredients and heat over medium heat. Stir occasionally until thickened. (Makes 1 1/2 cups) MIDGE WAKEFIELD

Pizza

First you make gooey dough with flour. Then make a circle with the dough. Next you put cheese on the dough. You can put sausage on it or hot dogs cut up. Put Chef Boy-Ardee sauce on the pizza. Cook the pizza in the oven for 7 minutes. Then you deliver it. You can take it home, cut it, put it on the table and then you eat it. MATTHEW, AGE 7

PORK

Seafood

SEAFOOD

Crab	199
Shrimp	200
Scallops	206
Fish	210

Crab and Noodles

1   cup half-and-half cream
1/2   cup butter
1   8-ounce package pimento cheese slices (Kraft)
1/4   cup dry vermouth
3/4   pound crabmeat
1 2   ounces wide egg noodles

In a saucepan, simmer cream and butter until butter is melted and thoroughly blended. Crumble slices of cheese into mixture while simmering and stir constantly until cheese melts. Add vermouth and simmer another 3-5 minutes. Add crabmeat to mixture, simmer another 10-15 minutes. Meanwhile, prepare noodles according to package directions. Drain; toss with above mixture. Let settle in baking dish, covered with foil, for 1-2 days in the refrigerator allowing flavors to blend. Then warm at 225-250° for approximately 1 hour (keep covered with foil).

KATHY DOYLE-SCHUELER

Crab Luigi

8   ounces small shell macaroni
1   tablespoon salad oil
4   hard-cooked eggs, chopped
1/3   cup diced celery
1/3   cup diced green pepper
1/4   cup sliced green onions
1   6-ounce package frozen crabmeat, thawed and shredded

Cook macaroni according to package directions. Rinse; drain well. In large bowl, toss with oil. Cover and chill. In a separate bowl, combine eggs, celery, green pepper, onions and crabmeat. Set aside. Make dressing.

DRESSING:
1   cup mayonnaise
1/3   cup chili sauce
1/4   cup sour cream
1   tablespoon lemon juice
1   teaspoon Worcestershire sauce
1/2   teaspoon salt

In a small bowl, combine all dressing ingredients; mix well. Toss dressing with macaroni, crabmeat and vegetable mixture. Cover and chill at least 3 hours before serving. ELLA M. ALLEN

Seafood Enchiladas

1	package Krab Delight chunks
2	cups shredded Monterey Jack cheese
1/4	cup minced onion
1	4-ounce can chopped green chiles
8	flour tortillas

Preheat oven to 350°. Mix Krab meat, cheese, onion and chiles. Soften tortillas in microwave (10 seconds). Fill tortillas with mixture, roll and place in a greased 9 x 12-inch baking dish. Make white sauce.

WHITE SAUCE:

4	tablespoons butter or margarine
4	tablespoons flour
21/4	cups milk
1/4	cup dry sherry
1/4	teaspoon Beau Monde seasoning

In a saucepan, melt butter; add flour and whisk vigorously to make a smooth paste. Add milk and sherry gradually, whisking continuously until thick. Add Beau Monde. Cook 5 minutes. Pour over enchiladas and bake 20 minutes. (4 servings) ANDREA WOO

Shrimp Scampi

11/2	pounds large shrimp
1/4	cup butter
2	cloves garlic, minced
2	tablespoons minced fresh parsley
1/8	cup lemon juice
1/4	teaspoon salt (optional)
1/8	teaspoon pepper
3	tablespoons bread crumbs

Clean shrimp. Melt butter in skillet. Sauté garlic on low for 1 minute. Add shrimp and sauté 5-8 minutes until lightly browned. Remove shrimp and put in baking dish. Add remaining ingredients to skillet. (More butter can be added at this point, if desired.) Pour over shrimp. Sprinkle bread crumbs over shrimp. Put under broiler about 2 minutes. (2 servings) GLORIA PROCHOWNIK

Tempura

3 0   prawns (or lobster)
1   cup flour
1   egg, slightly beaten
1   cup very cold water
        Cooking oil

Cut prawns into pieces, wipe with paper towel. Make a batter by mixing flour, egg and water together with a fork. Dip fish into mixture and fry in boiling oil that has reached a temperature of 300°. Drain on paper towel. Make the dipping sauce.

SAUCE:
11/2   cups soup stock
6   tablespoons mirin (or white wine or sake)
6   tablespoons soy sauce

GARNISH:
1   tablespoon grated Japanese daikon (radish)
1/2   teaspoon grated fresh ginger

In a small saucepan, combine soup stock, wine and soy sauce; bring to a boil. Cool. Serve sauce in small dishes with grated daikon and ginger.

TAMAE YOKOYAMA

Marinated Shrimp

30-35   fresh medium shrimp
1/2   cup olive oil
1/4   cup white wine vinegar
2   cloves garlic, minced
1   tablespoon Herbes de Province

Drop shrimp into boiling water and boil until pink. Rinse in cold water and remove shells. Mix remainder of ingredients and thoroughly coat the shrimp. Marinate overnight in refrigerator or at least three hours at room temperature. JANET GILSDORF

New Orleans-Style Barbecued Shrimp

1 4   large fresh shrimp (heads on)
6   tablespoons unsalted butter, cold and cut into cubes
11/2 teaspoons ground black pepper
1   teaspoon Creole seasoning (see below)
3   tablespoons Worcestershire sauce
1   teaspoon minced garlic
      Juice of 1 lemon
      French bread

CREOLE SEASONING:
1   cup salt
1/4   cup granulated garlic
2   teaspoons ground black pepper
1   teaspoon cayenne pepper
1   teaspoon oregano
1/4   cup paprika
1   tablespoon granulated onion

Preheat oven to 450°. Place shrimp, 3 tablespoons butter, pepper, Creole seasoning, Worcestershire and garlic in a saucepan large enough so that the shrimp are in one layer. Place shrimp in the oven for 2 minutes. Turn the shrimp and return to the oven for 2-3 minutes. Remove saucepan from the oven and begin to sauté over moderate heat. Add lemon juice and melt the remaining 3 tablespoons of cold butter by swirling pan and stirring with a fork. Serve shrimp in a bowl and pour the sauce over the shrimp. Garnish with hot French bread for dipping. Store remaining Creole seasoning in a sealed container. (2 servings) ROXANNE SCHIELKE

Summer Shrimp

1   cup mayonnaise
2   teaspoons salad herbs
1/4   cup crumbled feta cheese
1   cup fancy frozen vegetables, or fresh (cooked)
3/4   pound salad shrimp
1   cup bean threads, cooked*

Blend mayonnaise, herbs and feta in blender. Mix all ingredients together in a skillet. Heat gently and serve. (4 servings)

*COOK'S TIP: If bean threads are unavailable, may substitute 2 packages cooked Ramen noodles. DEBRA BOYER

202

Double Batch Shrimp Florentine

4	packages frozen chopped spinach
3	pounds uncooked shrimp
1/2	cup butter
1/2	cup flour
3	cups milk
1	cup dry white wine
1/2	cup chopped green onions
	Salt and pepper
	Paprika
1/4	cup grated Parmesan cheese

Preheat oven to 350°. Line two 9-inch pie pans with foil. Thaw and drain spinach. Spread half of spinach in each pie pan and top with shrimp. In a saucepan, melt butter; stir in flour. Gradually add milk, wine and green onions. Cook and stir constantly over low heat until sauce bubbles and thickens. Add salt and pepper to taste. Add paprika to give a rosy color. Pour sauce over shrimp; sprinkle with cheese. Bake one pie 35 minutes; freeze the other. (Later, bake frozen pie, uncovered, at 350°, 1 hour.) (4-6 servings each) SANDY MERINO

Baked Seafood Casserole

2	6-ounce cans crabmeat
2	cans shrimp
1	small green pepper, diced
1/2	cup chopped onions
1/2	can pimento
1	cup chopped celery
1	4-ounce can mushrooms
1	cup cooked rice

SAUCE:

1	cup salad dressing
1/2	teaspoon salt
1	cup half-and-half cream
1/8	teaspoon pepper
1	tablespoon Worcestershire sauce
1/2-3/4	cup bread crumbs

Preheat oven to 375°. Mix seafood, vegetables and rice together and set aside. Blend all sauce ingredients together except bread crumbs. Mix with seafood/vegetable mixture and place in buttered baking dish. Sprinkle with bread crumbs and bake, uncovered, 30 minutes. ELLA M. ALLEN

Datta's Shrimp

1 2	extra-large fresh shrimp
2	cloves garlic, minced
	Salt and pepper to taste
1	large egg, beaten
	Ritz cracker crumbs
	Oil

OPTIONAL SAUCE:

21/2	tablespoons soy sauce
11/2	teaspoons sugar
1/4	teaspoon Accent

Mix sauce ingredients together until sugar is dissolved; set aside. Peel shrimp and devein. Split down the back, butterfly fashion, being careful not to cut all the way through. Tenderize by lightly chopping in a criss-cross fashion. When all are ready, peel garlic cloves; cut in half across the middle and put the pieces through a garlic press. Rub the pulp across the shrimp. Let shrimp stand for 3-5 minutes; scrape off excess garlic, if you wish. Sprinkle shrimp with salt and pepper to taste. Beat egg in a bowl. Dip shrimp in egg and then in cracker crumbs. At this stage you can put prepared shrimp between layers of waxed paper and refrigerate (until 5 minutes before mealtime). At the last moment, heat vegetable shortening in a small skillet (to a depth of 1/2 inch or so) until quite hot. Fry shrimp (it should only take a couple of minutes) until golden brown, turning once. Serve at once with soy sauce mixture or any sauce to your liking.

COOK'S TIP: The shrimp can be prepared during your free time, even a day before. Save the shells from the shrimp. Add 3/4 cup water to the shells and bring to a boil briefly. Save the broth to add to soups, sauces, etc. P. DATTA

Hot and Spicy Shrimp with Noodles

1	cup fresh orange juice
2/3	cup chicken broth
1/4	cup soy sauce
2	tablespoons grated orange peel
2	teaspoons sugar
3	tablespoons peanut oil
2	small carrots, peeled and cut into thin strips
2	Anaheim chiles, seeded and cut into thin strips
1	red bell pepper, cut into thin strips
1	8-ounce package noodles or spaghetti
1	tablespoon sesame oil
6	slices peeled fresh ginger, minced
4	cloves garlic, minced
3	green onions, minced
3/4	teaspoon red pepper flakes
3/4	pound uncooked unpeeled large shrimp
21/2	teaspoons cornstarch (dissolved in 2 tablespoons chicken broth)

Combine orange juice, chicken broth, soy sauce, orange peel and sugar in a small bowl; stir to dissolve sugar. Heat 1 tablespoon peanut oil in a wok or large skillet over high heat. Add carrots, chiles and bell pepper; stir-fry about 4 minutes. Transfer vegetables to bowl. Cook noodles until al dente, about 3 minutes; drain well. Toss with sesame oil. Return to hot pot; cover to keep warm. Heat remaining peanut oil in wok over high heat. Mix in ginger, garlic, onions and pepper flakes. Add shrimp and stir until beginning to turn pink, about 1 minute. Add orange juice mixture and cook about 3 minutes, until shrimp are almost cooked. Return vegetables to wok and stir until heated. Pour cornstarch mixture into center of wok. Stir until sauce thickens. Serve shrimp mixture on top of noodles.
(2 servings) CHRIS IMAZUMI-O'CONNOR

Shrimp and Scallop Gruyère

3/4 cup plus 2 tablespoons margarine
3/4 cup flour
3 cups milk
1 2 ounces Gruyère cheese
1/4 teaspoon garlic powder
31/2 teaspoons salt
Pepper
1/4 teaspoon dry mustard
2 teaspoons tomato paste
3 teaspoons lemon juice
1 pound raw scallops
1/2 pound fresh mushrooms, sliced
1 pound cooked shrimp
Rice or patty shells

In a saucepan, make a cream sauce by combining 3/4 cup margarine, flour and milk. Cut cheese into small pieces and add to the sauce. Cook and stir until cheese melts. Add garlic powder, 3 teaspoons of salt, pepper, dry mustard, tomato paste and 2 teaspoons of lemon juice. Poach scallops for 10 minutes in water with remaining lemon juice and 1/2 teaspoon salt. Add 1/2 cup broth from scallops to the cream sauce. Sauté mushrooms in 2 tablespoons margarine and add to the sauce. Drain scallops and add with the shrimp to the sauce; heat. Serve on rice or in patty shells. (6 servings)
MARIEL PECK

Shrimp-Garlic Pasta

21/2 pounds fresh tomatoes
2 tablespoons olive oil
2 (or more) cloves garlic, minced
1/4 teaspoon hot pepper flakes
1 teaspoon oregano
1 tablespoon parsley
1/2 teaspoon Mrs. Dash seasoning
Pepper to taste
1/2 cup red wine
1 pound peeled shrimp
1 14-ounce can artichoke hearts, drained
1 pound spaghetti, cooked
2 tablespoons grated Parmesan cheese

Cook tomatoes in oil and garlic. Add spices and red wine. Add shrimp and artichoke hearts; toss with cooked pasta. Sprinkle Parmesan on top of each serving. (6 servings) PAT HABER

Shrimp and Crabmeat Madeira

1/2	pound shrimp
6	ounces cooked, drained crab
1/2	cup Madeira wine
3	tablespoons butter
2	tablespoons chopped shallots
3/4	cup sliced mushrooms
1/4	teaspoon tarragon
1	tablespoon lemon juice
2	teaspoons tomato paste
2	egg yolks
3/4	cup heavy cream
	Salt and pepper to taste
	Cooked linguine
	Chopped parsley

Marinate shrimp and crab in Madeira 20 minutes. Melt butter in saucepan. Add shallots and mushrooms; sauté until soft. Add shrimp and crab with Madeira. Cook until mixture is almost completely reduced. Add tarragon, lemon juice and tomato paste; mix thoroughly. Combine egg yolks with cream and very slowly add to saucepan, mixing constantly. Salt and pepper to taste. Heat completely. Serve on cooked thin linguine. Top with parsley. (2-3 servings) KATHY DOYLE-SCHUELER

Scallops Provencale

6	tablespoons oil (corn or olive)
1 1/2	pounds scallops
2	tablespoons flour
1/4	cup finely-chopped onions
1	teaspoon lemon juice
1	8-ounce can whole tomatoes
	Salt and pepper to taste
1/4	cup chopped parsley
2	tablespoons flour
	Rice

Heat oil in frying pan over medium heat. Dust scallops with flour and add to frying pan; cook 5 minutes until opaque. Add onion and cook 2 minutes. Add lemon juice, tomatoes, salt, pepper and parsley; simmer 3-5 minutes. Serve with rice. (4-6 servings) CAROLINE BLANE

Scallops with Red Pepper Cream

RED PEPPER CREAM:
1/4   cup unsalted butter
2   pounds red bell peppers, diced
2   tablespoons sugar
2   tablespoons cider vinegar
1   teaspoon paprika
1/2   teaspoon red pepper flakes
       Pinch salt

Melt butter in small saucepan over low heat. Stir in all ingredients. Cover and cook until peppers are very soft, stirring occasionally, about 50 minutes. Uncover pan. Increase heat to medium and stir until all liquid evaporates and peppers just begin to brown, about 10 minutes. Purée peppers in blender and discard skins. (Makes about 1 cup) (Can be stored in refrigerator 1 week or frozen.)

2   tablespoons unsalted butter
21/2   pounds sea scallops
       Salt and pepper
1   cup dry white wine
1/4   cup dry sherry
1   cup heavy cream
1/2   cup Red Pepper Cream

Heat butter in a large skillet over high heat. Add scallops, salt and pepper; stir until just opaque, 3-4 minutes. Transfer scallops to bowl. Add wine and sherry to skillet and boil until reduced to syrup, stirring frequently, about 7 minutes. Whisk in cream and any juices in scallop bowl. Boil until thickened, stirring occasionally. Whisk in Red Pepper Cream and heat through. Stir in scallops. Serve immediately. (6 servings)

CHRIS IMAZUMI-O'CONNOR

Scallops in Wine Sauce
(Coquilles Saint-Jacques)

2   pounds small scallops
1   pint white wine (Chablis)

WINE SAUCE:
4   tablespoons butter, melted
1   cup sliced mushrooms (about 1/2 pound)
4   green onions, chopped
1   tablespoon minced parsley
      Salt and pepper to taste
      Dash marjoram
      Dash thyme
11/2 tablespoons flour
4   tablespoons heavy cream
1/2   cup bread crumbs
2   tablespoons butter, melted
      Paprika

In a saucepan, simmer scallops in white wine 10 minutes until white; remove scallops. Cut scallops into small pieces and keep warm. Simmer liquid down to about 1 cup. In another saucepan, combine butter, mushrooms, green onions, parsley and seasonings. In a small bowl, make a smooth paste combining flour and 2 tablespoons of cream; slowly add to saucepan along with the scallop wine broth. Using a whisk, stir constantly to thicken. Add 2 more tablespoons of cream. Stir scallops into mixture; take pan off heat. Combine bread crumbs and butter with a fork. Pour scallops into individual scallop dishes. Sprinkle paprika on top; then sprinkle bread crumbs. Broil until the crust is golden brown. Serve immediately. (4 generous servings) *"This elegant entrée is one of our favorites."* ANN BETZ

Fettuccine with Shrimp and Scallops in White Wine Sauce

4	tablespoons butter
1	tablespoon olive oil
1/2	cup chopped shallots (or green onions)
1/2	pound medium shrimp, shelled and deveined
1/2	pound baby scallops (or bay scallops, cut in half)
1	tablespoon dill
1	teaspoon basil
1/2	cup white wine
1	cup half-and-half cream (or milk)
1	pound fettuccine, cooked al dente (regular or spinach)
1/2	cup grated Parmesan cheese

In a skillet, melt 2 tablespoons of butter and add olive oil. Sauté shallots until transparent, 2-3 minutes. Add shrimp and scallops; sauté until coated, about 1 minute. Add dill and basil; mix. Add white wine and cook over medium heat until liquid is reduced by half, about 20 minutes. Add cream and simmer until sauce is thickened, about 5 minutes. Toss cooked fettuccine with 2 tablespoons butter and Parmesan cheese. Top with shrimp and scallop mixture. CINDY MEYERS

Teriyaki Tuna Kabobs

MARINADE:

1/2	cup light soy sauce
2	tablespoons sugar
2	tablespoons dry sherry
1	tablespoon rice wine
2	cloves garlic, minced
1	tablespoon hoisin sauce
11/2	teaspoons grated fresh ginger
1	tablespoon sesame oil

KABOBS:

3/4-1	pound fresh tuna
1	bell pepper, cut in large pieces
1	medium onion, cut in large pieces
2	medium potatoes, cut in large pieces

Combine marinade ingredients. Prepare tuna and vegetables. Cut tuna into large chunks and marinate 30-60 minutes. Thread tuna and vegetables onto bamboo skewers that have been soaked in water. Grill 4-6 minutes, basting occasionally. (2-3 servings) JERI KELCH

210

Hot Tuna Ring with Cold Cucumber Sauce

1	can cream of mushroom soup
2	eggs, beaten
1/2	cup mayonnaise
1/2	teaspoon salt
1/4	teaspoon pepper
1/2	cup chopped onions
1/4	cup chopped green pepper
1	cup dry bread crumbs
2	61/2 ounce cans tuna, drained and flaked

Preheat oven to 350°. In a bowl, combine soup, eggs, mayonnaise, salt and pepper; whisk until smooth. Add onions, green pepper and bread crumbs. Fold in tuna. Pour into a 5-cup ring mold and bake 50 minutes. Serve with Cold Cucumber Sauce. (6-8 servings)

COLD CUCUMBER SAUCE:

1/2	cup mayonnaise
1/2	cup sour cream
1/2	cup chopped cucumber
2	tablespoons chopped onions
1/2	teaspoon dill

Blend all ingredients in a food processor. Place in a bowl in the center of tuna ring. (11/2 cups sauce) JAY MCDONALD

Tuna Melt

Put a piece of bread in a toaster. When it comes out, put tuna fish on the toast. Then put a piece of cheese on top. Then put in a microwave for 30 seconds. When it comes out, let it cool, then eat it. SARAH, AGE 7

Teriyaki Salmon

1/2   cup light corn syrup
1/2   cup light soy sauce
1/4   cup sake or gin
21/2   pounds salmon fillets

Heat a toaster oven to 400° (450° for a regular oven). In a small saucepan, combine corn syrup, soy sauce and sake. Heat to boiling. Cook 5 minutes, stirring frequently. Remove from heat; cool. Spoon some sauce over salmon. Cook 5-10 minutes, basting with additional sauce until fish just turns opaque. (4 servings) *This salmon is delicious served with spicy, Asian eggplant.* ROXANNE SCHIELKE

Salmon Fillets with Mustard Cream Sauce

1   cup plus 2 tablespoons chilled heavy cream
1   cup dry white wine
1/4   cup dry vermouth
3   green onions, minced
4   6-ounce salmon fillets, 1-inch thick

Whisk 2 tablespoons cream in a small bowl to soft peaks; cover and refrigerate. Combine wine, vermouth and green onions in a heavy skillet. Boil until liquid is reduced by half, about 5 minutes. Add 1 cup cream and bring to boil. Reduce heat to low. Add fish fillets. Cover and simmer until just cooked, about 10 minutes. Transfer fish to plates using slotted spatula. Tent with foil to keep warm.

CREAM SAUCE:
1/4   cup unsalted butter, cut into pieces
2   tablespoons Dijon mustard
1/4   cup chopped fresh chives
    Salt and pepper to taste

Place skillet with fish poaching liquid over high heat. Boil until reduced to 3/4 cup, stirring occasionally, about 5 minutes. Reduce heat to low. Gradually add butter, whisking until melted. Add mustard and chives and whisk to blend. Remove sauce from heat. Fold in chilled whipped cream. Season with salt and pepper. Spoon sauce over fish. (4 servings)
JANET GILSDORF

Salmon Rice Casserole

1   can cream of chicken soup
1   151/2-ounce can salmon, drained (reserve liquid)
2   teaspoons Dijon mustard
1   teaspoon seasoned pepper
11/2   cups (6 ounces) shredded cheddar cheese
1   10-ounce package frozen chopped broccoli,
        (thawed and drained)
3   cups cooked rice
        Paprika

Preheat oven to 350°. In a saucepan, stir together soup, 1/2 cup salmon liquid, mustard, pepper and 3/4 cup cheese. Stir until cheese is melted. In a mixing bowl, toss together broccoli and rice. Stir in half the soup mixture. Spoon into a greased, 2-quart baking dish. Top with flaked salmon. Pour remaining soup mixture over salmon and sprinkle with remaining cheese. Dust with paprika. Bake 20 minutes or until hot and bubbly. *"This may be frozen to use later. Simply complete casserole except for sprinkling with remaining cheese. Wrap and freeze. Thaw and sprinkle with cheese, dust with paprika and bake as directed."*

ELLA M. ALLEN

Salmon Celery Loaf

1   1-pound can salmon, drained and flaked
1/4   cup salmon liquid
1   can cream of celery soup
1   cup dry bread crumbs
2   eggs, slightly beaten
1/2   cup chopped onions
1   tablespoon lemon juice

Preheat oven to 375°. Combine above ingredients thoroughly. Pack into well-greased loaf pan. Bake 1 hour. May serve with sour cream sauce. (6 servings)

OPTIONAL SAUCE:
1   can cream of celery soup
1/3   cup sour cream
1/4   teaspoon dill

In a saucepan, combine sauce ingredients and stir until well blended. Serve with salmon loaf. KATHERINE KERSEY

213

Grilled Salmon with Herb Butter Sauce and Tomatoes

11/2   **pounds salmon fillet**
      Olive oil
      Salt and pepper to taste
      Garnish: 4 sun-dried tomatoes

HERB BUTTER SAUCE:
1	tablespoon olive oil
21/2	tablespoons minced shallots
3/4	teaspoon minced garlic
1	cup chopped tomatoes
	Salt and pepper to taste
4	sprigs parsley
2	sprigs tarragon leaves
3/4	cup chicken broth
1/2	cup heavy cream
1	cup butter, cut into 16 pieces
1	teaspoon thyme
2	tablespoons white wine
1	tablespoon chopped parsley
1	tablespoon chopped chives
1	tablespoon tarragon

To make the sauce: Heat olive oil in saucepan; add shallots and 1/2 teaspoon garlic and sauté 7-8 minutes. Add tomatoes, salt and pepper. Tie sprigs of parsley and tarragon into a bundle and add. Add chicken broth and bring to a boil; cook 30 seconds. Strain sauce; discard spice bundle. There should be about 1/2 cup of tomato pulp; set aside. Bring liquid to a boil in a saucepan and add cream. Cook over moderately high heat, stirring, about 3 minutes. Add butter, 2-3 pieces at a time. Cook until melted. Add reserved tomato pulp, remaining garlic, thyme and white wine. Bring to a slow simmer, stirring occasionally. Add parsley, chives and tarragon; stir. Cut salmon crosswise into 4 pieces. Brush lightly on both sides with olive oil and sprinkle both sides with salt and pepper. Brush the surface of a clean grill with olive oil and add salmon. Cook through. Pour equal portions of sauce onto 4 heated dinner plates. Place 1 piece of salmon on each plate. Garnish with sun-dried tomatoes.
(4 servings) PRUE ROSENTHAL

Sarah's Plate

GREEN BEAN MIXTURE:
1/4   cup hot French mustard
1/4   cup lemon juice
1/2   cup corn oil
       Salt and pepper to taste
1   pound fresh green beans, stems removed

ARRANGE ON A PLATE:
4   large lettuce leaves
1/2   pound smoked salmon
1   lemon, cut in wedges
1 6   cherry tomatoes
1   cucumber, sliced
       Green Bean Mixture

In a small bowl, combine all ingredients except green beans and whisk until well blended. Cook green beans 10 minutes until tender but still crisp and green. Plunge into cold water to cool. Coat green beans with dressing. *"This can be used as a first course or as a whole light meal."*

CAROLINE BLANE

Fish Sticks and Macaroni

Fish sticks first! You get them out of the freezer and pop them in the microwave for 15 minutes. Then eat them. Now we make the macaroni and cheese. First you boil the water and then when it's all boiled, you put the macaroni in. Then the bubbles keep turning when you keep spinning the spoon. You put the macaroni in the sink to get all of the water out. Then you put the cheese in. Then it's all done. KENNY, AGE 7

Crumb-Top Flounder

2   flounder fillets (about 1/2 pound)
2   tablespoons grated Parmesan cheese
1   tablespoon butter
3   tablespoons fine Ritz cracker crumbs

Preheat oven to 425°. Line shallow pan with foil; butter the foil. Put fillets in a single layer in pan and sprinkle each with 1 tablespoon of cheese. In a skillet, melt butter; stir in crumbs. Sprinkle over fillets. Bake 5 minutes. Broil a few minutes to brown the crumbs. (2 servings) BETTY CHAPIN

Broiled Rainbow Trout

2   14-ounce whole dressed trout
1/2   cup butter
1/4   teaspoon salt
1/8   teaspoon freshly-ground pepper

SAUCE:
1/2   cup butter, melted
1/4   cup dry white wine
2   tablespoons finely-minced parsley
1/8   teaspoon garlic powder
1/8   teaspoon paprika
2   tablespoons Grand Marnier liqueur

Wash fish thoroughly with cold water. Dry with paper towels. Melt butter. Baste inside and outside of fish heavily with butter. Season with salt and pepper. Combine all sauce ingredients except Grand Marnier and simmer a few minutes. Broil fish 10 minutes on each side, basting with sauce after turning. (Make sure not to overcook.) Sprinkle fish with Grand Marnier and top with wine sauce before serving. (4 servings)

COOK'S TIP: Put two fillets together (meat sides). Skin may look burned after grilling. MARTIE BAKER

Stuffed Flounder

1/4	cup chopped onions
1/4	cup butter or margarine
1	3-ounce can chopped mushrooms, drained (reserve liquid)
1	71/2 ounce can crabmeat, drained and cartilage removed
1/2	cup coarse saltine cracker crumbs
2	tablespoons snipped parsley
1/2	teaspoon salt
	Dash pepper
2	pounds flounder fillets (8)
3	tablespoons butter
3	tablespoons flour
1/4	teaspoon salt
	Dash pepper
	Milk
1/3	cup dry white wine
4	ounces (1 cup) shredded Swiss cheese
1/2	teaspoon paprika

Preheat oven to 400°. In a skillet, sauté onions in butter until tender, but not brown. Combine drained mushrooms, crab, cracker crumbs, parsley, salt and pepper. Spread mixture over flounder fillets. Roll fillets and place seam side down in a 9 x 12-inch baking dish. In a saucepan, melt 3 tablespoons butter. Blend in flour and salt. Add enough milk to mushroom liquid to make 11/2 cups. Add with wine to saucepan. Cook and stir until mixture thickens and bubbles. Pour over fillets. Bake 25 minutes. Sprinkle with cheese and paprika. Return to oven. Bake 10 minutes longer or until fish flakes easily with fork. (8 servings)

GEORGE CARIGNAN

Sole Casserole

1/4	cup butter
1/4	cup lemon juice
	Salt and pepper to taste
1	cup cooked rice
1/2-1	package chopped broccoli, thawed
1/2	cup shredded cheddar cheese
1	pound flounder fillet or sole

Preheat oven to 375°. Melt butter and add lemon juice, salt and pepper. Combine rice, broccoli and cheese. Mix half of butter mixture with broccoli mixture; spread on bottom of baking dish. Lay fish on top and sprinkle remaining butter mixture. Bake 30 minutes; broil 5 minutes to brown the top. (4 servings) PRUE ROSENTHAL

217

Stuffed Fillet of Sole

11/2	tablespoons butter
1	tablespoon flour
1/2	teaspoon salt
1/2	teaspoon lemon juice
1/2	teaspoon horseradish
1/8	teaspoon Worcestershire sauce
	Dash onion powder
	Dash hot pepper sauce
1/8	teaspoon Accent
	Dash pepper
1/3	cup milk
1/2	cup crabmeat
1/2	cup shrimp
4	fillets of sole
2	tablespoons butter
11/2	teaspoons lemon juice
	Paprika
	Lemon wedges

Preheat oven to 350°. In a saucepan, melt butter. Stir in flour and add salt, lemon juice, horseradish, Worcestershire, onion powder, hot pepper sauce, Accent and pepper. Blend in milk; cook until thick, stirring continuously over medium heat. Remove from heat. Add crab and shrimp; mix well. Arrange 2 fillets in a greased shallow baking dish. Pour mixture over fillets and top with 2 more fillets. In a mixing bowl, combine butter and lemon juice; pour over top. Sprinkle with paprika. Bake 30 minutes. Serve with lemon wedges. (4 servings) KATHY DOYLE- SCHUELER

Fantastic Fish

1   teaspoon salt
2   tablespoons fresh lemon juice
4   4-6 ounce white fish fillets, scrod or sole (skin removed)
1   cup milk
11/2 cups bread crumbs
3/4   cup mayonnaise
3/4   cup sour cream
1   bunch fresh green onions, chopped (including green tops)
       Paprika

Preheat oven to 375°. Sprinkle salt and lemon juice over fish. Soak fish in milk for 3 minutes; drain slightly. Lightly coat top and bottom with bread crumbs. In a bowl, combine mayonnaise, sour cream and onion. Spread mixture on top of fish. Dust with paprika. Bake 20-25 minutes until sauce is thick, bubbly and browned. Serve immediately with baby redskins and fresh green beans. (4 servings) *This can be put together up to four hours in advance of baking.* DICK REEDY

Soufflé Baked Fish

11/2 pounds fresh or frozen fish fillets, thawed
1   teaspoon salt
1/4   teaspoon pepper
2   egg whites
1/4   cup mayonnaise
1   tablespoon pickle relish, drained
3   tablespoons green onions, chopped
1   tablespoon chopped parsley
1/4   teaspoon salt
2   drops red pepper sauce

Preheat oven to 425°. Place fish in greased baking dish. Sprinkle with salt and pepper. Bake 10 minutes. In a medium bowl, beat egg whites until stiff peaks form. Blend in mayonnaise, drained relish, green onions, parsley, salt and red pepper sauce. Spread over fish, covering completely. Continue baking 10-15 minutes longer until the topping is well puffed and fish flakes easily with a fork. (4 servings) BETTY CHAPIN

Vegetables

VEGETABLES

Boston Baked Beans

1	pound navy beans
1	teaspoon baking soda
2	small cubes (1 x 1 inch) salt pork
21/2	tablespoons brown sugar
1/3	cup molasses
1	teaspoon dry mustard
1/8	teaspoon pepper
1	small onion, cut into 4 pieces
2	teaspoons vinegar
1/8	cup ketchup

Soak beans overnight covered in water. Add baking soda and simmer 20 minutes. Remove water and rinse. Preheat oven to 325°. In another pot, boil salt pork in 2 cups water 10 minutes. Drain and rinse. Combine beans, pork and all other ingredients; mix well. Cover mixture with boiling water. Bake 5-6 hours. Remove salt pork after baking and discard. (6 servings)

COOK'S TIP: Beans must always be covered with water while baking. Check every hour, stir and add water as needed, but do not add during the last hour. Towards the end of baking, the beans turn brown, look moist, not dry. DENISE PROCHOWNIK

Special Baked Beans

1	pound bacon, cut up
3-4	onions, sliced thin
1	teaspoon garlic powder
1/2	teaspoon dry mustard
1	cup brown sugar
1/2	cup vinegar
2	15-ounce cans red kidney beans
1	can butter beans
1	28-ounce can B&M baked beans

Preheat oven to 325°. Fry bacon in a skillet; drain on paper towel. Sauté onions in drippings. Drain off as much grease as possible. Make sauce by combining garlic powder, mustard, brown sugar and vinegar. Pour over onions and simmer 20 minutes. Mix in all beans. Pour into baking dish and bake, uncovered, 50 minutes. MARY SWANSON

Lake Five Beans

1   pound dried Great Northern beans
4   tablespoons Honey Cup mustard
1/3   cup white wine vinegar
1/3   cup maple syrup
2   cups water
1   tablespoon salt
1   tablespoon coarsely-ground pepper
1   pound smoked sausage links, cut into 1-inch pieces

In a large bowl, soak beans overnight in enough water to cover. The next day, drain off water. Preheat oven to 350°. Add mustard, vinegar, syrup, water, salt and pepper to beans. Mix well. Add sausage. Add more water as needed to cover beans. Bake 2 hours. Turn oven down to 250° and cook 10 hours, adding water as necessary to keep beans moist. *"I make this every summer on vacation at Lake Five, Minnesota."* JANET GILSDORF

Homemade Refried Beans (Frijoles Refritos)

1   pound pinto beans
2   onions, chopped
2-4   teaspoons chili powder (or to taste)
2-4   cloves garlic, minced
2   teaspoons salt
1   teaspoon pepper
1   teaspoon oregano
1/2   teaspoon cumin
1/2   cup hot bacon drippings, margarine or lard
      Shredded cheese, optional
      Sour cream, optional

Soak beans in 5-6 cups water in a saucepan overnight. Drain. Add fresh water to cover. Add remaining ingredients except bacon drippings. Cook covered, over low heat, for 3 hours or until tender. Mash beans. Heat drippings in large frying pan over medium-high heat. Add beans and cook until thickened, stirring frequently. Sprinkle shredded cheese and spoon sour cream on top of each serving. Serve immediately. (6 servings) *"I like to make these so I can control the amount of fat used. These can be used as a filling for tortillas or as a sidedish."* NANCY FROST COLLINS

Broccoli

First you cook it. Then put cheese on it. Let the cheese melt. Then you eat it. It tastes good when you eat it. QUATAVIUS, AGE 6

Italian Broccoli Casserole

2	10-ounce packages frozen chopped broccoli
2	eggs, beaten
1	can condensed cheddar cheese soup
1/2	teaspoon dried oregano
1	8-ounce can stewed tomatoes, cut up
3	tablespoons grated Parmesan cheese

Cook broccoli per package directions; drain well. Preheat oven to 350°. Combine eggs, soup and oregano. Stir in broccoli and tomatoes. Pour into a 10 x 6-inch baking dish. Sprinkle with cheese. Bake, uncovered, 30 minutes, or until heated through. (6-8 servings) MOLLY GATES

Broccoli Soufflé

1	20-ounce package frozen broccoli
2	cans cream of mushroom soup
1	cup shredded cheddar cheese
1/2	cup milk
2	beaten eggs
1/2	cup mayonnaise

CRUMB TOPPING:

2	tablespoons butter, melted
1/2	cup bread crumbs

Cook broccoli according to package directions. (Do not add salt.) Drain. Preheat oven to 350°. Put broccoli in bottom of 9 x 12-inch baking dish. Stir soup and cheese together and gradually add milk, eggs and mayonnaise until blended. Pour over broccoli. Mix butter and crumbs together. Sprinkle crumb mixture over top. Bake 45 minutes. Let set before serving. (8 large servings) *"This recipe is great for preparing ahead of time and freezes well."* JOYCE HERSHENSON

225

Sweet and Sour Brussels Sprouts

1	package frozen Brussels sprouts, cooked
2	tablespoons cooking oil
1/4	cup vinegar
1	tablespoon sugar
1/2	teaspoon salt
1/4	teaspoon pepper
2	tablespoons grated Parmesan cheese

Preheat oven to 350°. Arrange sprouts in a shallow buttered baking dish. Combine ingredients (except the cheese) and pour over sprouts. Sprinkle with cheese. Cover and bake 15 minutes. (6 servings) BETTY CHAPIN

Braised Red Cabbage

1	medium head red cabbage (2-21/2 pounds)
4	tablespoons butter, cut into small pieces
1	tablespoon sugar
1	teaspoon salt
1/3	cup water
1/3	cup vinegar
1/4	cup red currant jelly
2	tablespoons grated apple

Preheat oven to 325°. Wash cabbage and remove tough outer leaves. Cut away core and slice cabbage very finely. (There should be approximately 9 cups.) Combine butter, sugar, salt, water and vinegar in a heavy stainless steel or enameled 4-5 quart baking dish. When butter has melted, add shredded cabbage and toss thoroughly. Bring to a boil and cover tightly. Place in center of oven to braise for 2 hours, checking liquid level occasionally. (Add a little water if it seems necessary.) About 10 minutes before cabbage is finished, stir in jelly and grated apple. Replace cover and complete the cooking. (6 servings) *"Serve hot as an accompaniment to a stuffed loin of pork or goose."*

COOK'S TIP: The piquant taste of red cabbage will improve if allowed to rest for a day in the refrigerator and then reheated in a 325° oven.

ROXANNE SCHIELKE

Carrots with Sour Cream and Dill

6   medium carrots, cut into thick slices
2   tablespoons water
1/4   cup chopped onions
1/2   teaspoon salt
1/2   teaspoon pepper
1/4   teaspoon dill
1   tablespoon brown sugar
1/4   cup sour cream

In a 11/2-2 quart casserole, combine carrots and water. Cover; microwave on high 7-8 minutes. Stir at half-time. Drain, reserving 1 tablespoon liquid. Combine with remaining ingredients and stir into cooked carrots. Cover; microwave on high 1-2 minutes. (4-6 servings) NANCY DHUE

Cauliflower-Olive Spread (for Muffaletta Sandwiches)

1   28-ounce can olives with pimentos
1/2   bunch celery, coarsely chopped
1/2   head cauliflower
3   carrots, coarsely chopped
1   onion
1/3   cup capers
1/2   bunch parsley
3   cloves garlic, minced
    Salt and pepper to taste
1   cup olive oil
1/2   cup vinegar

In a food processor, coarsely chop olives and transfer to a large bowl. Chop remaining vegetables and add to olives. Add capers, parsley, garlic, salt and pepper, oil and vinegar. May store in refrigerator for up to two weeks. JANET GILSDORF

Antipasto

1	small cauliflower (2 pounds)
4	red peppers
4	green peppers
2	cups Mazola oil
4	20-ounce bottles ketchup (use good quality)
2	jars sweet pickle onions (can leave whole if small)
1	2-quart jar dill pickles
3	4-ounce cans mushrooms, cut up
2	pounds carrots, cut up
1	head celery, cut up
3	16-ounce cans black pitted olives, drained
3	16-ounce jars green pimento olives
5	cans green beans, cut up
3	cans tuna fish
1	large can anchovies
1/2	cup vinegar
	Salt to taste

In a canner, boil cauliflower slightly, 3-4 minutes. Slice and cut peppers and sauté in oil. Pour ketchup in pot; add cauliflower, onions, pickles, mushrooms and peppers. Boil 5 minutes, stirring often. Add rest of the ingredients. Bring to boil. Pack in sterilized jars. Process 15 minutes. *"You may serve antipasto on crackers or small pieces of bread. It can also be used as an omelette filling."* (Makes approximately 20 pints)

COOK'S TIP: Do not use a food processor to cut the vegetables; it flakes them and you get mush (average-size pieces are best). This will keep for a very long time in the refrigerator, once the jar is opened. You can pack the antipasto in quart or pint jars. The cost per pint to make this is approximately $1.50 to $2.00, not including cost of jars and lids.

ENA HOBELAID

Onion-Olive Spread

2	green onions, chopped fine
1/4	cup chopped black olives
1/4	cup chopped pecans
1/4	cup whipped cream cheese
2	English muffins, cut in half

In a small bowl, combine onions, olives, pecans and cream cheese. Mix well using a fork. Spread onto toasted English muffins. ANN BETZ

Corn Pudding

1	8-ounce can corn, drained
2	eggs, beaten
2	tablespoons sugar
2	tablespoons soft butter
2	cups scalded milk
	Pepper to taste
1	cup Grapenuts cereal

Preheat oven to 325°. Combine all ingredients except Grapenuts in a baking dish. Sprinkle Grapenuts on top. Bake 30 minutes. (6 servings)

DOROTHY WARDELL

Corn Casserole

1	8-ounce can corn, drained
1	8-ounce can creamed corn
1	cup sour cream (or cottage cheese)
2	eggs, slightly beaten
4	tablespoons minced onions
1	box Jiffy cornbread mix
1/4	cup margarine, melted

Preheat oven to 350°. Mix corn, sour cream, eggs and onions together. Add dry cornbread mix and margarine. Stir vigorously and pour into greased 8 x 8-inch pan. Bake 45 minutes to 1 hour. NADINE KORC

Fried Corn

1/4	cup butter
2	cups corn (4-5 large ears or 1, 10-ounce box frozen)
1/2	cup chopped ham or bacon
1/2	cup chopped onions
1/2	cup diced green pepper
	Salt to taste
	Freshly-ground black pepper to taste
3	tablespoons cream, milk or water

Heat butter in medium skillet until hot, but not smoking. Add corn, ham, onions and green pepper. Sauté, stirring often until onions and green pepper are crisp-tender, about 5 minutes. Stir in salt, pepper and cream. Cook 20 minutes, stirring several times until thickened. *"Fresh corn is the best to use. Scraping corncob to get all of the milk from the corn is important."* KATHERINE KERSEY

Eggplant Szechwan

1-11/2 pounds eggplant
1/4   cup vegetable oil
3   green onions, chopped
1   large clove garlic, minced
1/2   teaspoon grated fresh ginger
2   tablespoons cornstarch
4   tablespoons water

SEASONING MIXTURE I:
1/2   teaspoon Szechwan bean paste or crushed red pepper
1   tablespoon soy sauce
2   tablespoons mirin or sherry
1   tablespoon sugar
1   cup chicken broth
1   tablespoon vegetable oil
1/4-1/2 pound pork butt, minced

SEASONING MIXTURE II:
1   tablespoon white vinegar
1/4   teaspoon sesame oil

Trim ends off eggplant and cut into eighths, lengthwise. Cut each section into 1/4-inch slices and cut slices into 2-inch lengths. Lightly sprinkle with salt and dry with paper towels. Mix together green onions, garlic and ginger. Separately combine ingredients for seasoning mixture I and II. Place wok over medium heat. When hot, add oil. Add eggplant and stir until lightly browned. Remove and set aside. Put pork in wok, add garlic-ginger-onion mixture and stir-fry 1 minute. Add seasoning mixture I, broth and eggplant. Cover and simmer 5 minutes. Mix cornstarch and water until smooth. Add seasoning mixture II and enough cornstarch and water mixture to thicken to desired consistency. Stir until sauce has thickened and serve. CHRIS IMAZUMI-O'CONNOR

Vegetable Pizza

2	cans crescent rolls
2	8-ounce packages cream cheese, room temperature
1	package ranch dressing mix
1	cup plain yogurt or mayonnaise
1	cup sliced broccoli
1	cup cauliflower, separated
4-5	mushrooms, sliced
1	green pepper, sliced
1/4	cup sliced olives
1	carrot, sliced
1	tomato, diced

Preheat oven to 350°. Spread crescent roll dough on cookie sheet. Seal all seams. Bake 8 minutes. Mix together cream cheese, ranch dressing mix and yogurt. Spread mixture on cooled crescent rolls. Combine all vegetables. Sprinkle veggies over cream cheese, press lightly and refrigerate. Cut in squares to serve. BARBARA COLWELL

Spicy Asian Eggplant

4	Asian or 2 young Italian eggplants*
2	tablespoons peanut oil
1	1/2-inch piece fresh ginger, peeled and minced
3	garlic cloves, minced
1/2-1	teaspoon crushed red pepper flakes
1/3	cup light soy sauce
1	tablespoon sesame oil
2	green onions, thinly sliced
1/2	cup cilantro (fresh coriander) leaves (or 1/4 cup minced fresh parsley)

Cut eggplant into 1/2-inch slices. Place in colander over boiling water. Cover tightly and steam 5 minutes or just until tender. Remove eggplant to serving dish. Meanwhile, heat peanut oil in a small saucepan over medium heat. Add ginger, garlic and crushed red pepper; sauté 3 minutes but do not brown. Add soy sauce and heat to boiling. Remove from heat; stir in sesame oil. Scatter green onions on top of eggplant. Pour hot sauce over eggplant and garnish with cilantro or parsley. (4 servings)

*COOK'S TIP: Use long, thin, bright purple Asian eggplants if you can find them. If not, the young Italian ones are a good substitute; simply cut them lengthwise into quarters and proceed. ROXANNE SCHIELKE

Mushroom Stroganoff

1/8	cup dried mushrooms
2	tablespoons sherry or marsala wine
1/4	cup boiling water
2/3	cup plain low-fat yogurt
2	teaspoons Dijon mustard
2	teaspoons poppy seeds
1/2	teaspoon tarragon
3/4	pound mushrooms, thinly sliced
3	teaspoons olive oil
2	teaspoons margarine
1	medium onion, thinly sliced
1	clove garlic, minced
1/4	teaspoon salt
	Freshly-ground black pepper to taste
3	cups medium egg noodles, cooked
1/4	cup minced parsley

Soak dried mushrooms in sherry and boiling water for 30 minutes. Cut into smaller pieces; reserving liquid. Stir together yogurt, mustard, poppy seeds and tarragon. Sauté fresh mushrooms in 2 teaspoons olive oil and margarine until soft and brown. Remove from skillet and set aside. Heat remaining oil in the skillet and sauté onions and garlic, about 10 minutes. Return sherry mushrooms with the liquid and stir 2 minutes. Add sautéed fresh mushrooms, salt and pepper; cook 3 minutes. Remove from heat. Stir some hot mixture into yogurt mixture. Add yogurt back into mushrooms, stirring to combine. Drain noodles. Pour stroganoff mixture over noodles and add parsley; stir to combine. (6 servings) DEBBIE ZIES

Roasted Marinated Peppers

1	each red, green and yellow bell peppers
1/2	tablespoon balsamic vinegar

Scorch peppers over gas burner or in electric broiler until skin is burned on all sides. Place scorched peppers in a paper bag for 10 minutes. Remove peppers; under running cold water, peel away burned skin. Slice peppers into strips and place into serving bowl. Toss with vinegar. (4-6 servings) JANET GILSDORF

Onion Tart

CRUST:
3   cups flour
1   teaspoon salt
1   cup unsalted butter, chilled and cut in pieces
1/4   cup plus 2 tablespoons ice water

In a food processor, combine flour and salt. Add butter and process until mixture resembles coarse meal. Add ice water, a tablespoon at a time, and process just until dough forms a ball. Divide in half. Roll out each half to about 12-inch circles and line 9-inch pie pans. Freeze one for future use.

FILLING:
2   tablespoons unsalted butter
4   cups thinly-sliced sweet red onions
1/2   cup dry white wine
1/4   cup minced fresh parsley
2   cups shredded Swiss cheese

Preheat oven to 450°. In a large skillet, melt butter and sauté onions over medium-low heat 15 minutes, until wilted. Add wine and parsley and simmer 15 minutes more, until liquid is almost evaporated. Layer 1 1/2 cups cheese on bottom of tart shell and top with 1 1/2 cups of onion mixture. Layer remaining cheese and onions. Bake just long enough to melt cheese and brown crust. Cut into wedges and serve with black olives, pickles and/or cherry tomatoes. (8 servings) JANET GILSDORF

Scalloped Tomatoes

2   cups canned tomatoes
1   tablespoon sugar
3   tablespoons quick-cooking tapioca
1/2   cup chopped onions
1   cup chopped celery
1   teaspoon salt

TOPPING:
4   tablespoons butter, melted
1   cup crushed cornflakes

Preheat oven to 350°. Combine tomatoes, sugar, tapioca, onions, celery and salt. Mix well. Pour into greased 1-quart baking dish. Set aside. Combine butter and crumbs until crumbs are moist. Sprinkle over tomato mixture. Bake 45 minutes. (4 servings) BETTY CHAPIN

233

Squash Casserole

11/2	pounds yellow summer squash (cooked and puréed)
1	2-ounce jar chopped pimento
1	small onion, grated
2	large carrots, grated
1	can cream of chicken soup, undiluted
1	cup sour cream
1	package Pepperidge Farm cornbread stuffing
1/2	cup margarine, melted

Preheat oven to 350°. Combine squash, all other vegetables, soup and sour cream; set aside. Mix stuffing and margarine; pour on bottom of baking dish (reserve some for top). Spoon squash mixture over this and top with remaining stuffing. Bake 30 minutes. (12 servings)

MRS. HOMER LACKEY

Spinach with Raisins and Pine Nuts

1/4	cup raisins
2	tablespoons olive oil
3	tablespoons pine nuts
1	onion, finely chopped
1	clove garlic, minced
2	pounds fresh spinach
	Salt and pepper to taste

Soak raisins in boiling water to plump, then drain. Sauté pine nuts in olive oil until golden; set aside. Sauté onions and garlic. Rinse spinach. Cook in a covered pan, with only the water clinging to the washed leaves, for a few minutes, turning leaves a couple times from top to bottom. Drain, pressing out liquid and chop. Stir chopped leaves into onions and garlic; add raisins and nuts. Season with salt and pepper. (4-6 servings)

JANET GILSDORF

Tomato-Cheese Pie

PIE CRUST:
11/2   cups flour
1/4   teaspoon salt
1/4   pound butter
5   tablespoons ice water

Preheat oven to 375°. Combine flour and salt. Cut up cold butter into small pieces. Blend butter into flour and salt. Add ice water a tablespoon at a time. Mix with a fork, make into a ball with fingers, blending in butter further. Refrigerate at least 1 hour, preferably overnight. Roll out dough and place in 10-inch quiche dish or other flat, shallow pan. Prick bottom and sides. Place foil inside pie crust to hold in place. Bake 10-15 minutes.

FILLING:
3-4   fresh tomatoes, cut into 1/2-inch slices
3/4   pound Gruyère cheese, sliced
1   teaspoon basil
1   tablespoon grated Parmesan cheese
1   tablespoon butter, melted

One-half hour before baking, sprinkle tomatoes with salt and place on paper towels to absorb water. Place Gruyère cheese on bottom of partially-cooked pie crust. Place drained tomatoes on top of cheese. Sprinkle basil and Parmesan over tomatoes. Drip melted butter over top. Bake about 1/2 hour at 375° until cheese is melted. Let stand 5 minutes before slicing. (6 servings) SUZANNE F. GREFSHEIM

Quick and Healthy Veggie Quiche

1   unbaked pie crust
1   package frozen Stouffer's spinach soufflé (thawed)
4   eggs, beaten (throw one yolk out)
2   cups fresh broccoli (or cauliflower or any vegetable)
1   cup low-fat milk
8   ounces cheese of choice, sliced thin
   Leftover chicken, rice or pasta (optional)

Preheat oven to 375°. Mix spinach soufflé, eggs, vegetables, milk and cheese in a bowl. Pour into crust. Bake 45 minutes. Allow to sit for 5 minutes. CATHY MALETTE

Swiss Vegetable Medley

1	16-ounce bag frozen broccoli, carrots and cauliflower
1	can cream of mushroom soup
1	cup shredded Swiss cheese
1/3	cup sour cream
1/4	teaspoon pepper
1	4-ounce jar chopped pimentos, drained (optional)
1	2.8-ounce can French-fried onions

Preheat oven to 350°. Combine all ingredients except for half of the cheese and half of the onions; place in a 1-quart baking dish. Cover and bake 30 minutes. Add rest of cheese and onions to top and bake, uncovered, 5 minutes longer. SANDI LIBKE

Mixed Vegetable Curry

2	tablespoons vegetable oil
2	teaspoons mustard seeds
6	cloves garlic, minced
1	2-inch piece fresh ginger, diced (optional)
1	teaspoon turmeric
1	medium onion, sliced lengthwise
2	cups diced tomatoes
1	cup diced potatoes
1	cup green peas (preferably fresh)
1	cup shredded cabbage
1	cup diced zucchini
1	cup diced yellow squash
1	cup chopped green bell pepper
2	teaspoons salt
2	teaspoons coriander powder
2	teaspoons cumin powder

Heat oil in a large, cast-iron pot. Add mustard seeds, garlic and ginger; stir. When mustard seeds begin to pop, add turmeric and stir until it changes color. Add onions and lightly fry until golden. Add all remaining ingredients, cover and cook mixture in its own steam until done. (Some water may have to be added.) Vegetables should have plenty of gravy at time of serving. *"A curry containing an assortment of fresh vegetables is delicious served over plain rice."*

VARIATION: Almost any vegetable can be used: okra, eggplant, various types of green beans, pumpkin, squash and green leafy vegetables such as spinach. Submitted by HEMALATA C. DANDEKAR, reprinted with permission from Beyond Curry: Quick and Easy Indian Cooking.

Mixed Vegetables

2   16-ounce packages frozen vegetables
1   pound Velveeta cheese
1   can cream of celery soup
2   tablespoons grated onions
2   cups crushed Ritz crackers
1/2 cup butter or margarine, melted
1/2 cup grated Parmesan cheese
1/2 cup shredded cheddar cheese

Preheat oven to 350°. Put frozen vegetables in the bottom of a 12 x 13-inch baking dish. Melt cubed Velveeta cheese. Pour over vegetables. Pour undiluted soup and onions over this. Mix crushed crackers with cheeses and butter. Sprinkle over top. Bake, uncovered, 30-40 minutes. (12-16 servings) *"Can be made a day ahead and refrigerated. I use the mixed vegetables of broccoli, cauliflower and carrots."* MARGARET TAPPING

Tarragon-Vegetable Medley

4   cups cauliflower flowerets
2   medium carrots, julienned
2   medium onions, cut into thin wedges
4   tablespoons water
2   medium green peppers, cut into 1-inch squares
2/3 cup pitted ripe olives, halved

DRESSING:
4   tablespoons white wine vinegar
2   tablespoons sugar
2   tablespoons cooking oil
1   teaspoon tarragon
1/2 teaspoon salt
     Garnish: Walnut halves

In a 2 1/2-quart baking dish, combine cauliflower, carrots, onion wedges and water. Place in microwave and cook, covered, on 100% power (high), about 7 minutes or until vegetables are almost tender, stirring once. Add green pepper. Cover and cook on high 2 minutes more or until green pepper is tender. Add olives. Stir together vinegar, sugar, oil, tarragon and salt. Stir oil mixture into vegetables. Cover and cook on high 30 seconds more. Garnish with walnut halves. (8 servings) *"You may serve this as a hot vegetable or let the vegetables marinate in the oil and vinegar dressing and serve cold."* ANN HANTON

VEGETABLES

Desserts

DESSERTS

Cookies

You put in some sugar and some water and some flour and put it in the oven for 10 minutes. Take them out. Eat 'em up. JERRY, AGE 7

Snickerdoodles

1	cup butter
11/2	cups sugar
2	large eggs
23/4	cups flour
2	teaspoons cream of tartar
1	teaspoon baking soda
1/4	teaspoon salt
1/4	cup sugar mixed with 1 tablespoon cinnamon

Cream butter and sugar until fluffy. Slowly add eggs and then flour, cream of tartar, baking soda and salt. Beat thoroughly. Wrap dough in plastic and chill for at least 1 hour.

Preheat oven to 400°. Roll small chunks of dough about the size of a large gumball and roll in sugar/cinnamon mixture. Place about 2 inches apart on ungreased cookie sheets. Bake 8-10 minutes or until lightly browned, but still soft. Center of cookie should still be soft. SUSAN HURWITZ

Italian Pizzelles

3/4	pound butter
2	cups sugar
8	eggs
2	teaspoons vanilla*
8	cups sifted flour
6	teaspoons baking powder
2	teaspoons salt

Cream together butter, sugar, eggs and vanilla. Add dry ingredients slowly; mix to dough consistency. Cut into 1 x 1 x 1/2-inch cubes and cook in pizzelle iron (about 30 seconds, until golden). Cool on a flat surface. (Makes about 10 dozen)

*COOK'S TIP: May substitute almond, orange, bourbon, etc. for vanilla flavoring. BARB LANESE

241

COOKIES

Sweetheart Cookies

1/2	cup shortening
1/2	cup sugar
1/4	cup brown sugar
1	egg
1/2	cup sour cream
1/2	teaspoon vanilla
21/2	cups flour
1/2	teaspoon baking powder
1/2	teaspoon baking soda

Preheat oven 350°. Cream shortening, sugars, egg, sour cream and vanilla. Add dry ingredients. Refrigerate one hour. Roll out on floured board and cut into desired shapes. Bake on ungreased cookie sheets 6-8 minutes or until golden. (Makes 4 dozen)

COOK'S TIP: You may sprinkle with sugar prior to baking or frost when cool. DEBBIE LOWN

Scottish Butter Cookies

1	cup unsalted butter, room temperature
2/3	cup sugar
2	cups flour
2	teaspoons vanilla
1/4	teaspoon salt
	Powdered sugar

Preheat oven to 350°. In a large bowl, cream butter with sugar until smooth. Gradually blend in flour, vanilla and salt; mix thoroughly. Pat mixture evenly into ungreased 10 x 15-inch jelly roll pan (can also use 9 x 12-inch cake pan). Sprinkle top with powdered sugar. Bake until golden (16-18 minutes). Cool 5 minutes; then cut into squares while still warm. Store in airtight container. (Makes 4 dozen) *These are great with ice cream.* JANET GILSDORF

M & M's

First you melt chocolate chips and shape them any way you want. Then put them in the freezer on a cookie sheet overnight. Then in the morning you take them out. Then you put sugar and a light color of dye and dip the chocolate in. KIRSTIN, AGE 8 AND LINDSEY, AGE 7

242

Stir and Drop Cookies

2	eggs
2/3	cup oil
2	teaspoons vanilla
3/4	cup sugar
2	cups flour
2	teaspoons baking powder
1/2	teaspoon salt

Preheat oven to 350°. Beat eggs, oil, vanilla and sugar. Add flour, baking powder and salt; mix thoroughly. Drop by teaspoonsful onto ungreased cookie sheets, about 2 inches apart. (The cookies may be decorated with sugar at this time.) Bake 10-12 minutes. JANINE MOURGUET

Nutmeg Cookie Logs

3	cups sifted flour
1	teaspoon nutmeg
1	cup butter or margarine (or half and half)
2	teaspoons vanilla
2	teaspoons rum flavoring
3/4	cup sugar
1	egg, unbeaten

Preheat oven to 350°. Sift together flour and nutmeg; set aside. Cream together butter, vanilla and rum flavoring. Add sugar to butter mixture; cream well. Blend in egg. Add flour mixture gradually. Shape pieces of dough into long narrow rolls (1/2-inch diameter) on a lightly-floured surface. (This dough usually doesn't need to be refrigerated to shape). Cut into 3-inch lengths and place close together on an ungreased baking sheet. Bake 12-15 minutes. Cool and frost.

FROSTING:

3	tablespoons margarine
1/2	teaspoon vanilla
1	teaspoon rum flavoring
21/2	cups powdered sugar
2-3	tablespoons evaporated milk

Combine margarine, vanilla and rum flavoring. Add powdered sugar and evaporated milk. Spread a little frosting on the cookies and score with a fork to resemble bark. Sprinkle with more nutmeg before icing sets.

MARJORIE BEST

243

Pecan Crunch Cookies

1	cup butter
1/2	cup sugar
1	teaspoon vanilla
1/2	cup crushed potato chips
1/2	cup chopped pecans
2	cups flour

Preheat oven to 350°. Cream butter, sugar and vanilla. Add potato chips and pecans. Stir in flour. Form into small balls. Place on ungreased cookie sheet. Press balls flat with bottom of a glass dipped in sugar. Bake 15-18 minutes. BETTY CHAPIN

Date Nut Balls

3/4	cup margarine
1	cup sugar
1	8-ounce package chopped dates
1	cup chopped nuts (pecans or walnuts)
2	cups Rice Krispies cereal
	Powdered sugar

In a large skillet over low heat, melt margarine. Add sugar, dates and nuts, stirring constantly. Remove from heat, add cereal and stir. Let cool just enough to roll into small balls. Dust in powdered sugar.

COOK'S TIP: When rolling balls, it helps to butter your hands to avoid sticking. KATHY DUNN FINGER

Pecan Balls

1	cup margarine
2	cups flour
1	cup plus 2 teaspoons powdered sugar
1/2	teaspoon vanilla
2	cups finely-chopped pecans

Preheat oven to 300°. Cream margarine until light and fluffy. Gradually beat in flour, 2 teaspoons powdered sugar and vanilla; mix in pecans. Shape into balls the size of small walnuts. Bake on ungreased cookie sheet 50 minutes. Carefully roll hot cookies in 1 cup powdered sugar. Store in covered container. (Makes 3 dozen) FRANK MOLER

Macadamia Nut Cookies

11/2   cups butter or margarine
2   cups sugar
2   eggs
4   cups flour
1   teaspoon baking soda
1   teaspoon cream of tartar
2   teaspoons vanilla
1   cup chopped macadamia nuts

Preheat oven to 400°. Cream butter with sugar. Add eggs and beat. Sift dry ingredients together; add to creamed mixture. Add vanilla and nuts, blending well. Roll into small logs, about 12 inches long, on waxed paper. (Dough will be soft, so refrigerate until firm.) Slice about 1/4-inch thick and place about 1 inch apart on ungreased baking sheets. Bake 10 minutes or until brown. (Makes about 8 dozen)

Poppy Seed Cookies

        Peel of 1 orange
1   egg yolk
1   cup sugar
1   cup (2 sticks) unsalted butter, room temperature (cut into 8 pieces)
1/2   teaspoon salt
1/2   teaspoon nutmeg
1   cup flour
1   cup cake flour
1/4   cup poppy seeds

Using a food processor, mince orange peel. Add egg yolk and sugar; mix 1 minute. Add butter, salt and nutmeg and mix until light and fluffy, about 1 minute. Add remaining ingredients and mix using 4 or 5 on/off turns (do not overprocess). Divide dough into 4 equal portions. Arrange each on sheet of plastic wrap. Using plastic as aid, shape dough into 2 x 4-inch rolls. Seal and refrigerate until firm, 1 hour. (Can be frozen at this point.)

Preheat oven to 350°. Cut dough into 1/4-inch slices. Arrange on baking sheet, 1 inch apart. Bake until edges are lightly browned, 8-10 minutes. Cool and store in airtight container. (Makes 5 dozen cookies)

CHRIS IMAZUMI-O'CONNOR

COOKIES

Gingersnaps

2 1/4 cups flour
1   cup packed brown sugar
3/4   cup cooking oil
1/4   cup molasses
1   egg
1   teaspoon baking soda
1   teaspoon ground ginger
1   teaspoon freshly-grated ginger
1   teaspoon ground cinnamon
1/2   teaspoon ground cloves
1/4   cup sugar

Preheat oven to 375°. In a mixing bowl, combine half of the flour, brown sugar, oil, molasses, egg, baking soda, both gingers, cinnamon and cloves. Beat until thoroughly combined. Beat in remaining flour. Shape dough into 1-inch balls. Roll in sugar. Place 2 inches apart on an ungreased cookie sheet and bake 8 minutes (no more). Cool cookies on a wire rack. (Makes 48 cookies)

COOK'S TIP: Make sure not to overbake. A little underdone makes them chewy on the inside. Store in a container with a piece of bread to keep them moist if they are not all eaten at once! LISA M. STOCK

Ranger Cookies

1   cup margarine
1   cup brown sugar
1   cup sugar
2   eggs
1   teaspoon vanilla
2   cups flour
1   tablespoon baking soda
1   cup oats
1   cup coconut
3   cups Rice Krispies cereal
1   cup chocolate chips

Preheat oven to 350°. Cream margarine, sugars and eggs. Mix in vanilla. Add flour and baking soda; mix well. Stir in oats, coconut, cereal and chips. Drop onto cookie sheet and bake 8-10 minutes. (Makes 3-4 dozen)

COOK'S TIP: For variety, add butterscotch chips and/or nuts. Store cookies in an airtight container. Freeze well. KELLY THOMAS

Peanut Butter Crunchies

1	12-ounce package chocolate chips
1	4-ounce cake paraffin
1	1-pound box powdered sugar
1/2	cup margarine
2	cups peanut butter
3	cups Rice Krispies cereal

Melt chocolate chips and paraffin in top of a double boiler. In a large bowl, mix together powdered sugar, margarine and peanut butter with your hands. Add cereal and mix well. Form into walnut-size balls and dip in mixture of chocolate chips and paraffin. Let dry on wax paper. DEB REISER

Double Chocolate Chewy Cookies

1/3	cup vegetable oil
4	ounces unsweetened chocolate
12/3	cups sugar
4	large eggs
13/4	teaspoons vanilla
1/8	teaspoon almond extract
13/4	cups flour
11/2	teaspoons baking powder
1/4	teaspoon salt
3/4	cup chocolate chips
	Powdered sugar

Combine oil and chocolate in saucepan and warm over low heat, stirring occasionally until chocolate melts. Remove from heat and stir in sugar using a wooden spoon. Add eggs and blend. Add vanilla and almond. Place flour, baking powder and salt in bowl and pour into chocolate mixture. Stir until mixed well. Add chocolate chips and stir until distributed. Cover and refrigerate at least 48 hours.

Preheat oven to 350°. Grease 2 baking sheets. Roll dough into balls (11/4-inch diameter). Place 2 inches apart on baking sheets. Bake 10-12 minutes or until just beginning to get firm in center. Remove from oven; let stand 1 minute. Transfer to wire racks to cool. Lightly sprinkle with powdered sugar. SUSAN HURWITZ

Chocolate Chip Cookies

First wash your hands. Put the one cup of powder, 8 pieces of chocolate chips, 3 cups of milk, sugar, 2 eggs in a bowl. Then take a spoon. Take some dough. Put in on a pan. Put it in the oven at 7°. You take it out and eat it. MARGARET, AGE 6

Peanut Butter Cookies

1	cup shortening
1	cup sugar
1	cup brown sugar
2	eggs
1	cup peanut butter
1	teaspoon vanilla
3	cups flour
1/2	teaspoon salt
2	teaspoons baking soda

Preheat oven to 375°. Cream shortening and sugars; add eggs. Stir in peanut butter and vanilla, then dry ingredients. Form tiny balls. Place on greased cookie sheet. Press with back of fork to make criss-cross. Bake 10 minutes. (Makes 50-60 small cookies) KATHERINE KERSEY

The Best Chocolate Chip Cookie

1/2	cup butter
1/2	cup margarine
1	cup sugar
1	cup brown sugar
1	teaspoon vanilla
2	eggs, at room temperature
21/2	cups oat bran flour
1	teaspoon baking soda
1	teaspoon baking powder
2	cups flour
6	ounce Hershey bar, grated
1	12-ounce package chocolate chips
1	cup chopped pecans

Preheat oven to 350°. Cream together butter, margarine, sugar, brown sugar, vanilla and eggs. Slowly add oat bran flour, baking soda, baking powder and flour. Stir in chocolate and pecans. Roll into balls and bake 12 minutes. (Makes 40 cookies) BARB LANESE

Rita's Oatmeal Cookies

1	cup shortening
1	cup brown sugar
1	egg
11/2	cups flour
1	teaspoon baking soda
1	teaspoon salt
2	teaspoons cream of tartar
11/2	cups oatmeal
1/2	cup grated coconut
1/2	cup chopped almonds, optional
1/2	cup chopped nuts, optional
1	12-ounce package chocolate chips, optional

Preheat oven to 350°. Cream shortening, brown sugar and egg together. Sift flour, baking soda, salt, cream of tartar and oatmeal together. Combine shortening and flour mixtures. Add coconut and, if desired, nuts and chocolate chips. Roll or drop from teaspoon onto greased cookie sheet. Bake 10-12 minutes. NORAH KARSCH

Oatmeal Cookies

1	cup shortening
1	cup brown sugar
1	cup white sugar
2	eggs, lightly beaten
1	teaspoon vanilla
13/4	cups flour
1/2	teaspoon salt
1	teaspoon baking soda
1	teaspoon baking powder
2	cups oatmeal
1/2	cup coconut
1/2	cup chopped nuts
1	cup cornflakes

Preheat oven to 350°. Cream together shortening and sugars. Add eggs and vanilla; mix well. In a separate bowl, combine flour, salt, baking soda, and baking powder. Combine shortening mixture with flour mixture, stirring well with a fork. Add oatmeal and stir. Add coconut, nuts and cornflakes and mix. Make into small balls. (Chill for 1/2 hour if batter gets too soft.) Bake about 10 minutes. (Makes 4-5 dozen)

NANCY LIVERMORE AND LAURIE HENDRICK

COOKIES

Spiced Apple-Raisin Cookies

3/4	cup butter, softened
1	cup packed brown sugar
1	egg
1	teaspoon vanilla
11/2	cups flour
1	teaspoon baking powder
1/2	teaspoon baking soda
1/2	teaspoon salt
1/2	teaspoon cinnamon
1/2	teaspoon nutmeg
11/2	cups quick-cooking oats, uncooked
1	cup finely-chopped, unpeeled apple
1/2	cup raisins
1/2	cup chopped nuts

Preheat oven to 350°. In a large bowl, cream butter. Gradually add sugar; beat until light and fluffy. Beat in egg and vanilla. In a separate bowl, combine flour, baking powder, baking soda, salt and spices. Gradually add flour mixture to creamed mixture; blend well. Stir in oats, apple, raisins and nuts. Drop dough by rounded teaspoonfuls 2 inches apart onto lightly-greased cookie sheets. Bake 10-12 minutes or until lightly browned. Cool completely on wire racks. (Makes about 5 dozen)

SUE GAUSS

Chocolate Chip Cookies

First you mix sugar and then you put flour and milk to thin the dough. Then you put two cups of vanilla in the batter. Add 44 chocolate chips. Put the cookies on a cookie sheet and bake them for 10 minutes. The degrees are 15. Then it's ready to eat. DAVID, AGE 7

No-Bake Cookies

2	cups sugar (white, brown or combination)
3	tablespoons cocoa
1/4	cup butter or margarine
1/2	cup milk
1/2	cup crunchy peanut butter
1	teaspoon vanilla
3	cups rolled oats

Optional: Coconut, peanuts, M&M's or marshmallows

Place sugar, cocoa, butter and milk in a saucepan and just bring to a rolling boil (cook no longer than 1 minute). Remove from heat and stir in peanut butter and vanilla. Stir in rolled oats and mix thoroughly. Add anything else you wish. Roll into balls. Put on wax paper to dry. *"These are great for kids to help make with adult help."* DEB REISER

Almond Apricot Delights

1 1/2	cups coarsely-chopped dried apricots
2	tablespoons cognac
1/2	cup almond paste
1/2	cup powdered sugar
2	teaspoons dry instant coffee
2	teaspoons cocoa
1/4	cup powdered sugar
1	teaspoon cocoa

Combine first 6 ingredients in food processor or blender and puree. Combine 1/4 cup powdered sugar and 1 teaspoon cocoa. Roll apricot mixture into marble-size balls and shake in the powdered sugar mixture. Store in an airtight container with the leftover powdered sugar mixture to prevent them from sticking. (Best kept in the freezer.) (Makes 50 balls) Reprinted with permission, MEDSPORT, HIGH FIT - LOW FAT™, REGENTS OF THE UNIVERSITY OF MICHIGAN

Lemon Cookies

1   box lemon cake mix
1   small container Cool Whip
1   egg, beaten
     Powdered sugar

Preheat oven to 350°. Mix egg with Cool Whip. Combine with cake mix. Roll into balls the size of a walnut and cover with powdered sugar. Bake 10-12 minutes. (Makes about 40 cookies) *"Quick and easy!"* KAREN RITZ

Venetian Cookies

1/2   cup sugar
1/2   cup butter
1/2   cup shortening
3   egg yolks, beaten
       Grated zest of 1 lemon
21/2   cups flour
       Jam of your choice

Preheat oven to 375°. Cream sugar, butter and shortening together. Mix in egg yolks and lemon zest; add flour gradually. Make balls the size of a large marble. Place on greased cookie sheets. Indent with thumb and fill with jam of your choice. Bake 12-15 minutes. *"We make these at Christmas only and the jam of choice is always raspberry."* SALLY CAYLEY

Caramel Bars

2   cups flour
1   cup margarine, melted
2   cups quick oatmeal
11/2   cups brown sugar
1   teaspoon baking soda
       Chopped nuts
1   14-ounce package caramels
1   cup heavy cream (or evaporated milk)

Preheat oven to 350°. Mix flour, margarine, oatmeal, 1/4 cup cream, brown sugar, soda and nuts together. Spread all but 3/4 cup of mixture into a 9 x 13-inch pan. Melt caramels with 3/4 cup of heavy cream slowly on top of the stove. Pour melted caramel mixture on top of crust. Sprinkle remaining topping over caramel mixture and bake 15 minutes. Let stand several hours. CAROL ZIEGLER

Layered Chocolate Bars

BARS:
11/2   cups margarine, room temperature
3   cups sugar
6   eggs
21/4   cups flour
1   cup cocoa
1   teaspoon salt
11/2   cups chopped walnuts

FIRST ICING:
1/2   cup margarine, room temperature
2   cups powdered sugar
3   tablespoons milk
2   tablespoons instant vanilla pudding (dry)

SECOND ICING:
1/2   cup margarine, room temperature
2   cups powdered sugar
3   tablespoons milk
2   tablespoons cocoa
1   teaspoon vanilla

Preheat oven to 350°. Mix together bar ingredients. Bake 25-30 minutes in greased and floured 9 x 13-inch pan. Cool. Cream together all ingredients for first layer of icing. Spread on brownies; then refrigerate. Cream together all ingredients for second layer. Spread over vanilla icing; then refrigerate. Serve cold. *"Freezes very well. Don't overcook! Very rich - tastes almost like fudge."* SUSAN GOOCH

Peanut Butter Bars

2   cups graham cracker crumbs
3/4   cup margarine, melted
11/2   cups peanut butter
2   cups powdered sugar
1   large package chocolate chips

Preheat oven to 350°. Combine above ingredients, except chocolate chips. Press mixture in a 9 x 13-inch pan. Top with chocolate chips. Bake until chips are melted; then spread chocolate evenly. Refrigerate just long enough to set chocolate. CAROL ZIEGLER

COOKIES

Pumpkin Cheesecake Bars

CRUST:
1   16-ounce package pound cake mix
1   egg
2   tablespoons margarine or butter, melted
2   teaspoons pumpkin pie spice

FILLING:
1   8-ounce package cream cheese, room temperature
1   14-ounce can Eagle sweetened condensed milk
2   eggs
1   16-ounce can pumpkin
2   teaspoons pumpkin pie spice
1/2 teaspoon salt
1   cup chopped nuts

Preheat oven to 350°. In large mixing bowl, combine crust ingredients until crumbly. Press onto bottom of 15 x 10-inch jelly roll pan. In another bowl, beat cream cheese until fluffy. Beat in condensed milk, then eggs, pumpkin, pumpkin pie spice and salt; mix well. Pour over crust and sprinkle with nuts. Bake 30-35 minutes or until set. Let cool, then chill. Cut into bars. Store, covered, in refrigerator. (48 bars) CHRISTINE ADAMS

Butterscotch Brownies

1/2 cup margarine
2   cups light brown sugar
2   eggs
2   cups flour
2   teaspoons baking powder
1   teaspoon salt
1   teaspoon vanilla
1   cup chopped pecans
1   package butterscotch chips

Preheat oven to 350°. Melt margarine in large saucepan. Add brown sugar. Cool mixture. Stir in eggs. Add flour, baking powder, salt, vanilla, nuts and butterscotch chips. Bake in 9 x 13-inch pan 35 minutes.
CATHERINE MCDOWELL

Pumpkin Bars

4	eggs
1	small can pumpkin
2	cups sugar
1	cup oil
2	cups flour
2	teaspoons baking powder
1/2	teaspoon salt
2	teaspoons cinnamon
1/4	teaspoon cloves
1	teaspoon baking soda

FROSTING:
1	tablespoon milk
21/2	cups powdered sugar
6	tablespoons margarine
1	teaspoon vanilla
1	3-ounce package cream cheese, room temperature

Preheat oven to 350°. Beat eggs, pumpkin, sugar and oil together. Add flour, baking powder, salt, cinnamon, cloves and baking soda and beat well. Put on greased cookie sheet and bake 20-30 minutes. ELLA M. ALLEN

Apricot Squares

1	cup sugar
1	cup butter
2	egg yolks
2	cups flour
1/2	cup chopped nuts (optional)
1 2	ounces apricot preserves (or apricot filling)

Preheat oven to 325°. Cream butter and sugar together until fluffy. Stir in egg yolks, flour and nuts; mix thoroughly. Spread half of dough on a greased 9 x 13-inch pan and pat down. Spread preserves over dough. Crumble rest of dough on top of preserves. Bake 35 minutes. When cool, cut into squares. SHARON SMITH

Date Bars

3	cups chopped dates
1/8	teaspoon salt
2	cups boiling water
1/3	cup brown sugar
1/2	teaspoon vanilla
3	cups oatmeal
2	cups flour
1/2	teaspoon salt
1	teaspoon baking powder
1/2	cup brown sugar
1/2	cup butter
1/2	cup shortening

Preheat oven to 325°. Cook dates, salt and water until thick, stirring so they will not burn. Add brown sugar and vanilla. Mix well and cool. Put oatmeal in a large mixing bowl. Sift flour, salt and baking powder over oatmeal. Add brown sugar; mix well. Mix butter and shortening into this until crumbly. Combine with date mixture. Pour into greased 9 x 13-inch pan and bake 40 minutes. JOAN DOOP

Gumdrop Bars

1	cup gumdrops (use red and green for Christmas)
2	eggs
1	cup sugar
1	teaspoon vanilla
1	cup flour
1	teaspoon salt
1/2	cup chopped almonds, toasted and blanched

Preheat oven to 325°. Cut up gumdrops, divide in half and set aside. (Cut big ones into fourths. Don't use spicy gumdrops.) Beat eggs until foamy. Beat in sugar and vanilla. Stir together flour and salt. Mix in almonds and 1/2 cup gumdrops. Spread in a well-greased and floured 9-inch square baking dish. Sprinkle remaining gumdrops over top of batter. Bake 30-35 minutes. Cut into squares while warm, but don't remove from pan until cool. (The crust will crack, but don't worry about it.) MARJORIE BEST

256

Pecan Pie Squares

CRUST:
3   cups flour
1/4   cup plus 2 tablespoons sugar
3/4   cup margarine or butter, softened
3/4   teaspoon salt

Heat oven to 350°. Grease 15 x 10-inch jelly roll pan. Beat flour, sugar, margarine and salt on medium speed until crumbly (mixture will be dry). Press firmly in pan. Bake until light golden brown, about 20 minutes. Prepare filling.

FILLING:
4   eggs, slightly beaten
1 1/2   cups sugar
1 1/2   cups Karo corn syrup (light or dark)
3   tablespoons margarine or butter, melted
1 1/2   teaspoons vanilla
2 1/2   cups chopped pecans

Mix all filling ingredients except pecans until well blended. Stir in pecans. Pour over baked layer; spread evenly. Bake until filling is set, about 25 minutes; cool slightly. While still warm, cut into 1 1/2-inch squares. (Makes 70 squares) SHERYL IKEMOTO

S'More Bar Cookies

1/2   cup margarine
1/2   cup packed brown sugar
3/4   cup flour
1/2   cup graham cracker crumbs
1   7-ounce milk chocolate bar, melted
2   cups miniature marshmallows

Preheat oven to 375°. Beat margarine and sugar until light and fluffy. Add flour and crumbs; mix well. Press onto bottom of greased 9-inch square pan. Bake 15-18 minutes or until golden brown. Spread chocolate over crust. Top with marshmallows. Broil 4 inches from heat source, 1-2 minutes, or until marshmallows are lightly browned. Cool; cut into bars. (Makes 16 bars) NANCY JOHNSON

Rocky Road Fudge Bars

BASE:

1/2	cup butter
1	square unsweetened chocolate
1	cup sugar
1	cup flour
1/2-1	cup chopped walnuts (optional)
1	teaspoon baking powder
1	teaspoon vanilla
2	eggs

Preheat oven to 350°. Grease and flour a 9 x 13-inch pan. In a large saucepan, melt butter and chocolate over low heat. Add remaining ingredients; blend well. Spread in prepared pan.

FILLING:

1	8-ounce package cream cheese, room temperature (reserve 2 ounces for frosting)
1/2	cup sugar
2	tablespoons flour
1/4	cup butter, room temperature
1	egg
1/2	teaspoon vanilla
1/4	cup chopped walnuts (optional)
1	cup (6-ounce package) semisweet chocolate chips
2	cups miniature marshmallows

In a small bowl, combine 6 ounces cream cheese with next 5 filling ingredients. Blend until smooth and fluffy. Stir in nuts. Spread over base mixture. Sprinkle with chocolate chips. Bake 25-35 minutes, until toothpick inserted in center comes out clean. Sprinkle with marshmallows, bake 2 minutes longer.

FROSTING:

1/4	cup butter
1	square unsweetened chocolate
2	ounces cream cheese (reserved from filling)
1/4	cup milk
3	cups (1 pound) powdered sugar
1	teaspoon vanilla

In large saucepan, melt butter, chocolate, remaining 2 ounces of cream cheese and milk over low heat. Stir in powdered sugar and vanilla; blend until smooth. Immediately pour over marshmallows; swirl together. Cut into bars. Store in refrigerator. (Makes about 4 dozen bars)

CYNDI BOERSMA

Special K Bars

1	cup sugar
1	cup Karo syrup
11/2	cups peanut butter
1	teaspoon vanilla
6	cups Special K cereal
1	6-ounce package chocolate chips, optional
1	6-ounce package butterscotch chips, optional

Heat sugar and syrup until sugar is dissolved. (Do not boil or heat too long as bars will become too hard.) Add peanut butter and vanilla. Stir well and pour over cereal. Mix and spread in a small cake pan. If desired, melt chocolate and butterscotch chips and spread on bars. JOAN DOOP

Snowcap Brownies

1	cold egg, separated*
1/2	cup sugar
1/2	teaspoon vanilla
3/4	cup flour
1	teaspoon baking powder
1/2	teaspoon salt
1/2	cup margarine
21/2	squares unsweetened chocolate
11/4	cups sugar
1	teaspoon vanilla
1/2	teaspoon red food coloring, optional
2	eggs
1	cup chopped nuts

Preheat oven to 325°. Beat egg white in a small bowl until stiff peaks form. Gradually (1 tablespoon at a time) blend in sugar and vanilla; set aside. Mix together flour, baking powder and salt. In a 2-quart pan, over low heat, melt margarine and chocolate; let cool. Blend into chocolate mixture sugar, vanilla and food coloring. Add 2 unbeaten eggs and remaining egg yolk. Stir in dry ingredients along with chopped nuts. Spread in a well-greased 10 x 15-inch cookie sheet or jelly roll pan. Drop meringue onto batter by teaspoonfuls. Draw the tip of a knife through the batter lengthwise, then crosswise to make a design. (Don't mix the meringue into the batter, it should show on top.) Bake 25-30 minutes.

*COOK'S TIP: Eggs should be separated when they're cold, just out of the refrigerator. Egg whites should always be at room temperature before beating. MARJORIE BEST

Frosted Applesauce Brownies

1	cup shortening
4	1-ounce squares unsweetened chocolate
2	cups sugar
4	eggs
2	teaspoons vanilla
1	cup applesauce
2	cups flour
2	teaspoons baking powder
1	teaspoon salt
1	cup chopped nuts

Preheat oven to 350°. Melt shortening and chocolate; stir in sugar, eggs, vanilla and applesauce. Sift flour, baking powder and salt together. Combine two mixtures. Add nuts. Spread batter into greased 10 x 15-inch rimmed cookie sheet. Bake 25-30 minutes. Cool. Frost, if desired.

CHOCOLATE CREAM CHEESE FROSTING:

1	3-ounce package cream cheese, room temperature
1	square unsweetened chocolate, melted
2	cups powdered sugar
1	teaspoon vanilla
1 - 2	teaspoons milk or cream

Blend cream cheese with chocolate. Gradually mix in powdered sugar, vanilla and enough milk to make a smooth frosting. Spread on brownies.

LYNN SORRELLS

Better Than S.E.X. Brownies

1	box brownie mix (any brand)
1	12-ounce package semisweet chocolate chips
1	8-ounce package cream cheese, room temperature

Prepare brownie mix according to package instructions. Add chocolate morsels. Cut cream cheese into 1-inch cubes and stir into mixture. Pour into greased 9 x 13-inch pan. Bake according to package instructions or until center is slightly firm to the touch. Cool and cut into squares. (Be careful not to overcook the brownies!) (Makes approximately 24 brownies)

VARIATION: Use one 6-ounce package chocolate chips and 10-12 caramels cut in half, in place of 12-ounce package of chips. KATHY WARNER

Deluxe Chocolate Walnut Squares

6	ounces semisweet or bittersweet chocolate, cut into pieces
1/2	cup plus 2 tablespoons butter, cut into pieces
5	tablespoons dark rum
4	large eggs, separated
3/4	cup sugar
3/4	cup chopped walnuts
1/4	cup sifted flour
1/4	teaspoon cream of tartar
	Powdered sugar and/or unsweetened cocoa powder (to dust the top

Preheat oven to 375°. Line bottom of a 8-inch square cake pan with a square of parchment or waxed paper. Melt chocolate and butter in a small double boiler, stirring occasionally until melted and smooth. Remove from heat. (Or, microwave on medium, 50%, about 2 minutes). Stir in rum; set aside. Beat egg yolks with 1/2 cup sugar until pale and thick. Stir in warm chocolate mixture, nuts and flour; set aside. In another mixing bowl, beat egg whites and cream of tartar at medium speed until soft peaks form. Gradually add remaining 1/4 cup sugar and continue to beat at high speed until stiff but not dry. Fold one quarter of egg whites into chocolate batter. Fold in remaining whites. Turn batter into prepared pan. Bake 30-40 minutes, or until a toothpick inserted into center shows moist crumbs. Allow to cool completely in pan on a rack.

When cool, cake will settle in the center, leaving a higher rim around edges. Press edges gently with your fingers to flatten and level cake. Run a small knife around the edge of pan and unmold upside down onto a cutting board. (Cake may be prepared to this point, wrapped well and refrigerated up to 3 days or frozen up to 3 months.) Cut into 2-inch squares. Use a fine strainer to dust with powdered sugar or cocoa. Stencil a simple pattern, if desired. Serve at room temperature.

CHRIS IMAZUMI-O'CONNOR

261

Chocolate Marble Squares

1/2	cup butter or margarine
1/4	cup plus 2 tablespoons sugar
1/4	cup plus 2 tablespoons packed brown sugar
1/2	teaspoon vanilla
1	egg
1	cup flour
1/2	teaspoon baking soda
1/2	teaspoon salt
1	cup chocolate chips

Preheat oven to 375°. Mix butter, sugars and vanilla. Beat in egg. Blend in flour, baking soda and salt. Spread in greased 9 x 13-inch pan. Sprinkle chips over top of dough. Place in oven 1 minute until chips melt. Remove and cut through chocolate and dough with a knife to make a marble effect. Return to oven 12-14 minutes. Cool and cut into bars or squares. (Makes 24 squares) JOYCE HERSHENSON

Ultimate Brownies

4	eggs
2	cups sugar
4	squares unsweetened chocolate
2/3	cup margarine
2	teaspoons vanilla
11/3	cups flour
1	teaspoon baking powder
1/2	teaspoon salt
1	cup semisweet chocolate chips

Preheat oven to 350°. Beat eggs until light. Gradually mix in sugar. Melt chocolate and margarine in a double boiler; add vanilla. Stir into sugar mixture. Combine flour, baking powder and salt; add to chocolate mixture. Stir until well blended. (Do not overmix.) Stir in chocolate chips. Spread batter into a greased 9 x 13-inch baking dish. Bake approximately 25 minutes. Cool and cut into pieces. (Makes 40 brownies) *"These are intensely chocolate brownies - for chocolate lovers only."*
ED GOLDMAN

262

Nancy's Brownies

2	cups sugar
2	cups flour
1	cup water
1/2	cup margarine
1/2	cup shortening
31/2	tablespoons cocoa
2	eggs
1/2	cup buttermilk
1	teaspoon baking soda

FROSTING:

1/2	cup margarine
1/3	cup milk
3	tablespoons cocoa
1	1-pound box powdered sugar
1	teaspoon vanilla
1	cup chopped pecans or walnuts

Preheat oven to 375°. In a large bowl, mix sugar and flour; set aside. In a saucepan, mix water, margarine, shortening, cocoa and bring to a boil. Add to sugar and flour mixture. Add eggs, buttermilk and baking soda; mix well. Pour into a 11 x 17-inch cookie sheet. Bake 20 minutes or until done.

FROSTING: About 5 minutes before cake is done, combine in a saucepan, margarine, milk and cocoa; bring to a boil. Remove from heat; add powdered sugar, vanilla and nuts. Pour over cake as it comes from oven. (Makes 20 bars) JOYCE TREPPA

One Egg Cake

13/4	cups unbleached wheat flour
21/2	teaspoons double-acting baking powder
1	teaspoon salt
1/3	cup margarine, room temperature
11/4	cups sugar
1	teaspoon vanilla
1	egg, beaten, room temperature
1	cup milk, room temperature

Preheat oven to 350°. Sift together flour, baking powder and salt. Mix margarine, sugar and vanilla until smooth. In a small bowl, mix egg and milk. Add one-third flour mixture to margarine mixture; then add one-third milk mixture. Repeat with another one-third of each until all are mixed together. Bake in greased and floured baking pans about 25 minutes until done. Frost when cool. PAUL MELTZER

Eggnog Cake

2	cups flour
2	teaspoons baking powder
1/2	teaspoon nutmeg
1/2	teaspoon salt
4	eggs
4	tablespoons butter, melted
11/2	cups sugar
11/2	cups eggnog
2	tablespoons rum (or 1/2 teaspoon rum extract)
2	tablespoons butter
1/2	cup sliced almonds

Preheat oven to 350°. Combine flour, baking powder, nutmeg and salt; set aside. In mixer bowl, beat eggs, 4 tablespoons butter and sugar until thick and lemon colored (about 5 minutes). Add eggnog and rum. Fold dry mixture into wet mixture. In a small bowl, blend 2 tablespoons butter and almonds together. Press into a 10-inch Bundt pan. Pour batter into pan and bake 45-55 minutes. Cool in pan 10 minutes, then invert cake onto rack to cool completely. (10-12 servings) CHRIS IMAZUMI-O'CONNOR

Walnut Torte

1	cup finely-chopped walnuts
2	cups graham cracker crumbs
1	tablespoon baking powder
1/4	teaspoon salt
3/4	cup soft butter
11/2	cups sugar
3	eggs
1	teaspoon vanilla
11/2	cups milk

Preheat oven to 350°. In a mixing bowl, combine nuts, crumbs, baking powder and salt. In a food processor or blender, put butter, sugar, eggs and vanilla; mix 45 seconds. Pour milk in as motor is running. Add to dry mixture and stir. Turn into two greased 9-inch cake pans. Bake 30-35 minutes.

GRAND MARNIER WHIPPED CREAM FROSTING:

1	pint heavy cream
1	teaspoon sugar
2	tablespoons powdered sugar
1/4	cup Grand Marnier liqueur

Whip cream, sugar and powdered sugar until stiff peaks form. Add Grand Marnier and mix again.

FROSTING VARIATION:
Mocha Frosting: Substitute 1/2 cup sugar, 1 teaspoon coffee and 1 teaspoon vanilla in place of powdered sugar and Grand Marnier.
Cocoa Frosting: Substitute 2 tablespoons cocoa and 3 teaspoons sugar in place of powdered sugar and Grand Marnier.
Peppermint Frosting: Substitute 3 tablespoons powdered sugar and 1/2 teaspoon peppermint extract in place of powdered sugar and Grand Marnier. DOROTHY WARDELL

Mimi's Ice Cream Sherbet Cake

4	pints assorted ice creams and sherbets (strawberry, orange, raspberry, pistachio, etc.)
1	gallon vanilla ice cream
2	cups chopped pecans
2	cups coarsely-chopped chocolate (chocolate chips or good semisweet chocolate)
1	pint heavy cream
1	pint strawberries
	Green food coloring
	Flowers or ivy, for decoration

Make small balls with each of the sherbets or ice creams. Place balls on chilled jelly roll pan and freeze until very firm. Soften vanilla ice cream and put into large bowl. Beat until smooth. Fold in nuts and chocolate. Make 2-inch layer of vanilla ice cream mixture in the bottom of an angel food cake mold. Quickly arrange a layer of different colored frozen balls. Spoon more vanilla ice cream mixture on top. Add another layer of frozen balls and spoon rest of ice cream on top. Tap pan to remove air bubbles and return to freezer. Early on the day to be served: Remove cake pan from freezer. Run knife around edges of pan and inner tube. Quickly dip pan in and out of hot water and unmold on a plate which can go in the freezer.

About 2 hours before serving: Whip cream, add a few drops of green coloring and quickly frost frozen cake. Return to freezer until serving time. To serve: Decorate with strawberries and ivy leaves or flowers. Let set a few minutes before cutting.

COOK'S TIP: Can be made up to 1 week ahead. Very colorful and elegant. (12-18 servings) ANN SCHRIBER

Poppy Seed Cake

1	package yellow cake mix
1	13/4-ounce box vanilla pudding
4	eggs
1	cup sour cream
1/2	cup butter, melted
1/2	cup cream sherry
1/3	cup poppy seeds

Preheat oven to 350°. Butter and flour Bundt cake pan. Beat all ingredients together for 5 minutes. Bake 1 hour. Cool completely.

DOROTHY FARHAT

Ice Cream Cake

3 0	Oreo cookies
3/4	cup butter or margarine
1	16-ounce can Hershey's chocolate syrup
1	can Eagle sweetened condensed milk
1/2	gallon vanilla ice cream
1	12-ounce container Cool Whip
	Peanuts, optional
	Maraschino cherries, optional

In food processor, blend cookies until fine crumbs. Melt 1/2 stick margarine and mix in crumbs. Pat into 9 x 13-inch baking dish. Freeze half an hour. In a saucepan, combine remaining stick of margarine, chocolate syrup and milk; bring to boil, then simmer 5 minutes. Remove from heat and cool. Slice semi-softened ice cream to fit on top of cookie mixture. Freeze 45 minutes. Pour cooled chocolate syrup mixture on top. Freeze 1 hour. Top with Cool Whip, and if desired, peanuts and cherries. Freeze until ready to serve. "*A family favorite.*" DENISE BROOKS

Cheesecake Pie-ettes

6 0	vanilla wafers
2	8-ounce packages cream cheese, room temperature
2	eggs
3/4	cup sugar
1 1/2	teaspoons vanilla
1	cup sour cream
1/3	cup sugar
1	1 pound, 5-ounce can cherry pie filling

Preheat oven to 350°. Place miniature muffin cup liners in miniature muffin tins. Place one vanilla wafer in each cup; set aside. In large bowl, mix together cream cheese, eggs, sugar and vanilla. Spoon atop vanilla wafer. Bake 10 minutes; cool. Mix together sour cream and sugar; blend well. Spoon onto pie-ette. Top with a spoonful of cherry pie filling. (Makes 60) STEPHANIE METCALFE

CAKES

Nancy's Cheesecake

CRUST:

2	cups graham cracker crumbs
1/2	cup sugar
3/4	cup (12 tablespoons) unsalted butter, melted

FILLING:

3	8-ounce packages cream cheese, room temperature
1	cup heavy cream
1	cup sugar
5	eggs
1/2	cup sour cream
1	teaspoon vanilla or almond extract (or to taste)

Preheat oven to 400°. Combine crust ingredients. Press onto bottom and sides of springform pan. Bake 10 minutes. Turn heat in oven down to 320°. Soften cream cheese with electric mixer. Add ingredients in above order, mixing at medium speed for at least 3 minutes after each addition. Scrape bottom of bowl occasionally to make sure all the cream cheese is blended in. Pour into crust and bake 11/2 hours. (Cheesecake will continue to set after removed from oven.) Wait at least 1 hour before removing from pan.

CAKE FLAVOR VARIATIONS:
Hazelnut Cheesecake: Brush melted chocolate over bottom of crust and sprinkle with chopped hazelnuts. Add 1/4 to 1/2 cup coarsely-ground hazelnuts and 1/4 cup Frangelico liqueur to batter.
Chambord Cheesecake: Add 1/4 to 1/2 cup raspberries and 1/4 cup Chambord liqueur to batter.
Fruit Cheesecake: Add strawberries, raspberries or blueberries to batter.
Chocolate Chip Cheesecake: Use a chocolate crust (see below) and add 1/2 to 1 cup mini chocolate chips.

Chocolate Crust: Add 1/4 to 1/2 cup cocoa to crust ingredients, or spread 4 ounces melted bittersweet chocolate over bottom of crust. Add chopped nuts to crust, if desired. NANCY FROST COLLINS

Cheesecake

CRUST:
1 1/4   cups graham cracker crumbs
2   tablespoons sugar
1/4   cup butter, melted

CAKE:
1 2   ounces cream cheese, room temperature
1/2   cup sugar
2   eggs
1   teaspoon vanilla
1   cup crushed pineapple, drained well

Preheat oven to 350°. Combine crust ingredients and pat into a 9 x 9-inch baking dish. Blend cream cheese, sugar, eggs and vanilla until smooth. Add pineapple and stir. Pour mixture over crust and bake 25 minutes.

TOPPING:
1/2   pint sour cream
3   tablespoons sugar
1   teaspoon vanilla
1   2-ounce package slivered almonds

Blend sour cream, sugar, and vanilla until smooth. Spread on top of hot cheesecake. Sprinkle with almonds. Let sit in warm oven 5 minutes with door open. Refrigerate. Serve cool. (12 servings) MAGGIE BROWNRIDGE

Gooey Butter Cheesecake

CRUST:
1   yellow cake mix (or lemon or pineapple)
1/2   cup soft butter or margarine
1   egg, slightly beaten

CAKE:
1   1-pound box powdered sugar
2   8-ounce packages cream cheese, room temperature
2   eggs, slightly beaten

Preheat oven to 350°. Mix crust ingredients using fork. Put in greased 9 x 13-inch baking dish and pat down with fork. Mix cake ingredients together for 3 minutes. Pour over crust and bake 60 minutes. (Do not overbake; sometimes 50 minutes is enough if top is nicely browned.)
BARB LANESE

CAKES

Pumpkin Swirl Cheesecake

CRUST:
2   cups crushed vanilla wafer crumbs
1/4   cup margarine, melted

CAKE:
2   8-ounce packages cream cheese, room temperature
3/4   cup sugar
1   teaspoon vanilla
3   eggs
1   cup canned pumpkin
11/2 teaspoons cinnamon
1/2   teaspoon nutmeg

Preheat oven to 350°. Combine crumbs and margarine; press into 9-inch springform pan. Blend cream cheese, 1/2 cup sugar and vanilla together. Add eggs, one at a time. Reserve 1 cup cream cheese mixture. Add pumpkin, remaining sugar and spices to remaining cream cheese mixture. Mix well. Layer half of the pumpkin mixture and half cream cheese mixture over crust. Repeat layers. Cut through batter with knife for marble effect. Bake 55 minutes. Cool and serve. MARTHA JAMES

Helen's Lemon Pound Cake

2   cups sugar
1   cup margarine
2   cups flour
5   eggs
1   1-ounce bottle lemon extract

Preheat oven to 350°. Cream sugar and margarine until smooth. Alternating, add 1/2 cup flour and egg, ending with egg. Mix well. Add lemon extract; beat well. Pour into greased and floured Bundt pan (may also be made in 2-3 small loaf pans). Bake approximately 45-60 minutes. Let cool and glaze. (May be frozen for later use.)

GLAZE:
     Juice of one lemon
1/2   box powdered sugar

In a saucepan, blend lemon juice and powdered sugar until smooth; bring to a boil. Drip the glaze onto cooled cake. CANDACE TERHUNE

270

Mary's Cheesecake

CRUST:
3/4   cup graham cracker crumbs
3/4   cup finely-chopped nuts
4   tablespoons butter, melted

CAKE:
4   8-ounce packages cream cheese, room temperature
4   eggs, room temperature
11/4   cups sugar
2   teaspoons vanilla
       Juice of 1 lemon, room temperature

Preheat oven to 350°. Combine crumbs, nuts and butter. Press into a 9 or 10-inch springform pan. Beat cake ingredients together (mixture may be lumpy). Pour on top of crust and bake 50-55 minutes for 9-inch pan or 45-50 minutes for 10-inch pan. Remove from oven and let cool 15 minutes.

TOPPING:
16   ounces sour cream
1/4   cup sugar
1   teaspoon vanilla

Blend sour cream, sugar and vanilla. Spoon over cake and return to oven for 5 minutes. (12 servings) *"This is one of the easiest cheesecakes I've ever made and never fails."* MOLLY GATES

Mom's Fast Goodie Cupcakes

1   package chocolate cake mix
1   8-ounce package cream cheese, room temperature
1   egg
1/2   cup sugar
1   8-ounce package chocolate chips

Make cake according to package directions; set aside. In a separate bowl, blend cream cheese, egg and sugar together and add chocolate chips. Put cake mixture into cupcake pan and top with spoonful of creamed mixture. Bake according to cake mix directions. *"Best without icing."*
MARY LOUISE GOOD

Bailey's Irish Cream Cheesecake

CRUST:

1 0	whole graham crackers, broken into pieces
11/4	cups pecans
1/4	cup sugar
6	tablespoons unsalted butter, melted

Preheat oven to 325°. Finely grind graham crackers, pecans and sugar in food processor. Add butter and blend (using on/off turns). Press crumbs on bottom and 2 inches up sides of lightly-buttered 9-inch springform pan. Refrigerate 20 minutes.

FILLING:

3	8-ounce packages cream cheese, room temperature
3/4	cup sugar
3	eggs
1/3	cup Bailey's Irish cream liqueur
1	teaspoon vanilla
3	ounces white chocolate, broken into pieces

Using electric mixer, beat cream cheese and sugar in large bowl until smooth. Whisk eggs, Bailey's and vanilla in medium bowl. Beat egg mixture into cream cheese mixture. Finely chop chocolate in food processor. Add to cream cheese mixture. Pour into crust. Bake until edges of filling are puffed and dry and center is just set, about 50 minutes. Cool on rack.

TOPPING:

1-1/2	cups sour cream
1/4	cup powdered sugar
11/2	ounces white chocolate, grated
24-30	pecan halves

Mix sour cream and powdered sugar in small bowl. Spread onto cooled cake. Refrigerate until well-chilled, about 6 hours. Sprinkle grated chocolate over cake and place pecans around edge. DEBBIE LOWN

Pound Cake Squares

1   package pound cake mix
1/2 cup butter or margarine, melted
4   eggs
1   8-ounce package cream cheese, room temperature
1   teaspoon vanilla
1   1-pound package powdered sugar
1/2 cup chopped nuts

Preheat oven to 350°. Blend cake mix, butter and 2 eggs. Spread in greased 9 x 13-inch baking dish. Combine cream cheese, remaining 2 eggs, vanilla and powdered sugar (reserve 3 tablespoons powdered sugar and set aside). Beat until smooth. Spread mixture over cake batter. Sprinkle nuts over top. Bake 45-50 minutes. Cool about 25 minutes, then sift remaining powdered sugar over top. Cool completely and cut into squares. (Makes 48-60 squares) *"Freezes well. Tastes delicious refrigerated or still frozen."* JERRI JENISTA

Cottage Cheese Cheesecake

CRUST:
10 graham crackers, crushed (set aside a little for top)
1/3 cup sugar
1/3 cup butter, melted
1   teaspoon cinnamon

CAKE:
1/2 cup cold water
2   packages gelatin
2   eggs, separated
1/2 teaspoon salt
1/2 cup milk
1   cup sugar
1   pound carton cottage cheese
1/2 teaspoon vanilla
1   pint heavy cream

Combine crust ingredients and press into large cake pan. Pour cold water in bowl; sprinkle gelatin into water. Beat egg yolks and place in saucepan with salt, milk and sugar. Cook until shiney and thick (be careful it will scorch easily). Stir gelatin into hot mixture. Add cottage cheese and vanilla; beat until light and fluffy. Whip cream until stiff. Beat egg whites until stiff and fold mixture into yolk mixture. Pour over crust. Sprinkle reserved graham cracker crumbs on top. Place in refrigerator to set. *"Really good, light and low fat."* VERMA LOLMAUGH AND NORMA WEGNER

273

CAKES

Oreo Cheesecake

CRUST:
2 5   Oreo cream sandwich cookies
4   tablespoons butter, melted

FILLING:
4   8-ounce packages cream cheese, room temperature
11/2   cups sugar
2   tablespoons flour
4   large eggs, room temperature
3   large egg yolks, room temperature
1/3   cup heavy cream
2   teaspoons vanilla
11/4   cups Oreo cookie crumbs (about 15 cookies)
2   cups sour cream

Preheat oven to 450°. To make crust: Process cookies in food processor. Mix with butter and press firmly on bottom and 2/3 way up the sides of 10-inch springform pan. Place in freezer while preparing filling. In a large bowl, beat cream cheese on medium speed until smooth. Add 11/4 cups sugar and beat until light and fluffy, about 3 minutes. Mix in flour. While beating continuously, add eggs and egg yolks and mix until smooth. Beat in cream and 1 teaspoon vanilla until well blended. Pour half the batter in prepared chilled pan. Sprinkle evenly with coarsely-chopped cookies and cover with remaining batter. Smooth with spatula. Bake 15 minutes. Reduce heat to 225° and bake an additional 50-60 minutes until center of cake is set. (Don't worry if top cracks.) Meanwhile in medium bowl: beat together sour cream, remaining 1/4 cup sugar and remaining teaspoon of vanilla. Remove cheesecake from oven when set and spread evenly with sour cream mixture. Set oven temperature at 350° and bake an additional 7-10 minutes or until sour cream starts to set. Place on wire rack and cool to room temperature. Refrigerate and chill overnight. (12-15 thin slices)

NANCY BERNEMAN

274

Quick Blueberry Cheesecake

CRUST:
11/2   cups vanilla wafer crumbs
1/4   cup margarine, melted

CHEESECAKE:
1   envelope unflavored gelatin
1/4   cup cold water
2   8-ounce packages cream cheese, room temperature
1   tablespoon lemon juice
1   7-ounce jar marshmallow creme
1   8-ounce container frozen whipped topping, thawed
2   cups blueberries*
    Garnish: Whipped topping and lemon peel (optional)

Combine crumbs and margarine; press onto bottom of 9-inch springform pan. Chill. Soften gelatin in cold water; stir over low heat until dissolved. In a mixing bowl, gradually add gelatin to cream cheese mixing at medium speed with electric mixer until well blended. Blend in lemon juice. Beat in marshmallow creme. Fold in whipped topping. Purée blueberries and fold into cream cheese mixture. Pour over crust. Chill until firm. Garnish with whipped topping and lemon peel, if desired. (10-12 servings)

*COOK'S TIP: You may substitute strawberries or raspberries.

NATALIE NOTHMAN

Sour Cream Pound Cake

1   cup butter
3   cups sugar
6   eggs, separated
1/4   teaspoon baking soda
1   cup sour cream
3   cups flour
1   teaspoon almond extract
1   teaspoon vanilla

Preheat oven to 300°. Cream butter and sugar. Add egg yolks, one at a time. Beat well after each addition. Stir baking soda into sour cream. Add flour and sour cream alternately to the egg yolk mixture and blend well. Add flavorings and fold in stiffly-beaten egg whites. Pour into a greased and floured tube pan. Bake 1 hour and 30 minutes. Cool 10-15 minutes and then remove from pan. PEGGY JOHNSON

Dutch Apple Brandy Cheesecake

CINNAMON CRUST:
11/4   cups graham cracker crumbs
1/3   cup margarine, melted
1/2   teaspoon cinnamon
1/3   cup ground walnuts or pecans

CHEESECAKE:
4   8-ounce packages cream cheese, room temperature
1   cup sugar
3   tablespoons apple brandy (or apple cider)
1   teaspoon cinnamon
1/2   teaspoon vanilla
1/8   teaspoon nutmeg
4   eggs
1   cup chunky applesauce
1/4   cup heavy cream

Preheat oven to 350°. Combine crust ingredients and press on bottom and 11/2 inches up sides of 10-inch springform pan. Bake 10 minutes or until golden. Cool. Beat cream cheese until smooth. Gradually add sugar, beating well. Add brandy, cinnamon, vanilla and nutmeg; blend well. Add eggs, one at a time, beating just until combined. Stir in applesauce and cream. Pour into cooled crust. Bake 50 minutes or until center appears nearly set. Meanwhile prepare crumb topping.

CRUMB TOPPING:
3/4   cup packed brown sugar
1/3   cup margarine, melted
1/4   teaspoon nutmeg
3/4   cup flour
1/2   teaspoon cinnamon

Combine all ingredients until crumbly. Sprinkle crumb topping over cake. Bake 10 minutes more or until cake is just set. Cool 5 minutes on wire rack. Loosen sides of cake. Cool 30 minutes. Remove sides of pan. Cover and chill thoroughly. (16 servings) IRENE ANN PALUCH

Lemon-Aniseed Pound Cake

3/4	cup unsalted butter, room temperature
21/2	cups sugar
3	eggs, separated, room temperature
5	teaspoons finely-grated lemon peel
11/2	teaspoons aniseed
1	teaspoon vanilla
1	tablespoon lemon juice
21/4	cups flour
2	teaspoons baking powder
1/2	teaspoon salt
3/4	cup milk, room temperature
	Pinch salt
	Pinch cream of tartar
1	tablespoon instant espresso powder

Preheat oven to 350°. Grease and flour loaf pan. Using electric mixer, cream butter and sugar in large bowl until light and fluffy. Beat in yolks, one at a time. Blend in lemon peel, aniseed, vanilla and lemon juice. Sift together flour, baking powder and salt. Mix dry ingredients into batter alternately with milk. Using electric mixer, beat egg whites with salt and cream of tartar in large bowl until stiff but not dry. Fold half of whites into batter to loosen. Fold in remaining whites. Spoon half of batter into prepared pan. Sprinkle evenly with espresso powder. Spoon in remaining batter. Bake until golden brown, about 11/2 hours. Cool 20 minutes in pan. Invert onto rack and cool completely. Chill overnight. Bring to room temperature before slicing. CHRIS IMAZUMI-O'CONNOR

Turtle Cake

1	package German chocolate cake mix
1	14-ounce package caramels
1/2	cup evaporated milk
6	tablespoons butter
1	cup chopped pecans
1	cup chocolate chips

Preheat oven to 350°. Prepare cake mix according to package directions. Pour half of batter into greased and floured 9 x 13-inch baking dish. Set remaining batter aside. Bake 15 minutes. Meanwhile, in medium saucepan, combine caramels, milk and butter. Stir occasionally, until caramels are melted. Stir pecans into caramel mixture. Pour caramel/nut mixture over cake. Sprinkle with chips and pour reserved batter over top. Bake 15-20 minutes or until cake springs back when pressed with fingertips. JOAN DOOP AND CYNDI BOERSMA

CAKES

German Chocolate Cheesecake

CRUST:
1 1/2   cups graham cracker crumbs
3   tablespoons sugar
1/3   cup butter

CAKE:
9   ounces cream cheese, room temperature
3/4   cup sugar
        Dash salt
2   ounces semisweet chocolate, melted
2   eggs
1   teaspoon vanilla

Preheat oven to 325°. Mix crust ingredients and press into a greased 9-inch cake pan. Beat cream cheese, sugar and salt until smooth. Add chocolate, eggs and vanilla. Pour batter into crust. Bake 45 minutes or until toothpick comes out clean.

TOPPING:
3   tablespoons butter
5   tablespoons evaporated milk
1/2   cup brown sugar
1/2   cup coconut
1/4   cup chopped nuts

Melt butter in heated evaporated milk. Add brown sugar and cook until melted. Add coconut and chopped nuts. Pour topping over baked cake. Refrigerate until firm. *"Tastes better after 24 hours."* MAGGIE J. SLATTERY

Mint Cake

1   package white cake mix
6   tablespoons crème de menthe
1   16-ounce can Hershey's chocolate syrup
9   ounces Cool Whip

Make cake according to package directions, except substitute 3 tablespoons crème de menthe for water and bake in 9 x 13-inch cake pan. Punch holes in top of cake and pour chocolate syrup over top. (The end of a wooden spoon works well for making holes.) Cover with Cool Whip which has been mixed with 3 tablespoons crème de menthe. Store in refrigerator.
BARB LANESE

278

Chocolate Cream Cake

1   cup boiling water
2   ounces unsweetened chocolate
1/2   cup soft butter or margarine
1   teaspoon vanilla
13/4   cups firmly-packed brown sugar
2   eggs
13/4   cups plus 2 tablespoons flour
1   teaspoon baking soda
1/4   teaspoon salt
1/2   cup sour cream

Preheat oven to 325°. Pour boiling water over chocolate squares in bowl. Let stand until cool. Cream butter and vanilla. Add brown sugar and blend well. Add eggs, one at a time, beating well after each addition. In a large mixing bowl, mix flour with soda and salt until blended. Stir blended dry ingredients into creamed mixture. Mix well. Blend in sour cream and chocolate/water mixture. Pour into greased waxed paper-lined 9 x 5-inch aluminum loaf pan. Bake 1 hour and 15 minutes or until cake pulls away from sides of pan. Cool on rack for 10 minutes. Turn cake out of pan and remove waxed paper. Frost with your favorite chocolate fudge frosting.

MRS. CONWAY ADAMS

Chocolate Pudding Cake with Sauce

1   cup flour
3/4   cup sugar
1/2   cup chopped nuts, if desired
2   tablespoons unsweetened cocoa
2   teaspoons baking powder
1/2   teaspoon salt
1/2   cup milk
2   eggs, slightly beaten
2   tablespoons oil
1   teaspoon vanilla
3/4   cup finely-packed brown sugar
1/4   cup unsweetened cocoa
13/4   cups water
        Whipped cream

Preheat oven to 350°. In a large bowl, combine first 10 ingredients. Mix at medium speed until well-blended. Spread in ungreased 8 x 9-inch square pan. In a small bowl, combine brown sugar, cocoa and water. Pour over batter. Bake 40-45 minutes or until cake is set. Serve warm or cool, topped with whipped cream. KAREN ALLEN

"Better Than Sex" Cake

1	cup flour
1	cup chopped nuts
1/2	cup butter, softened
1	8-ounce package cream cheese, room temperature
1	cup powdered sugar
2	8-ounce containers whipped dessert topping
3	cups milk
2	31/2-ounce packages instant chocolate pudding mix

Preheat oven to 350°. In medium bowl, combine flour, nuts and butter; mix thoroughly and press into bottom of a greased 9 x 13-inch baking dish. Bake 20 minutes. Cool on wire rack. In medium mixer bowl, combine cream cheese, powdered sugar and one carton of the dessert topping with electric mixer. Beat until well combined and spread over cooled cake; refrigerate. In large bowl with electric mixer, combine milk and chocolate pudding mix; beat 3 minutes at low speed until thickened and glossy. Spread evenly over cream cheese layer. Refrigerate until pudding is set. Spread remaining carton of dessert topping over chocolate layer and refrigerate until serving time. (16 servings) CYNDI BOERSMA

Peggy's Mocha Fudge Cake

1 8	ounces good dark chocolate, preferably semisweet
13/4	cups sugar
2	cups butter
1	cup plus 2 tablespoons strong coffee (liquid)
9	eggs
	Sweetened whipped cream

Preheat oven to 250°. Line a 10-inch springform pan with foil and spray with Pam. In a very large saucepan, melt chocolate, sugar, butter and coffee together over low heat. Whisk in eggs, one at a time. Pour into prepared pan and bake 2 hours or until set. Allow to cool completely; loosen sides of pan and refrigerate at least 24 hours. Serve with sweetened whipped cream. NANCY SCHLEICHER

Black Magic Cake

13/4	cups flour
2	cups sugar
3/4	cup cocoa
2	teaspoons baking soda
1	teaspoon baking powder
1	teaspoon salt
2	eggs
1	cup strong black coffee (liquid)
1	cup buttermilk or sour milk*
1/2	cup vegetable oil
2	teaspoons vanilla

Preheat oven to 350°. Mix all dry ingredients in bowl. Add eggs, coffee, milk, oil and vanilla. Beat for 2 minutes. Greased and flour 9 x 13-inch baking dish, bake 35-40 minutes.

FROSTING:

1	pint heavy cream
1	small package instant pudding mix

Whip cream and pudding mix until smooth. Spread on cooled cake.

*COOK'S TIP: To make sour milk: Mix 1 tablespoon vinegar with 1 cup milk; let stand for 1 minute. CHRISTINE WANG

Chocolate Mousse Torte

CRUST:

2	cups chocolate wafer crumbs
8	tablespoons butter

FILLING:

1	12-ounce package chocolate chips*
5	egg yolks
3	tablespoons brandy or crème de menthe
11/2	cups heavy cream, sweetened

Combine crumbs and butter; mix well. Line bottom and sides of 9-inch springform pan with mixture. Chill. In food processor or blender, combine chips, yolks and brandy. Bring whipping cream just to boil. With motor running slowly, add cream to chip mixture. Blend until completely smooth, about 1-2 minutes. Pour into crust and chill at least 6 hours. (8-10 servings) *"*If you prefer crème de menthe, substitute mint chocolate chips.*" NANCY WHITE

Tarte au Chocolat

CRUST:

1	cup flour
1/8	teaspoon salt
1/3	cup sugar
6	tablespoons unsalted butter, chilled and cut into pieces
1	small egg, slightly beaten

Place flour, salt, sugar and butter in bowl of food processor with metal blade. Process until mixture resembles coarse crumbs, about 10 seconds. Add egg and pulse until pastry begins to hold together, about 9 times. (The dough will be soft and supple, like cookie dough.) Turn into a 10 1/2-inch springform pan with removable bottom. Using a spatula and working quickly, evenly distribute the dough in pan. (To avoid problems with shrinkage as the pastry bakes, build the dough a bit higher than the height of the pan.) Prick bottom of shell with fork. Chill, uncovered, 1 hour.

Preheat oven to 375°. Line shell loosely with foil, pressing into edges of pan. Fill with rice or beans (for weight, to prevent shrinkage). Bake until pastry begins to brown around edges, about 20 minutes. Remove foil and weights and continue baking until pastry is light brown, about 10 minutes. Cool for 10 minutes before adding filling.

FILLING:

5	ounces bittersweet chocolate
1	egg
2	egg yolks
2	tablespoons sugar
1	teaspoon powdered sugar for garnish

Melt chocolate in double boiler; set aside. In a mixing bowl, combine egg, egg yolks and sugar; beat until thick and lemon-colored. Add chocolate and whisk until combined. Pour mixture into prebaked, cooled tart shell, spreading evenly. Bake until the filling is set, about 10 minutes. When tart has cooled, sprinkle with powdered sugar. (8 servings)

PRUE ROSENTHAL

Chocolate Cake

We need stuff from a box and put it in a bowl. Then we take 2 eggs and crack them on the side of the bowl. Then you have to stir it. Put it in a heart pan and put it in the oven. You take it out after awhile. Then you put the frosting on. Put it in the refrigerator till it's time to eat. CARRIE, AGE 7

Chocolate Torte

```
1      cup strong coffee (liquid)
2      tablespoons sugar
2-3    tablespoons brandy or Grand Marnier liqueur
12     ounces chocolate chips
1/2    pound butter
2      eggs
1      box vanilla wafers
```

In a mixing bowl, cream together coffee, sugar and brandy. Melt chocolate chips in double boiler. Cream butter and eggs; add to chocolate. Line loaf pan with foil, overlapping the edges. Put a layer of vanilla wafers on bottom of pan, sprinkling generously with coffee mixture. Next, layer cookies, coffee mixture and melted chocolate mixture. Finish with cookies. Cover top with foil and put weighted pan of equal size on top. Refrigerate 12-16 hours. Remove and frost.

FROSTING:
```
1      pint heavy cream
2-3    tablespoons brandy
1      tablespoon sugar
```

Whip cream, brandy and sugar until stiff peaks form. Frost cooled cake.

CHRIS IMAZUMI-O'CONNOR

Chocolate Cake

```
1      package chocolate cake mix
1      teaspoon almond extract
2      eggs
1      21-ounce can cherry pie filling
```

GLAZE:
```
6      ounces chocolate chips
1/3    cup milk
1      cup sugar
6      tablespoons butter
```

Preheat oven to 350°. Beat all crust ingredients together (will be lumpy). Pour into 9 x 13-inch greased cake pan. Bake 25-30 minutes. Cool slightly. Melt all glaze ingredients together in a small saucepan. Pour on top of cake. CHRIS IMAZUMI-O'CONNOR

283

Chocolate Roll

6   eggs, separated
1   cup sugar
2   heaping tablespoons flour
2   heaping tablespoons cocoa

FILLING:
1   pint heavy cream
2   tablespoons sugar

Preheat oven to 400°. Lightly butter and flour cookie sheet. Beat egg yolks slightly, then add sugar gradually. Add flour and cocoa; mix well. Beat whites until stiff but not dry; fold into chocolate mixture. Spread batter on cookie sheet. Bake 7-8 minutes. Let stand in oven a few minutes before taking out. Set cookie sheet on wet towel. Run spatula around and under cake. Turn out onto a dish towel sprinkled with sugar; roll up until ready to fill. Whip heavy cream with sugar until stiff peaks form. Spread onto cake. Roll cake up.

CHOCOLATE FROSTING:
11/2   squares unsweetened chocolate
1-11/2 tablespoons butter
11/2   cups powdered sugar
1/2   teaspoon vanilla
2-3   tablespoons milk

Melt chocolate and butter in double boiler. Add powdered sugar, vanilla and enough milk to make desired consistency; beat until smooth. Drizzle or spread onto chocolate roll. ELLEN VAN HOFTEN

Chocolate Gâteau with Port

1/2   cup port wine
1/2   cup butter
3   ounces semisweet chocolate
3   eggs, separated
1   cup sugar
3/4   cup flour
1/8   teaspoon salt

Preheat oven to 325°. In a small saucepan, bring port to a boil. Reduce heat immediately to warm setting. Add butter and chocolate. Blend when melted with a wire whisk and set aside to cool. In a bowl, beat egg yolks and sugar until well blended. Alternately add flour and cooled port mixture in three parts until well blended. In another bowl, beat egg whites with salt until stiff. Fold them into batter. Turn batter into a well-greased 10-inch cake pan and bake 30 minutes. Cool. *"This cake is very rich and needs no icing or topping. However, an icing of chocolate butter cream can be devastating, or a dusting of powdered sugar over a patterned paper doily can be pretty."* CHRIS O'CONNOR

Sour Cream Apple Squares

2   cups flour
2   cups firmly-packed brown sugar
1/2   cup butter or margarine, softened
1   cup chopped nuts
1-2   teaspoons cinnamon
1   teaspoon baking soda
1/2   teaspoon salt
1   cup sour cream
1   teaspoon vanilla
1   egg
2   cups finely-chopped, peeled apples
    Whipped cream, optional

Preheat oven to 350°. In large bowl, combine flour, sugar and butter; blend until crumbly. Stir in nuts. Press 23/4 cups of mixture firmly into ungreased 9 x 13-inch baking dish. To remaining mixture, add cinnamon, baking soda, salt, sour cream, vanilla and egg; blend well. Stir in apples and spoon evenly over base. Bake 25-35 minutes. Cut into squares. Serve with whipped cream, if desired. (Makes 12-15 squares)

DORIS NIETHAMMER AND BRENDA OSBORNE

Apple-Michigan Dried Cherries Tatin

4   tablespoons butter
1/2   cup sugar
6-8   small cooking apples (or 5 Granny Smith), peeled, and
        quartered
1/2   cup Michigan dried cherries
        Garnish: Whipped cream

Preheat oven to 450°. Melt butter in 12-inch cast iron skillet. Add sugar. Arrange apples, round side down, in pan and cook over moderate heat until apples are soft and syrup is thick. Add cherries. Set aside.

CRUST:
13/4   **cups flour**
21/2   **teaspoons baking powder**
1/4   **teaspoon salt**
1   **tablespoon sugar**
6   **tablespoons butter, cut into small pieces**
1   **cup milk**

In food processor, blend flour, baking powder, salt, sugar and butter just until crumbly. Add milk and process just to blend. Spread crust mixture evenly over top of apples. Bake about 15 minutes, or until brown on top. Let rest 5 minutes; then invert onto a large round serving plate. Cut into wedges and serve with whipped cream. (6-8 servings) *"This is like a coffee cake."* JANET GILSDORF

Apricot Pecan Fruit Cake

1/3   **cup sugar**
1/3   **cup brown sugar**
1/2   **cup margarine**
2   **eggs**
1   **teaspoon vanilla**
2   **tablespoons apricot brandy (optional)**
1   **cup flour**
1/3   **teaspoon baking powder**
2   **cups dried whole apricots**
2   **cups whole pecans**

Preheat oven to 300°. Cream sugars and margarine. Add eggs, vanilla and brandy; mix well. Add flour and baking powder; mix well. Stir in apricots and pecans. Pour mixture into buttered 9-inch loaf pan and bake 11/2 hours. *"Will keep in the refrigerator for months."* CAROLINE BLANE

Knobby Apple Cake

Vegetable cooking spray
1/4 cup raisins
1 cup boiling water
3 tablespoons soft margarine
3/4 cup sugar
2 egg whites
1 teaspoon vanilla
1 cup flour
1 teaspoon baking soda
1/2 teaspoon cinnamon
1/2 teaspoon nutmeg
3 cups chopped tart apples (about 5 medium apples)
1/4 cup chopped nuts
1/4 cup wheat germ

Preheat oven to 350°. Spray 8-inch baking dish with cooking spray. Add raisins to water for 5 minutes or until plump; drain. In medium bowl, cream margarine and sugar until smooth. Add egg whites and vanilla; mix well. In separate bowl, sift together flour, baking soda, cinnamon and nutmeg. Add flour mixture to creamed mixture. Stir in apples, nuts, raisins and wheat germ. Pour batter into pan. Bake 40-45 minutes. *"Only 244 calories per serving!"* JUDY DUNTON

Pumpkin Pie Cake

1 28-ounce can pumpkin (or 31/2 cups fresh)
1 cup sugar
3 eggs
1 13-ounce can evaporated milk
3 teaspoons pumpkin pie spice
1/2 teaspoon salt
1 box yellow cake mix
3/4 cup (11/2 sticks) margarine
1 cup chopped pecans
Whipped cream, optional

Preheat oven to 350°. Mix pumpkin, sugar, eggs, milk, spice and salt together. Pour into well-greased 9 x 13-inch baking dish. Sprinkle dry cake mix evenly on top of pumpkin mixture. Melt margarine; pour over top of dry cake mix. Spread evenly. Sprinkle nuts on top. Bake 1 hour or until lightly browned. Cool and cut into small squares. Top with whipped cream, if desired. BARBARA WRANESH

287

Prize-Winning Applesauce Cupcakes

2	cups flour
1	teaspoon nutmeg
1	teaspoon cinnamon
1	teaspoon salt
1/8	teaspoon cloves
1/2	cup shortening
1	cup sugar
1	egg white, slightly beaten
1 1/2	cups applesauce, unsweetened
2	teaspoons baking soda
1	cup raisins

Preheat oven to 375°. In a large mixing bowl, combine flour, nutmeg, cinnamon, salt and cloves. In a separate bowl, cream shortening and sugar until smooth. Add egg white. In a small saucepan, heat applesauce until hot and mix baking soda into it (it will foam up). Add hot mixture to the sugar and shortening. Blend in flour mixture, reserving a tablespoon to dredge over raisins. Then add raisins. Fill cupcake pans about two-thirds full and bake 20 minutes. Frost with a simple chocolate frosting.

COOK'S TIP: Whenever you add raisins or other dried fruit (or nuts) to batter, dredge them in 1 tablespoon of the flour mixture so they will be distributed evenly through the batter. Otherwise, they will sink to the bottom of the pan. MARJORIE BEST

Rhubarb Cake

3/4	cup butter
1 1/2	cups sugar
1	egg, beaten
1	cup buttermilk
2	cups flour
1	teaspoon salt
1	teaspoon baking soda
1	teaspoon vanilla
2	cups diced fresh rhubarb
1/2	cup sugar
1	teaspoon cinnamon
	Garnish: Whipped cream and fresh strawberries

Preheat oven to 350°. Cream butter and sugar. Add egg and buttermilk. Add flour, salt, baking soda and vanilla; beat again. Fold in rhubarb. Place in a greased 8 x 12-inch cake pan. In a small bowl, combine sugar and cinnamon. Sprinkle over cake. Bake 40 minutes. JOAN DOOP

Banana Split Cake

CRUST:
1/2   cup margarine
2   cups graham cracker crumbs

FILLING:
2   eggs
2   cups powdered sugar
3/4   cup margarine
3-4   large bananas
1   16-ounce can crushed pineapple, drained well
1   container Cool Whip
    Nuts (optional)
    Chopped red cherries

Melt margarine in 9 x 13-inch baking dish. Add cracker crumbs. Mix well in bottom of pan; pat down. Mix eggs, powdered sugar and margarine 15 minutes with electric mixer. Spread over crust. Slice bananas over sugar mixture. Spread pineapple over bananas. Cover with Cool Whip. Sprinkle nuts and cherries over top. Chill overnight. (12 servings)

KELLY FEARER

Christmas Cake

21/2   cups raisins
11/2   cups cherries
4   ounces orange peel
1/2   cup pecans
1/2   cup brandy
1   cup brown sugar
1   cup corn oil margarine
4   eggs
1/2   cup molasses
11/2   cups flour
1/2   teaspoon baking soda
1   teaspoon allspice
1   teaspoon cinnamon
1/2   teaspoon cloves

Mix fruit and nuts with brandy; marinate in refrigerator 12-24 hours before making cake. Preheat oven to 275°. Cream sugar and margarine. Add eggs and molasses. Combine flour, soda and spices; mix in. Add fruit mixture with its juice. Pour into baking dish. Put a pan of water in the oven to keep cake from drying out. Cook for 31/2 hours. After cooling, wrap well in plastic wrap and store in cool place. Will keep well for 2 months. (12 servings) CAROLINE BLANE

Pear Upside-Down Spice Cake

3	tablespoons plus 1/3 cup butter or margarine
2/3	cup brown sugar
1	29-ounce can pear halves
1	cup chopped walnuts
1	egg
1/2	cup sugar
11/4	cups flour
11/2	teaspoons baking powder
1	teaspoon baking soda
1/2	teaspoon salt
1/2	teaspoon cinnamon
1/2	teaspoon nutmeg
1/4	teaspoon cloves

Preheat oven to 350°. Melt 3 tablespoons butter in a 9-inch layer cake pan. Add brown sugar and heat until it begins to melt. Remove from heat. Slice each pear half into 5 fan-like pieces, using all but 1 half. Arrange pear slices in pan and sugar and scatter walnuts. In a mixing bowl, cream remaining butter, egg and sugar. Mix together flour, baking powder, baking soda, salt, cinnamon, nutmeg and cloves. Stir into creamed mixture and spoon evenly over pears. Bake 40-45 minutes. Cool slightly. Invert onto a plate, arrange remaining pear half on middle and serve while still slightly warm. (8 servings) CHRIS IMAZUMI-O'CONNOR

Strawberry Cake

First put two eggs in a pot. Then add 3 pounds of milk. Stir in 2 pounds of sugar and 1 pound of salt. Put in 10 pounds of flour. Mix this all together. Mix in 10 pounds of strawberries. Put the mixture into a cake pan and bake it for 1 hour at 2°. This cake will feed my whole family and my neighbors, too . . . at least 10 people. TANISHA, AGE 7

Cherry Crêpe Cake
(Gâteau de Crêpes aux Cerises)

CRÊPES:

2	cups milk
11/2	cups flour
6	eggs
4	tablespoons sugar
3	tablespoons butter, melted
3	tablespoons kirsch liqueur
1	tablespoon vanilla
1/4	teaspoon salt
	Butter (for frying crêpes)

Combine all ingredients except butter and beat until smooth, about 1 minute. Cover and refrigerate until batter has thickened to consistency of whipping cream (about 1-2 hours). Heat 10-inch skillet or crêpe pan over medium-high heat. Add about 1 teaspoon butter, swirling until sizzling but not brown. Pour off excess. Hold pan away from heat with one hand and with the other pour in 1/3 cup batter. Rapidly tilt pan back and forth to distribute batter evenly on bottom and part way up sides; pour excess back into bowl. Return pan to heat, shaking rapidly so crêpe does not stick. When top of crêpe looks dry and edges are lightly browned, remove from heat and flip onto a towel; (Do not brown on both sides). Cool on towel, then transfer to waxed paper. Continue with remaining batter, stacking each crêpe between waxed paper.

FILLING:

3	pounds fresh tart black cherries, pitted (or 3, 17-ounce cans pitted cherries packed in heavy syrup)
1/2	cup sugar (exclude if using canned cherries)
1	tablespoon grated lemon peel
1/4	cup kirsch liqueur
1/2	cup butter, melted
1/4	cup sugar

Preheat oven to 350°. If using fresh cherries: combine in heavy saucepan with sugar and lemon peel. Cook over medium heat until sugar is melted, stirring occasionally to prevent burning. Simmer until cherries are tender, about 5 minutes. Remove cherries with slotted spoon to mixing bowl. Turn heat to high and boil juice until reduced to about 1/2 cup. Remove from heat and stir in kirsch. Add to cherries. If using canned cherries: drain syrup into small saucepan and add lemon peel. Put cherries in a mixing bowl. Boil syrup over high heat until reduced to 1/2 cup. Stir in kirsch. Add to cherries. Lightly brush a round 2 x 11-inch baking dish, with melted butter. Center crêpe browned side up in the bottom. Spoon some cherries with syrup over top. Press another crêpe firmly on top and brush with butter. Continue layering, ending with a crêpe. (To prevent lopsided gâteau, stagger cherries on the crêpes and press firmly to flatten and balance.) Brush top with melted butter and sprinkle with 1/4 cup sugar. Bake until heated through, about 10-15 minutes.

CREAM SAUCE:

4	cups heavy cream
6	tablespoons sugar
1	teaspoon cinnamon
1	cup slivered almonds

Combine cream, sugar and cinnamon in small saucepan and boil until reduced to about 1 cup. Remove gâteau from oven. Pour half of cream sauce over top and sprinkle with nuts. Serve warm, cut into wedges, with a pitcher of remaining cream sauce. *"This was obtained while visiting in France. An incrediby delicious and elegant dessert. It takes awhile to make, but is definitely worth it!"* PAT DEARDORFF

Almond Cake with Raspberry Sauce

CAKE:

3/4	cup sugar
1/2	cup unsalted butter, room temperature
1	cup almond paste
3	eggs
1	tablespoon kirsch or Triple~Sec liqueur
1/4	teaspoon almond extract .
1/4	cup flour
1/3	teaspoon baking powder
	Powdered sugar

Preheat oven to 350°. Generously butter and flour 8-inch round cake pan. Combine sugar, butter and almond paste in medium mixing bowl and blend well. Beat in eggs, liqueur and almond extract. Add flour and baking powder, beating until just mixed (do not overbeat). Bake 40-50 minutes. Let cool. Invert onto serving platter and dust lightly with powdered sugar.

RASPBERRY SAUCE:

1	pint (2 cups) fresh raspberries or 1,12-ounce package frozen (thawed)
2	tablespoons sugar (or to taste)

Combine raspberries with sugar in processor or blender and puree. Gently press sauce through fine sieve to remove seeds. Serve sauce as an accompaniment to Almond Cake. (12 servings) CHRIS IMAZUMI-O'CONNOR

Date and Nut Cake

1	pound dates, chopped into small pieces
1	cup chopped pecans
3/4	cup butter
11/2	cups packed brown sugar
1	teaspoon baking soda
1	cup boiling water
1	cup flour
2	eggs, beaten
1/3	cup rum

Preheat oven to 325°. Place dates, pecans, butter and brown sugar in a large bowl. In a separate bowl, combine baking soda and boiling water. (Be careful, it bubbles.) Add to other ingredients; mix well. Add flour, eggs and rum; beat until smooth. Spoon into greased and floured 9 x 13-inch baking dish. Bake 40-50 minutes. Let cool.

FROSTING:

1/4	cup butter
2	cups powdered sugar
1-2	tablespoons rum

Cream butter and powdered sugar. Add rum to desired consistency. *"This cake freezes very well but leave off frosting."* JANE WILSON COON

293

Peach Torte

1/2	cup butter
3/4	cup powdered sugar
4	eggs, separated
1	cup flour
1	teaspoon baking powder
1/4	teaspoon salt
3	teaspoons milk
11/2	cups sugar
4	tablespoons sliced almonds
2	cups peaches, peeled and sliced (or raspberries or strawberries)
1	cup heavy cream (may flavor with amaretto)
	Toasted almonds for top (optional)

Preheat oven to 325°. Grease and flour two 9-inch cake pans. In a large bowl cream butter and powdered sugar. Beat in egg yolks one at a time. In another bowl sift together flour, baking powder and salt. Add to the creamed mixture, alternating with milk. Divide the batter between the cake pans. In a mixing bowl beat egg whites to soft peaks. Add 1 cup sugar and continue beating until peaks form. Spread this meringue mixture on top of batter. Sprinkle each pan with 1 teaspoon sugar and 2 tablespoons almonds. Bake 30 minutes. Cool pans on racks and then remove cake from pans. Sprinkle peach slices with 2 tablespoons sugar. Place one layer of cake on a serving plate, meringue side down. Whip cream and add remaining sugar. Spread the bottom layer with about 1/3 of the whipped cream. Pile the peaches on top of the whipped cream saving some for garnish. Place the second layer, meringue side up, on the peaches. Mound remaining whipped cream on top and around the edges of the torte. Garnish with peach slices. Refrigerate until ready to serve. (10-12 servings) ANN SCHRIBER

Crumb-Topped Apple-Mince Pie

1	unbaked 9-inch pie crust
1/4	cup butter or margarine
1/2	cup packed brown sugar
3/4	teaspoon cinnamon
1/3	cup flour
3	apples, peeled and sliced
2	cups prepared mincemeat*

Preheat oven to 425°. Line 9-inch pie plate with pastry; make fluted edge; chill. Mix butter, sugar, cinnamon and flour with fork until crumbs are size of peas. Slice apples into pie shell. Top with mincemeat. Sprinkle on crumbs. Bake 30-35 minutes or until apples are tender.

*COOK'S TIP: Mincemeat with rum and brandy is best. DOROTHY HILTON

Agnes' Lemon Pie

1/2	cup lemon juice
	Grated rind of 2 lemons
1	cup sugar
4	egg yolks, slightly beaten
5	tablespoons cornstarch
1 1/2	cups milk
1	tablespoon butter
1/2	teaspoon salt
1	baked pie crust

Preheat oven to 400°. Place all ingredients in the top of a double boiler in order listed. Place over boiling water and stir constantly until mixture thickens. Add butter and salt; stir. Pour into baked pie shell.

MERINGUE:

4	egg whites, room temperature
8	tablespoons sugar
1/4	teaspoon cream of tartar

When egg whites are at room temperature, beat to a foamy consistency. Add sugar gradually; then add cream of tartar. Spoon meringue directly onto the hot pie filling, spreading it to the edge and making sure it touches the pastry all around. Sealing it to the pastry like this anchors it and helps to prevent shrinkage. Bake 8-10 minutes. GRACE JORDISON BOXER

Soufflé Lemon Pie

4	eggs, room temperature, separated
3/4	cup sugar
1/4	cup lemon juice
2	tablespoons hot water
1	teaspoon grated lemon rind
1/8	teaspoon salt
1	baked 9-inch pie crust

Preheat oven to 325°. In medium bowl, beat egg yolks and 1/2 cup sugar on medium speed until very thick and lemon-colored. Place on top part of double boiler. Stir in lemon juice, hot water and lemon rind. Stirring constantly, cook over simmering water until mixture has thickened, 7-10 minutes. Remove from heat; let cool while preparing egg whites. In small bowl, beat egg whites and salt on high speed until soft peaks form. Reduce speed to medium. Gradually add remaining 1/4 cup sugar, one tablespoon at a time. Continue beating until whites form stiff peaks. Do not overbeat. Gently fold whites into egg yolk mixture. Pour into baked pie shell. Bake 20-25 minutes until puffed and golden brown. (Pie will shrink while cooking.) Serve with Raspberry Sauce at room temperature or refrigerated. (8-10 servings)

RASPBERRY SAUCE:

1	10-ounce package frozen raspberries, thawed
3	tablespoons sugar
11/2	teaspoons cornstarch
1/2	teaspoon lemon juice
1/4	teaspoon almond extract

In blender, purée raspberries. Strain through sieve, discarding pulp. Reserve 1/4 cup of juice. Place remaining juice and sugar in small saucepan. Bring to boil over medium heat. Combine cornstarch with reserved juice. Gradually stir into berry mixture. Cook, stirring frequently, until thickened. Remove from heat; add lemon juice and almond extract. Serve at room temperature. (Makes 1 cup)

CHRIS IMAZUMI-O'CONNOR

Frozen Peach Pie

3 1/2   cups sugar
1/2   cup plus 2 tablespoons minute tapioca
1/4   cup lemon juice
2   teaspoons ascorbic acid
1   teaspoon salt
4   quarts peaches, peeled and sliced
2   unbaked pie crusts
1   tablespoon butter

Preheat oven to 425°. Combine sugar, tapioca, lemon juice, ascorbic acid and salt. Toss with peaches. Pour into pastry-lined 9-inch pie pan. Dot with butter. Arrange and seal top crust and flute edge. Slit top crust. Bake about 1 hour.

COOK'S TIP: You may freeze the peach mixture in a 1-quart freezer box to use at a later date. Thaw before pouring into pie shell. This filling also works well for peach cobbler. NANCY FROST COLLINS

Melt-in-Your-Mouth Pie

1   cup powdered sugar
1/4   cup margarine, softened
1   egg
1/4   teaspoon salt
1/2   teaspoon vanilla
1   baked pie crust, cooled
2   cups frozen whipped topping, thawed
3/4   cup chopped pecans
1   cup crushed pineapple, drained
1/2   cup chopped maraschino cherries
1   tablespoon milk

Cream sugar and margarine together. Add egg, salt and vanilla. Beat until smooth and creamy. Spread mixture into pie shell. Chill. Combine whipped topping, pecans, pineapple, cherries and milk until blended. Spread mixture over filling. Chill and serve. LIZ THOMAS

Pineapple-Orange Cream Pie

1	8-ounce package light cream cheese, room temperature
1	1-cup carton plain nonfat yogurt
1/2	cup sugar
1/2	teaspoon vanilla
1	9-inch graham cracker pie crust
1	can pineapple slices, drained
1	can mandarin orange pieces, drained

Preheat oven to 375°. In a saucepan, combine cream cheese, yogurt, sugar and vanilla; heat until smooth. Pour into pie shell. Bake 20 minutes or until just set; cool. Arrange fruit in circular pattern on chilled pie. (6-8 servings) *"Delicious low calorie dessert."* DONNA LOWRY

Strawberry Pie

1	cup sugar
3	tablespoons cornstarch
	Juice of half lemon
	Pinch salt
1	tablespoon butter, melted
2	boxes frozen strawberries, thawed
3/4	cup water
1	baked pie crust

TOPPING:

1/2	pint heavy cream
1/2	cup powdered sugar
1/4	teaspoon almond flavoring
	Garnish: Fresh strawberries

In a saucepan, combine sugar, cornstarch, lemon juice, salt and butter. Cook until clear. Add 1/2 cup crushed strawberries and water to saucepan. Bring to a boil. Cool mixture. Arrange remaining strawberries in a baked pie shell and pour cooked mixture over berries. Whip cream and gradually add powdered sugar and almond flavoring. Top pie with whipped mixture. Garnish with a few fresh berries halved. MARIAN FIFIELD

Strawberry Pie

GLAZE:
1/4 cup sugar
2 tablespoons cornstarch
1/2 cup water
1/2 cup grenadine syrup
1 tablespoon lemon juice

In a small saucepan, combine sugar and cornstarch. Blend in water, syrup and lemon juice. Cook on medium heat, stirring constantly until mixture thickens and bubbles. (If the mixture gets too thick, slowly add hot water.) Cover and cool at room temperature.

PIE:
11/4 cups milk
1 cup sour cream
1 33/4-ounce package instant vanilla pudding mix
1/3 cup sliced almonds, toasted
1 baked 9-inch pie crust
2 cups halved strawberries

Combine milk and sour cream; add pudding mix. Beat on low speed 1 minute. Sprinkle almonds on bottom of pastry. Immediately pour pudding over almonds. Spread 1/3 glaze on top of the filling. Arrange sliced berries on top. Spoon and spread remaining glaze over fruit. Chill until serving time. MARJORIE DUNN

Pecan Pie

1 cup dark Karo syrup
3 eggs
1 cup sugar
2 tablespoons butter or margarine, melted
1 teaspoon vanilla
1/8 teaspoon salt
1 cup chopped pecans
1/4 cup brandy, optional
1 unbaked pie crust

Preheat oven to 400°. Mix together syrup, eggs, sugar, butter, vanilla and salt. Stir in pecans. Pour into pie crust. Bake 15 minutes. Reduce oven to 350° and bake 30-35 minutes longer. (Outer edge of filling should be set with center slightly soft.) (8-10 servings) KATHERINE KERSEY

Angel Pie

6   egg whites, room temperature
1/4   teaspoon salt
2   cups sugar
1   tablespoon vinegar
1   pint strawberries or raspberries, sliced and sweetened
       Whipped cream

Preheat oven to 275°. Grease and flour a 9-inch pie plate. In a glass mixing bowl, beat egg whites with salt until stiff (never use a plastic bowl; the egg whites won't whip). Add 1 cup of sugar (1 tablespoon at a time). Dip a tablespoon into sugar and let sugar slowly fall over egg whites. Beat well. Gradually add remaining cup of sugar alternating with 1 drop of vinegar at a time. Beat well. Meringue should be very stiff and very glossy. Pile mixture into pie pan, mounding it high in the middle. Bake 30 minutes; then increase heat to 300° and bake 30 minutes. (Pie will be puffed up when it comes out of the oven but will fall and settle as it cools.) To serve, top with slightly sweetened fresh strawberries or raspberries; then top with swirled whipped cream. *"Angel Pie must be made at least one day ahead."* (6-8 servings) MARJORIE BEST

Pumpkin Pie

21/2   cups pumpkin purée
1/2   cup brown sugar
3/4   cup maple syrup
11/4   teaspoons cinnamon
1/4   teaspoon ground cloves
1/2 _   teaspoon nutmeg
1   teaspoon ground ginger (or more to taste)
1/2   teaspoon salt
2   eggs, lightly beaten
1   13-ounce can evaporated milk
1   unbaked pie crust

Preheat oven to 350 degrees. In a large bowl, combine all filling ingredients except eggs and milk; beat well. Stir in eggs and milk. Pour into pie crust. Bake 50-60 minutes or until knife inserted in center comes out clean. SUSAN HURWITZ

Black Bottom Pie

CRUST:
2 4   gingersnaps
5   tablespoons margarine, melted

PIE:
1   envelope unflavored gelatin
1/4   cup cold water
13/4   cups milk
1/2   cup sugar
1   tablespoon cornstarch
       Pinch salt
4   very cold eggs
11/2   squares unsweetened chocolate, melted
1   teaspoon vanilla
1/4   cup sugar
1   teaspoon rum flavoring
1/2   cup heavy cream, whipped
1/2   square grated unsweetened chocolate

Crush gingersnaps very fine and mix with margarine. Press into pie plate (bottom and sides). Put in freezer to chill. Soften gelatin in water for 5 minutes. Scald 11/2 cups milk in top of a double boiler. Combine sugar, cornstarch and salt; blend in remaining 1/4 cup milk. Add to hot milk. Separate eggs (set whites aside) and beat yolks slightly. Whisk a little hot milk mixture into yolks; pour into the rest of hot milk in double boiler. Cook, stirring constantly, until custard coats a metal spoon. Take mixture off heat and add softened gelatin. Stir until dissolved. Divide custard into two bowls. To one half, add 11/2 squares melted chocolate and vanilla. Chill in refrigerator slightly and pour into chilled gingersnap crust and put back in refrigerator until firm. Also chill (at least 15 minutes), second bowl of custard until it starts to set. Beat 4 egg whites (at room temperature) until stiff, gradually adding 1/4 cup sugar (1 tablespoon at a time) and rum flavoring. Fold egg white mixture into plain custard and chill until it mounds. Pile on top of chocolate mixture and chill. Spoon whipped cream in pretty peaks on top; sprinkle with grated chocolate. *"This takes time to make, but it's worth every sinful bite."* MARJORIE BEST

Eggnog Pie

1	envelope unflavored gelatin
1/4	cup cold water
4	eggs, room temperature
11/2	cups milk
1/2	cup sugar
1/8	teaspoon salt
2	teaspoons rum flavoring
1	baked pie crust (or graham cracker crust)
1/4	teaspoon nutmeg

Soften gelatin in water. Combine 3 beaten egg yolks (throw away extra yolk), milk, 1/4 cup sugar and salt in top of double boiler and cook until mixture is dissolved. Remove from heat and chill until slightly thickened. Beat 4 egg whites until frothy and add remaining 1/4 cup sugar gradually; beat until stiff. Fold into egg yolk mixture with rum flavoring. Pour into pie crust. Sprinkle with nutmeg. Chill until set.

TOPPING:

1	cup heavy cream
2	tablespoons powdered sugar
1	tablespoon rum
1/2	square unsweetened chocolate

When ready to serve, whip cream with powdered sugar and rum until stiff. Spread over pie filling. Shave chocolate curls over top. MARJORIE BEST

Yogurt Pie

2	8-ounce containers vanilla yogurt
1	9-ounce container Cool Whip
1	prepared graham cracker crust
	Topping: Fruit of choice

Combine yogurt and Cool Whip and pour into pie crust. Place in refrigerator. Can be flavored and garnished with any fruit. BARB LANESE

Chocolate Ice Cream Pie

1	cup chopped pecans
1/3	cup crushed vanilla wafers
1/2	cup margarine
1/2	gallon chocolate ice cream, softened
6	tablespoons crème de cacao

Preheat oven to 375°. Mix first 3 ingredients and press in 9-inch pie pan. Bake 8 minutes. Cool and fill with chocolate ice cream; freeze. Serve with 1 tablespoon crème de cacao on each piece. (6 servings) MERRY BREMER

The Queen's Chocolate Mousse Pie

1	3-ounce package cream cheese, room temperature
1/2	cup powdered sugar
1	4-ounce bar semi-sweet chocolate
2	eggs, well beaten
1/2	pint heavy cream
1	8-inch chocolate crumb pie crust
	Optional garnish: Whipped cream and chocolate

Beat cream cheese with sugar. Melt broken chocolate and blend into cheese. Add eggs and mix until smooth. Beat cream until soft peaks form (do not overbeat). Fold chocolate mixture, 1/3 at a time, into whipped cream. Spread into pie crust. Garnish with additional whipped cream and shaved chocolate, if desired. Freeze until firm. Thaw slightly before serving. Cut into wedges. PRUE ROSENTHAL

No Fail Fast and Easy Pie Crust

1	cup flour
1/2	teaspoon salt
1/3	cup cooking oil
2	tablespoons milk

Put flour and salt in pie pan and mix well. Mix together oil and milk. Pour milk mixture over flour mixture in pie pan and mix well. Press into pan. For 2-crust pie, double recipe and save half of mixture to sprinkle over top of filling. ELLEN TUBERGEN AND LAURIE HENDRICK

Perfect Pie Crust

4	cups flour
1	tablespoon sugar
2	teaspoons salt
13/4	cups Crisco (do not substitute oil, lard, margarine or butter)
1/2	cup water
1	tablespoon vinegar
1	large egg

Put flour, sugar, and salt in a bowl. Add Crisco and mix with a fork until crumbly. In a small bowl, using a fork beat water, vinegar and egg. Combine the two mixtures and stir with a fork until all ingredients are moistened. Wrap dough in plastic wrap or wax paper; chill for 1/2 hour. When ready to roll, flour dough lightly and roll on a lightly-floured pastry cloth. Bake pies or shells at the temperature and time your recipe calls for. (Makes enough dough for 2 double crusts or 4 single crusts) *"I divide the dough into 4 balls and freeze them. The individual balls can be defrosted and used when needed."* SUE MATTANO

Ritz Dessert

4	egg whites
1/4	teaspoon cream of tartar
1	cup sugar
1/2	teaspoon baking powder
1	teaspoon vanilla
1 4	Ritz crackers, crushed
1/2	cup chopped nuts
	Ice Cream

Preheat oven to 325°. Beat egg whites with cream of tartar and sugar until stiff but not dry. Add baking powder and vanilla; beat until mixed in. Fold in crushed crackers and nuts. Pour into 81/2 x 11-inch baking dish and bake 30-35 minutes. When cool, cut into squares. Serve with ice cream on top. MARJORIE DUNN

Crème Caramel

1/2	cup sugar
1/4	cup water
5	cups milk
8	eggs
2-3	tablespoons sugar
2	teaspoons vanilla

In a small saucepan, heat sugar and water over low heat, swirling pan occasionally, until sugar dissolves. Increase heat and bring to boil, brushing down sides of pan with pastry brush dipped in cool water. Reduce heat to medium and boil until syrup caramelizes and turns deep golden brown, about 25 minutes. Preheat oven to 300°. Pour caramel into a 6-7 cup mold, tilting mold from side to side making sure bottom is completely covered with caramel; set aside. In a saucepan, scald milk and set aside. In a large bowl beat eggs with sugar and vanilla. Carefully add scalded milk, whisking continuously as you add. Pour mixture through a strainer into the caramel-lined mold. Set mold in water-filled pan and bake about 1 hour. When just set, remove from oven and allow to cool. Chill before turning out onto serving dish. (12 servings)

CHRIS IMAZUMI-O'CONNOR

Lee's Cannoli Filling

4	cups milk*
1	cup Pet milk
3/4	cup sugar
	Pinch salt
1	cinnamon stick, broken up
	Big piece of orange rind or tangerine
71/2	heaping tablespoons cornstarch
1	teaspoon vanilla
	Almonds, toasted and chopped
	Milk chocolate, chopped
	Powdered sugar

In a saucepan, combine first 7 ingredients. Cook until thick, stirring constantly. When thick, take out orange rind and cinnamon stick pieces. (The mixture should have the consistency of pudding when it is fully cooked. If this sticks to the bottom of the pan, you need to change pans or it will be ruined.) Put in bowl and stir in vanilla. Let cool, then refrigerate. It will tend to collect moisture so put a paper towel or cheese cloth over it. Beat the filling before putting in shells.

To fill shells, remove some of the filling to a separate bowl. Add some chopped chocolate to the mixture. Fill the shells using a teaspoon. Make sure to fill the entire shell. Mix some toasted chopped almonds with finely chopped chocolate. Dunk each end of the filled cannoli shell in the mixture of almonds and chocolate. Sprinkle powdered sugar over all. (Makes filling for about 2 dozen cannoli shells)

*COOK'S TIP: Warm the milk in the microwave first, then add cornstarch. It saves on stirring time! You can purchase fresh cannoli shells at Maria's Bakery in Brighton. FRAN RUPP

Hot Fudge Ice Cream

You buy vanilla ice cream and fudge and you cook the fudge and you cook it for 20 or 30 minutes and eat it! MONICA, AGE 7

Copycat Chocolate Fudge Sauce

1/2	cup sugar
2	tablespoons cocoa
1/3	cup milk
1/4	cup light corn syrup
1	square (1 ounce) unsweetened chocolate, chopped
2	tablespoons butter
1/3	cup heavy cream
1	teaspoon vanilla

In a heavy 2-quart saucepan, stir together sugar and cocoa. Stir in milk and corn syrup until blended. Stirring constantly over medium heat, bring to a full boil for 8 minutes. Remove mixture from heat. Stir in chocolate and butter until melted. Gradually stir in heavy cream until blended. Stirring constantly over medium heat, bring to a boil for 2 minutes. Remove from heat and stir in vanilla. Cool. Store in a tightly-covered jar in the refrigerator. To reheat, uncover and set in a saucepan of almost simmering water until sauce is warm and spoonable. JOAN DOOP

Ice Cream Liquid

Do not use solid toppings. First get a spoon. Then get your ice cream. Then mash the ice cream with a spoon or a straw until it looks like water.
JORDAN, AGE 8

Nutty Fudge Sauce

1/2	pound butter
1	12-ounce package chocolate chips
1	cup coarsely-chopped nuts

In double-boiler or microwave, melt butter and chocolate chips. Stir until smooth. Stir in nuts. Serve hot. Hardens on ice cream. May be refrigerated. (Makes 2 cups) BARBARA WRANESH

Pots-de-Crème

1	6-ounce package chocolate chips
2	large eggs
2	tablespoons liquid black coffee (or 5 tablespoons Kahlua or crème de cacao)
3	tablespoons Kahlua
3/4	cup boiling water
	Dream Whip or Cool Whip

Put all ingredients (except Dream Whip) in a food processor; blend. Pour into pots-de-crème or demitasse cups (8-10). Put dab of Dream Whip in center. Let set in refrigerator a few hours or overnight. (Use demitasse spoons and serve with tea cookies.) *"Very fast and easy."* SALLY FLEMING

Pink Peppermint Dessert

2	cups vanilla wafer crumbs
1	cup coarsely-chopped almonds
3/4	cup butter
1 1/2	cups powdered sugar
3	squares unsweetened chocolate, melted
3	eggs, well beaten
1	teaspoon vanilla
1/2	gallon pink peppermint ice cream, softened

Preheat oven to 400°. Combine crumbs with almonds and toast in oven 8 minutes. Line bottom of 9 x 13-inch baking dish with little more than half of crumb mixture. Cream butter and sugar. Add chocolate, eggs and vanilla; mix well. Pour over crumbs and spread to cover. Spread ice cream over chocolate mixture. Top with remaining crumbs. Cover and freeze. (18-20 servings) MERRY BREMER

White Chocolate Mousse

1 2 ounces white chocolate
3 cups heavy cream
2 egg yolks
2 whole eggs
3/4 cup sugar
11/2 tablespoons unflavored gelatin

Chop white chocolate into small pieces and melt over hot water; cool. Whip cream until stiff, then refrigerate. Beat egg yolks and whole eggs together. Add sugar and beat until light lemon color. Stir a little of the egg mixture into the gelatin, then add gelatin to eggs and mix thoroughly. Beat melted chocolate slowly into mixture. Fold in whipped cream. Place in 8-cup mold and refrigerate 2 hours.

DARK CHOCOLATE LAYER:
2 4 ounces semisweet chocolate
11/2 cups heavy cream
5 tablespoons sugar
3 tablespoons butter
2 tablespoons Grand Marnier liqueur

Chop chocolate into small pieces. Combine cream, sugar and butter in saucepan and bring to a boil. Remove from heat. Add chocolate and mix until blended. Cool at room temperature 2 hours. Add Grand Marnier. Pour over top of white chocolate mold. Refrigerate 4 hours. Dip mold in warm water. Turn onto serving dish. (8-10 servings) *"A coveted recipe!"*

ENA HOBELAID

Puppy Chow

1/2 cup butter or margarine
1 cup peanut butter
1 12-ounce package semisweet chocolate chips
1 18-ounce box Crispix cereal
1 pound powdered sugar

Melt first 3 ingredients over medium heat. Pour over cereal in a large bowl. Mix until cereal is coated. Pour powdered sugar into large grocery bag. Add cereal mixture and shake well. Store in airtight box. Makes enough for 1 elementary school classroom for a snack! *"Very popular with kids and chocoholics and very quick to make."* JERRI JENISTA

Deep Dark Secret

4	eggs, separated
11/4	cups sugar
1	cup chopped dates
1	cup chopped pecans or walnuts
1/2	cup flour
1/4	teaspoon salt
1	teaspoon baking powder
11/2	teaspoons vanilla
11/2	pounds red seedless grapes, sliced
4	apples, cut in bite-size pieces
4	bananas sliced
2	cups oranges, cut in bite-size pieces
1	20-ounce can crushed pineapple with juice
1/2-1	pint heavy cream, whipped
	Chocolate chips, optional

Preheat oven to 350°. Beat egg yolks until light yellow. Add sugar and beat until thick. Add dates and nuts. Combine dry ingredients. Beat egg whites until stiff. Fold into mixture. Add vanilla. Pour into greased and floured 9 x 13-inch baking dish. Bake 30 minutes. When torte is cool, break into small pieces. Place 2/3 of pieces in a dish with shallow sides. Combine all the fruit. Place fruit on top of torte pieces. Use your hands to mix torte and fruit and to mold into a mound. Place remaining torte pieces on top and press into mound (like building a sand castle!). If there is juice around the mound, use it for basting the dessert. Cover with Saran wrap and refrigerate overnight. In the morning, whip the cream (use as much whipped cream as you like) and cover dessert. Return to refrigerator for the day. Before serving, decorate any way you choose. (We like it sprinkled with chocolate chips.) (12 servings) *"When you carry this to your table, be ready for compliments!"*

COOK'S TIP: You must prepare this one day in advance and put whipped cream on it the next morning. MARIEL PECK

DESSERTS

Apple Bread Pudding

2	loaves French or Italian bread (stale)
4-5	large apples (Granny Smith, Ida Red or both)
1/2	cup butter
3/4	cup plus 2 tablespoons sugar
1	teaspoon cinnamon
1/2	cup raisins
4	eggs plus 2 egg yolks
41/2	cups milk (or 1 cup cream plus 31/2 cups milk)
2	teaspoons vanilla
1/8	teaspoon salt
1/8	teaspoon nutmeg

Butter 9 x 13-inch oven-proof baking dish, at least 2 inches deep. If desired, remove crusts from bread. Slice 1/2-inch thick. Peel, quarter and core apples. Slice about 1/4-inch thick. Melt half stick of butter in large skillet. Add apples and 2 tablespoons sugar. Cook over medium heat for 2 minutes. Stir gently and cook about 6 more minutes, or less if apples soften so that they are floppy. Sprinkle cinnamon over apples and stir gently. Remove from heat. Place one layer of bread in baking dish, overlapping slices. Sprinkle with half of raisins. Spread apples and juice over top. Make another layer of bread. Set aside. In a mixing bowl, whisk eggs and egg yolks lightly. Add milk, vanilla, salt, nutmeg and 1/2 cup sugar, reserving 1/4 cup. Mix thoroughly and pour slowly over bread. Cover with wax paper and place in refrigerator with something heavy on top for up to 24 hours, so that liquid can be absorbed.

Preheat oven to 350°. Melt remaining half stick of butter and spread on top of bread. Sprinkle with 1/4 cup sugar. Place dish in larger, deeper pan and place in oven. Add water to larger pan to a depth of 1 inch. Bake 60-70 minutes. Knife stuck in center should come out clean. SUSAN HURWITZ

Caramel Dipped Apples

1	8-ounce package cream cheese, room temperature
11/2	cups brown sugar
1	teaspoon vanilla
1/2-3/4	cup crushed peanuts
	Apple slices

Mix all ingredients in blender. Serve with sliced apples. DIXIE COMSTOCK

DESSERTS

Spicy Apple Syrup

1	cup cold water
1/4	cup sugar
1/2	teaspoon cinnamon
1/2	cup unsweetened apple juice
11/2	tablespoons cornstarch
1/2	teaspoon vanilla

In saucepan, combine all ingredients. Stir until mixture simmers and is clear, about 10-12 minutes. Serve over ice cream, pancakes or crêpes.

CHARLOTTE BETZ

Easy Caramel Apple Dip

1	14-ounce can sweetened condensed milk
	Chopped walnuts
	Apples

Remove label and totally immerse milk can in pan of water. Bring to a boil, cover and reduce heat to simmer for 4 hours. Make sure can is always covered with water. Refrigerate until cold. Open both ends of can and push caramel out. Roll caramel in chopped nuts. Serve with apple slices. *"Use red and green apples at Christmas for a festive starter!"*

JOAN GREGORKA

Ozark Pudding

1	egg
3/4	cup sugar
1/3	cup flour
2	teaspoons baking powder
1/2	teaspoon salt
1	teaspoon vanilla
1/2	cup chopped nuts
1/2	cup chopped and peeled apples
	Whipped topping or ice cream

Preheat oven to 325°. Beat egg until fluffy. Sift dry ingredients together and add to egg. Mix thoroughly. Add vanilla, nuts and apples. Turn into greased 8-inch pie pan. Bake 30 minutes. Serve warm or cold with whipped topping or ice cream. (6 servings) BARBARA TREVETHAN

Monkey Tails

The cook should first: Wash hands, get the stuff you need, make it, enjoy it. You will need: 1 popsicle stick, 1 banana, 1 container of Hershey's chocolate syrup, a pan. Directions: Take your banana and put it on a stick (one stick per banana). Put it in your freezer for 1 hour. After 1 hour, take the container of Hershey's chocolate syrup and put it in a pan on the stove on high. Then wait til it bubbles. Then dip the banana in the chocolate. Then put it back in the freezer for another hour. Then take it out and enjoy!

VAL, AGE 8

Banana Split Dessert

1	package yellow Jiffy cake mix (1-layer box)
1	package instant vanilla pudding
1	8-ounce package cream cheese, room temperature
2	cups milk
1	20-ounce can crushed pineapple, drained
4	medium bananas
1	13-ounce tub Cool Whip
1/2	cup chopped nuts
1/2	cup maraschino cherries or strawberries

Bake cake according to package directions in 9 x 13-inch baking dish; cool Cream pudding, cream cheese and milk. Spread onto cake; chill 1 hour. Spread pineapple over pudding mixture, then layer bananas. Cover with Cool Whip. Scatter nuts on top. Add cherries for garnish. Chill 8-10 hours or overnight. (18-20 servings) KATHY CHAPIN

Crème de la Crème

1	envelope unflavored gelatin
2	cups heavy cream
3/4	cup sugar
1	tablespoon vanilla
2	cups sour cream
	Assorted fresh fruit

In a saucepan, mix together gelatin, sugar and cream. Let stand 5 minutes. Cook over low heat and stir until gelatin is dissolved. (Strain if necessary.) Remove from heat; cool. Add vanilla and sour cream, blending until smooth. Pour into a 11/2-quart mold. Refrigerate until firm (4-6 hours). Serve with diced fresh fruit in the center or around sides.

CAROL SEGALL

Light and Refreshing Blueberry-Peach Crisp

FILLING:
6   ripe peaches*
1   pint blueberries
1/4   cup brown sugar
1   teaspoon cinnamon
    Vegetable cooking spray

TOPPING:
1/4   cup brown sugar
1/2   cup oat bran
1   tablespoon Puritan oil
1/4   cup chopped pecans or almonds

Preheat oven to 400°. Peel and slice peaches, sort blueberries. Combine fruit with rest of filling ingredients, then arrange in 12-inch pie pan, coated with vegetable cooking spray. Combine topping ingredients and sprinkle evenly over fruit. Bake 30 minutes or until lightly browned and fruit is bubbly. Serve at room temperature. (8 servings)

*COOK'S TIP: If you use underripe peaches, increase sugar. Reprinted with permission, MEDSPORT, HIGH FIT - LOW FAT™, REGENTS OF UNIVERSITY OF MICHIGAN.

Cherry Blintz Soufflé

2   packages frozen cheese blintzes, thawed
1   package frozen cherry or blueberry blintzes, thawed
4   tablespoons butter

TOPPING:
6   eggs
11/2   cups plain yogurt
1/2   cup cottage cheese
1/2   cup sugar
1   teaspoon lemon juice
    Peel from 1/2 lemon (large size gratings)

Preheat oven to 350°. Melt butter in a 9 x 12-inch baking dish. Layer blintzes on bottom, alternating cheese and fruit blintzes. Beat eggs together; add remaining topping ingredients. Pour over blintzes. Bake, uncovered, 55-60 minutes until top starts to brown. (6-8 servings)

MONICA STARKMAN

Cherry Creek Crisp

1/4   **cup sugar**
11/2   **tablespoons cornstarch**
1/8   **teaspoon salt**
1   **10-ounce package frozen raspberries in syrup, thawed**
2   **teaspoons fresh lemon juice**
1   **16-ounce can tart, pitted cherries, drained**

Preheat oven to 375°. In a small saucepan, combine sugar, cornstarch and salt. Stir in raspberries with syrup and lemon juice. Heat to boiling and cook 1 minute, stirring. Remove from heat. If desired, press raspberry mixture through sieve, discarding seeds. Stir drained cherries into raspberry mixture and pour into lightly buttered 8 x 8-inch baking dish.

TOPPING:
4   **tablespoons butter, softened**
1/4   **cup sugar**
1/2   **cup flour**
1/8   **teaspoon salt**
         Vanilla ice cream

Cream butter and sugar in a small bowl. Blend in flour and salt until crumbly. Sprinkle crumbs over fruit. Bake 30-35 minutes or until lightly browned. Serve warm with ice cream. MARLENE HOLMES

Date Pudding

1/2   **cup crushed graham crackers**
1   **cup chopped dates**
1   **cup chopped English walnuts**
         Milk
1   **pint cream, whipped**

Mix together cracker crumbs, dates and walnuts. Moisten with enough milk to hold ingredients together. Put some of mixture in a 8 x 8-inch pan; alternate layers with whipped cream. KAREN RITZ

Lime Delight

1	141/2-ounce can evaporated milk
2	cups Nabisco chocolate wafer crumbs
1/2	cup margarine, melted
1	3-ounce package lime-flavored Jell-O
13/4	cups hot water
1	cup sugar
1/4	cup lime juice
2	teaspoons lemon juice
	Unsweetened or semisweet chocolate, grated

Pour milk into mixing bowl and chill in freezer until icy crystals form around edges. Combine wafer crumbs with margarine. Press into bottom of 71/2 x 111/2-inch baking dish. Dissolve Jell-O in hot water and chill until partially set. Whip gelatin mixture until light and stir in sugar, lime juice and lemon juice. In a large bowl, whip chilled milk until fairly stiff and fold into gelatin mixture. Pour over crumbs. Top with grated chocolate. Chill until firm.

COOK'S TIP: Don't try to splurge and use real whipping cream in this recipe; it just doesn't taste the same for some reason. MARJORIE BEST

Pavlova

7	egg whites
1	pound powdered sugar
1	teaspoon vanilla
1	teaspoon vinegar
2	teaspoons cornstarch
1/2	teaspoon cream of tartar
2	cups heavy cream, whipped
	Kiwi fruit, peeled and sliced

Preheat oven to 300°. Beat egg whites until stiff but not dry. Beat in powdered sugar, teaspoon by teaspoon. Add vanilla, vinegar, cornstarch and cream of tartar. Butter and flour baking dish (or line with greased waxed paper or foil). Turn stiffly-beaten meringue into center. With spatula, shape into a circle. Bake 2 hours. Turn off heat and allow to cool in oven. When cool, fill with whipped cream and top with kiwi fruit. *"A wonderful Australian/New Zealand dessert!"* MARILYN KIRKING

Orange Balls

1	12-ounce box vanilla wafers, crushed
1/2	cup frozen orange juice concentrate
3/4	cup powdered sugar
3/4	cup shredded coconut
1/2	cup chopped nuts
	Powdered sugar for coating

Combine all ingredients and mix with hands to smooth mixture. Shape into 1-inch balls and roll in the additional powdered sugar. Store in refrigerator or freezer in covered container. (Makes 2 dozen) *"Children can help make these; no baking."* KAREN VAINA

Baked Pineapple

1/2	cup sugar
2	tablespoons cornstarch
21/2	cups crushed pineapple, drained well (save juice)
3	eggs, well-beaten
1/4	cup butter
	Cinnamon

Preheat oven to 325°. Mix sugar and cornstarch with some pineapple juice. Add remaining ingredients. Pour into greased 8 x 8-inch baking dish. Dot with butter. Sprinkle with cinnamon. Bake 1 hour. (4-6 servings) *"This is an excellent side dish at Thanksgiving."* KATHRYN HAY

Frozen Pumpkin Dessert

1/2	cup sugar
1/2	teaspoon ginger
1/4	teaspoon nutmeg
1/2	cup chopped pecans
1	cup canned pumpkin
1/2	teaspoon salt
1/2	teaspoon cinnamon
1	quart vanilla ice cream, softened
	Gingersnaps, crushed
	Whipped Cream
	Pecan halves for garnish

Mix first seven ingredients together. Fold in ice cream. Butter a 9-inch square dish. Line dish with crushed gingersnaps. Pour pumpkin mixture over crumbs and sprinkle crumbs on top. Freeze. Cut into squares. Serve with whipped cream and a pecan half. (8 servings) LOIS NELSON

DESSERTS

Raspberry Applesauce

4	quarts apples (approximately 5-8 pounds)
1	quart fresh raspberries
1/2	cup water
1/2	cup brown sugar (or to taste)
2	tablespoons cinnamon (or to taste)

Peel and core apples. Place in a large stockpot. Add raspberries and 1/2 cup water. Cover and cook on very low heat until soft and mushy (1-2 hours, depending upon the apples). Remove from heat; mash apples. Add sugar and cinnamon; mix thoroughly.

COOK'S TIP: If you have a Foley food mill, no need to peel and core apples. Just cook the fruit and process fruit and juices through the mill.

JEROME GORSKI

Cheese Blintz Soufflé

6	tablespoons butter
1 2	cheese blintzes (keep frozen)
6	eggs
1/2	teaspoon salt
4	tablespoons sugar
4	tablespoons orange juice
2	cups sour cream
1	teaspoon vanilla
2	packages frozen strawberries, thawed

Preheat oven to 350°. Melt and spread butter on the bottom of 9 x 13-inch baking dish. Coat blintzes in butter and arrange in 2 rows in single layer. In blender, beat eggs well. Add salt, sugar, orange juice, sour cream and vanilla. Pour over blintzes and bake 45-50 minutes, or until brown. Serve a bowl of strawberries as topping. (12 servings) DEBBIE ZIES

318

Rhubarb Cream Delight

CRUST:

1	cup flour
1/4	cup sugar
1/2	cup butter or margarine

RHUBARB LAYER:

3	cups fresh rhubarb, cut in 1/2-inch pieces
1/2	cup sugar
1	tablespoon flour

CREAM LAYER:

12	ounces cream cheese, softened
1/2	cup sugar
2	eggs

TOPPING:

1	cup sour cream
2	tablespoons sugar
1	teaspoon vanilla

Preheat oven to 375°. Mix flour, sugar and butter; pat into 10-inch pie plate. Set aside. Combine rhubarb, sugar and flour; toss lightly and pour into crust. Bake about 15 minutes. Turn oven temperature to 350°. Beat together cream cheese and sugar until fluffy. Beat in eggs, one at a time, then pour over hot rhubarb layer. Bake about 30 minutes or until almost set. Combine topping ingredients; spread over hot layers. Chill. (12-16 servings) MARY DOYLE

Chocolate Dipped Fruit

3	ounces semisweet chocolate (use best quality Swiss or Belgian chocolate)
1	tablespoon unsalted butter
1	teaspoon cognac or brandy
	Perfect strawberries or perfect dried apricots

In a double boiler, combine chocolate, butter and cognac over moderate heat. Melt the mixture, stirring frequently, until smooth, about 5 minutes. Remove from heat. Dip fruit halfway into mixture and place on sheet of waxed paper. Refrigerate until set, about 10 minutes. (Don't store in refrigerator.) JANET GILSDORF

DESSERTS

Fruit Pudding

There's chocolate, strawberries, grapes, blueberries, just a little bit of orange and apples . . . and that's all. Now stir it for 2 minutes. Then put it in a large bowl. Heat it at 25° for 15 minutes on the stove. You can take it out and let it cool for 16 minutes and you're ready to eat it. ERIN, AGE 7

Strawberry-Rhubarb Cobbler

1	cup plus 1 tablespoon flour
2	tablespoons sugar
2	teaspoons baking powder
1/4	teaspoon salt
1/4	cup cold unsalted butter
1/2	cup half-and-half cream
21/2	cups sliced fresh rhubarb (or frozen unsweetened rhubarb, thawed and drained)
2/3	cup sugar
11/2	tablespoons quick-cooking tapioca
2	teaspoons lemon juice
21/2	cups halved fresh strawberries
2	tablespoons kirsch liqueur
	Whipped cream

Preheat oven to 425°. Sift flour, 2 tablespoons sugar, baking powder and salt in a large bowl. Cut in butter until mixture resembles coarse crumbs. Make a well in center; pour cream into well. Stir until moistened and dough cleans side of bowl. Combine rhubarb, 2/3 cup sugar, tapioca and lemon juice in medium-size saucepan. Heat to boiling. Reduce heat; simmer, stirring constantly, 2 minutes. Remove from heat; add strawberries and kirsch. Pour into buttered 6-cup baking dish. Gently spread dough over hot filling. Place dish on baking sheet. Bake until top is golden brown, 25-30 minutes. Cool 30 minutes; serve with whipped cream. (6-8 servings) DORIE SOUTHWELL

Strawberry Bavarian Cream

1	3-ounce package strawberry Jell-O
1/4	cup sugar
11/2	cups boiling water
1	10-ounce package frozen strawberries, thawed
1	pint Cool Whip

Mix Jell-O, sugar and water. Add strawberries. Set until thickened. Fold in Cool Whip. LIZ BARKER

Strawberry Frosted Squares

CRUST:
1	cup flour
1/2	cup chopped walnuts
1/4	cup brown sugar
1/2	cup butter, melted

Preheat oven to 350°. Combine flour, walnuts, brown sugar and melted butter. Spread in shallow 9-inch pan. Bake 20 minutes. Cool and crumble. Sprinkle two-thirds of crumbs into 9 x 13-inch baking dish.

FILLING:
2	egg whites
1	cup sugar
2	cups sliced fresh strawberries*
2	tablespoons lemon juice
1/2	pint heavy cream, whipped
	Strawberries for garnish

Beat egg whites until stiff, adding sugar slowly while beating. Add strawberries and lemon juice; continue to beat at high speed until berries are chopped. Fold in whipped cream. Spoon filling over crumb crust and sprinkle remaining crumbs over top. Freeze. Garnish with fresh strawberries. Thaw slightly before serving.

*COOK'S TIP: If using frozen strawberries, use 1/2 cup sugar.

JERI KELCH

Fruit Kabobs

1/4	cup orange juice
1/2	cup lemon juice
1/2	cup sugar
24	fresh strawberries
24	purple grapes
2	medium bananas, sliced
24	cantaloupe balls

DIP:
1	cup sour cream
3	tablespoons powdered sugar
1/2	teaspoon grated lemon rind

Blend juices and sugar. Pour over mixed fruit and chill. Alternate fruit on wooden skewers. Combine dip ingredients and chill. Serve with fruit kabobs.

Sweet Potato Flan

2	pounds sweet potatoes
2	cups sugar
2	cups water
2	cups heavy cream
6	eggs, room temperature
11/3	cups packed brown sugar
3	tablespoons dark rum
3	tablespoons brandy
1	tablespoon grated fresh ginger
2	teaspoons vanilla
1	teaspoon salt
1/2	teaspoon cinnamon
1/4	teaspoon ground allspice
1/4	teaspoon ground cloves

Preheat oven to 325°. Bake sweet potatoes until very soft, about 11/2 hours. Peel and purée in food processor until smooth. Press purée through sieve to remove any lumps. Heat 2 cups sugar and 1 cup water in heavy medium saucepan over low heat, swirling pan occasionally, until sugar dissolves. Increase heat and bring to boil, brushing down sides of pan with pastry brush dipped in cold water. Reduce heat to medium and boil until syrup caramelizes and turns deep golden brown, about 25 minutes. Immediately pour syrup into dry 2-3 quart glass loaf pan. Tip pan to coat bottom and sides evenly. Return excess caramel to saucepan. Mix 1 cup water into saucepan. Bring to boil, stirring until smooth syrup forms. Pour caramel sauce into bowl. Combine 2 cups sweet potato purée and all remaining ingredients in large bowl. Mix until just blended; do not overmix. Spoon into caramelized pan. Place loaf pan in baking pan. Add enough boiling water to come two-thirds way up sides of loaf pan. Bake until center of custard is firm when pan is jiggled, 11/2-2 hours. (Remove pan immediately if custard begins to puff.) Refrigerate at least 6 hours. Run knife around edge of pan. Invert custard onto platter. Cut into slices to serve. Pass caramel sauce separately. (6-8 servings) JANET GILSDORF

Gingered Fruit Compôte

2	pears, cut into chunks
1	cup Calimyrna figs, cut lengthwise in half
1/3	cup dark raisins
1/3	cup golden raisins
2	tablespoons minced crystallized ginger
1	cup orange juice
1	cup dried apricot halves
1	cup pitted prunes
1/2	orange, cut into chunks
1/4	cup Port wine

In medium saucepan over high heat, combine pears, figs, dark and golden raisins, crystallized ginger, orange juice and 1 cup water. Bring to boil. Reduce heat to low; cover and simmer, stirring occasionally, 5 minutes. Add remaining ingredients. Return to boiling. Reduce heat to low; cover and simmer, stirring occasionally, 5 minutes or until fruits are tender. Serve warm or chill slightly. If desired, serve compôte spooned over your favorite ice cream or slices of pound cake. KATHERINE KERSEY

Hot Fruit Compôte

1	1-pound 13-ounce can chunk pineapple
1	1-pound 13-ounce can peaches
1	1-pound 13-ounce can apricots
1	1-pound can sweet cherries
1	dozen crushed macaroon cookies
1/2	cup margarine
1/2	cup amaretto liqueur
1/2	cup slivered almonds

Drain pineapple, peaches, apricots and cherries well and mix. Add cookies to fruit mixture and toss lightly. Melt margarine and mix with amaretto. Pour mixture over fruit and cookie mixture. Place all ingredients in a 9 x 13-inch baking dish and sprinkle with almonds. Store fruit in refrigerator overnight, then bake, uncovered, in oven 30-45 minutes at 300°. (12 servings) RITA LAREAU

DESSERTS

Restaurant Recipes

From: Amadeus Cafe, Ann Arbor, MI

Salmon Mousse

1/2	pound smoked Nova salmon, ground
4	teaspoons finely-chopped fresh dill
1/4	onion, diced
	Dash pepper
1	pint heavy cream
1/4	ounce unflavored gelatin, prepared according to package directions

Combine and stir by hand, salmon, dill, diced onions and pepper; set aside. In a mixing bowl, whip cream with an electric mixer. Stop mixer and add salmon mixture. Whip for five more seconds. Add prepared gelatin; stir by hand. Pour mixture into well-greased mold pan; refrigerate 1 hour. "*Smacznego! Enjoy in Polish.*"

CHEF'S TIP: This looks wonderful when served on a bed of lettuce and garnished with thinly-sliced cucumbers, lemon and dill. We prefer to use smoked ground Nova salmon from Monahan's at Kerrytown.

From: Angelo's Restaurant, Ann Arbor, MI

Raisin Bread

3	pounds flour
3	eggs
1/4	pound sugar
2	tablespoons Crisco shortening
2	tablespoons salt
1/4	pound cake yeast
3	cups water
1 1/2	pounds raisins

Combine the above ingredients in a bowl and mix together. Transfer batter to tabletop and knead by hand 20 minutes. Let rise 20 minutes. Cut and shape into loaves; let rise another 20 minutes. Preheat oven to 350°. Place loaves on a greased pan (cookie sheet is fine) and bake 1 hour and 20 minutes. "*We recommend changing the position of the bread in the oven every 20 minutes. You also may want to vary the amount of water in the recipe to keep the batter dense and heavy.*" (Makes 4 healthy-sized loaves)

From: Arbor Farms, Ann Arbor, MI

Navy Bean Soup

23/4	cups dry navy beans
31/4	cups water
1	large onion, diced
13/4	cups shredded carrots
1	6-ounce package Fakin' Bakin' (or other soy bacon)
1/8	cup tamari
	Sea salt to taste

Soak beans overnight in enough water to cover. The next day, cook until tender; drain. Remove 3/4 cups of beans; purée and set aside. Add 3-1/4 cups water, onions and carrots to cooked beans. Sauté bacon and add to mixture. Cover and simmer, 1 hour. Turn off heat; add bean purée and seasonings. (Makes 4 quarts) SUSAN ROSE

Barbecue Marinade

1	cup safflower oil
1	cup toasted sesame oil
1/4	cup tamari
	Brown rice vinegar to taste
5	tablespoons grated fresh ginger
5	cloves garlic, minced
2	tablespoons honey

Combine all ingredients and mix well. Marinate meat overnight or at least 3 hours. Baste while barbecuing for extra flavor.

CHEF'S TIP: This is a good marinade for vegetable shish kebobs with tempeh. Only the tempeh is marinated overnight. The vegetables, such as onion, tomato, green pepper and corn are brushed with marinade while cooking. Shish kebobs can be barbecued, of course, and oven broiling works really well. You may also use this marinade for chicken, shrimp or scallops.

From: Argiero's, Ann Arbor, MI

Pepperonata Piccante

7	medium potatoes, sliced and then diced
5	cayenne peppers, finely chopped (or to taste)
1	large onion, finely chopped
3/4	cup olive oil
7	green peppers, diced
3	cups fresh tomatoes, peeled and chopped

Sauté potatoes, peppers and onions in olive oil 10 minutes. Add green peppers and tomatoes; cook another 15 minutes. Serve with a good crusty bread or over bread for an open-face sandwich. ROSA ARGIERO

From: Back Alley Gourmet, Ann Arbor, MI

Mexican Orzo and Shrimp Salad

3/4	pound orzo (rice-shaped pasta)
1 1/2	pounds peeled and deveined shrimp (remove tails)
1	red bell pepper, diced
1	green bell pepper, diced
1	ear of corn (cooked and removed from cob)
1	8-ounce can black beans (drained and rinsed)
1/2	bunch cilantro, minced

DRESSING:

	Juice of 1/2 lime
	Juice of 1/2 lemon
2	tablespoons minced garlic
2	teaspoons cumin
1	teaspoon chili powder
3/4	cup olive oil
2	tablespoons rice wine vinegar
	Pinch sugar
	Salt and pepper to taste

Cook orzo in boiling water until tender; drain and rinse. In a small saucepan, simmer shrimp in water until just firm; drain and rinse. In a mixing bowl, combine orzo, shrimp, peppers, corn, black beans and cilantro. Whisk all dressing ingredients together. Toss with salad. (8 servings) VICKI LOWE, CHEF

Thai Angel Hair Pasta Salad

3/4   pound uncooked angel hair pasta
1/3   pound snow peas (trim stem and blanch in boiling water)
3   green onions (sliced on the diagonal)
1   red bell pepper, julienned
1   carrot, julienned
3/4   cup cashews, roasted and unsalted

DRESSING:
1/2   cup peanut oil
1   teaspoon rice wine vinegar
      Pinch sugar
1   teaspoon turmeric
1   tablespoon red pepper flakes
1/4   cup soy sauce
1/2   bunch fresh basil, minced
      Salt and pepper to taste

Cook angel hair pasta in boiling water until tender. Drain and rinse. Place in bowls. Add vegetables and cashews to pasta. Mix ingredients. Whisk all dressing ingredients together. Toss with salad. TRICIA HILL, CHEF

Spicy Sesame Pasta Salad with Citrus Vinaigrette

1   8-ounce block tofu, cut into 1/2-inch slices
      Corn oil for frying
2   carrots (peeled)
1/4   head Napa cabbage, julienned
1   12-ounce package Al Dente spicy sesame pasta

CITRUS VINAIGRETTE:
1/2   cup peanut oil
2   tablespoons hot chili oil
2   cloves garlic, minced
      Zest and juice of 1/2 lemon
      Zest and juice of 1/2 lime
      Zest and juice of 1/2 orange
      Salt and pepper to taste

Place sliced tofu on paper towel. Heat oil in a sauté pan. Fry tofu slices on both sides until golden brown. Drain again on paper towels. When cool, cut into cubes and place in mixing bowl. Peel carrots down to core. Add peels and cabbage to tofu. Cook pasta until just tender. Add to bowl. Combine dressing ingredients and toss with pasta. ELYSA LEVINSOHN, CHEF

From: Bella Ciao Trattoria, Ann Arbor, MI

Couscous with Vegetables
(Cuscusi con Vegetali)

1	large eggplant
3	tablespoons salt
4	medium carrots
	Vegetable oil
2	large onions
2	medium zucchini
3	pints tomatoes, chopped (canned or fresh skinless tomatoes)
1/8	teaspoon red pepper
1	cinnamon stick
	Black pepper to taste
1	cup artichokes, cut into fourths
1	cup chick-peas
1/2	cup raisins
	Salt and white pepper to taste
1	box couscous*

Cut eggplant in half crosswise, then cut each half into eighths, top to bottom. Mix salt with 2 quarts of water. Soak eggplant in this mixture for two hours; drain. Peel carrots and onions; cut in half crosswise, then into fourths. Cut zucchini in half crosswise, then into fourths. Sauté carrots in hot oil 2 minutes. Add onions to the carrots; sauté until translucent. Add tomatoes, red pepper and cinnamon. Cover and simmer 30 minutes. Sauté eggplant. Season with black pepper and add to simmering vegetables. Sauté zucchini. Add to simmering vegetables and simmer 30-45 minutes. Add artichokes, chick-peas and raisins. Simmer 5 minutes. Adjust the seasoning with salt and white pepper. Cook couscous according to box directions. Serve each portion on top of 3/4 cup couscous. (6-8 servings)

*CHEF'S TIP: Couscous can be purchased at most food stores, health stores or bulk food stores. You may want to add 1 or 2 more pints of tomatoes depending on how moist you like this dish.

MARK EDWARD JUERGENS AND NEIL SENG, CO-CHEFS

RESTAURANT RECIPES

From: The Bagel Factory, Ann Arbor, MI

Vegetable Spread

1	8-ounce package cream cheese, room temperature*
11/2	tablespoons finely-chopped green onions
2	tablespoons grated carrot
2	tablespoons grated radish
3	tablespoons finely-chopped celery

Mix all ingredients together; refrigerate. Serve on bagels, crackers, vegetables, etc.

*CHEF'S TIP: This works best if you soften the cream cheese with the back of a large spoon or add a tablespoon of warm water.

From: Casey's Tavern, Ann Arbor, MI

Vegetarian Black Bean Chili

2	cups black beans
2	tablespoons vegetable oil
1	large onion, diced
1	red bell pepper, diced
3	cloves garlic, minced
2-3	teaspoons medium-hot chili powder
1	teaspoon cumin
1	teaspoon paprika
1	teaspoon allspice
1	teaspoon coriander
	Salt and pepper to taste
1	28-ounce can plum tomatoes, chopped with juices
1/4	cup balsamic vinegar
1	12-ounce bottle dark beer (such as Dos Equis)
2	bay leaves

Pick over and rinse black beans. Place in saucepan and fill with water 2 inches above level of beans. Add pinch of salt. Bring beans to boil over high heat and continue to cook until tender, about 1 hour. Add water as needed to keep beans covered until done. Set aside. In another large saucepan, heat oil over medium high heat. Add onions and bell pepper and sauté until tender. Add garlic and spices and sauté until fragrant. (A little salt and pepper here enhance flavors later.) Add tomatoes, vinegar, beer, bay leaves and beans (with their water). Bring chili to a boil, then reduce heat to low. Simmer to blend flavors and thicken, 30-40 minutes. Taste and adjust seasonings. (4-6 servings) RICHARD SCHUBACH, CHEF

332

Sweet Potato and Smoked Salmon Cakes

4	cups grated sweet potato
1	cup flaked smoked salmon*
1/4	cup cooked black beans
1/4	cup diced red bell pepper
1/4	cup diced green onions, green part only
1	tablespoon plus 1 teaspoon brown sugar
2	teaspoons chili powder
1	teaspoon cumin
	Pinch cinnamon
1	teaspoon salt
1	teaspoon pepper
3	tablespoons flour
2	eggs, beaten
2	tablespoons unsalted butter

Mix all ingredients together except butter in a large mixing bowl. Heat 1 tablespoon of butter in a large skillet or nonstick sauté pan over medium-high heat. Measure 1/2 cup potato mixture for each cake and form into 1/4-inch thick patties. Place in pan. Continue process until pan is full. Fry cakes until brown on bottom, approximately 4 minutes. Flip and cook another 3-4 minutes. Remove cakes from pan and keep warm. Fry remainder of mixture. Serve with brandied applesauce and creme fraiche or sour cream. (10-12, 3 inch cakes)

*COOK'S TIP: Almost any smoked meat or poultry can be substituted. Use what fits your taste or availability. TODD CALLIES, CHEF

Brandied Applesauce

6	Granny Smith or similar apples (peeled and diced)
6	tablespoons unsalted butter
1/4	cup brown sugar
1/3	cup brandy
1/2	teaspoon cinnamon
1/2	teaspoon nutmeg
	Pinch salt

In a large saucepan, melt butter over medium heat. Add apples and sauté 3-4 minutes or until soft. Stir in remaining ingredients. Lower heat and continue simmering until sauce is thick and apples have disintegrated, about 20 minutes. Stir often. Remove from heat and adjust seasonings. For a smooth sauce, allow mixture to cool and puree in a food processor (Makes 3-4 cups) TODD CALLIES, CHEF

RESTAURANT RECIPES

From: The Champion House, Ann Arbor, MI

Fried Pork Spareribs

1 pound pork spareribs

MARINADE:
1/2	teaspoon salt
1	teaspoon meat tenderizer
1	teaspoon baking soda
1	tablespoon soy sauce
1	tablespoon flour
1	tablespoon cornstarch
2	tablespoons cold water

SEASONING SAUCE:
5	cups oil
2	tablespoons oil
1	tablespoon A-1 sauce
1	tablespoon sugar
1	tablespoon Worcestershire sauce
1	tablespoon ketchup
2	tablespoons cold water

Chop spareribs into 1 x 2-inch long square pieces. Separate bone lengthwise into two pieces. Combine salt, meat tenderizer, baking soda, soy sauce, flour, cornstarch and cold water. Add to spareribs and coat thoroughly. Soak 2-4 hours. Heat oil in a frying pan until very hot. Deep fry ribs about 3 minutes over high heat until lightly browned and crispy. Drain oil from pan. Heat another 2 tablespoons of oil in frying pan. Combine seasoning sauce ingredients. Pour in seasoning sauce. Cook until boiling. Remove from heat. Add spareribs and mix well. Serve on a platter and decorate with a flower-shaped scallion or pineapple slices.

334

From: The Common Grill, Chelsea, MI

Black Bean Soup

2	pounds black beans, soaked overnight
1	gallon water
1/2	pound bacon, medium chopped
1/2	cup medium-chopped onions
1/2	cup medium-chopped celery
1	teaspoon minced garlic
1/2	teaspoon cayenne pepper
1/2	teaspoon black pepper
1	pound ham, medium chopped
1/2	pound tomatoes, diced

TOPPING (per bowl):
1	tablespoon salsa
1	teaspoon sour cream
1	teaspoon green onions

Soak beans overnight and rinse. Place beans into pot with water and simmer. Sauté bacon, onions, celery and garlic in a pan until crisp. Cook until translucent. Add cayenne and black pepper; mix well. Add ham and cook 1 minute. Add mixture to beans. Add tomatoes and cook 2 hours or until beans are tender. Place the soup in bowls and garnish with salsa, sour cream and green onions. (12 servings) CRAIG COMMON

Salmon with Papaya, Mango and Lime Salsa

4	6-ounce salmon fillets
3/4	cup olive oil
1/4	teaspoon salt

SALSA:
1	papaya, diced 1/4 inch
1	mango, diced 1/4 inch
1	red bell pepper, diced 1/4 inch
1/2	cup finely-chopped cilantro
1/4	cup lime juice
1	clove garlic, minced
2	drops Tabasco sauce

Combine all salsa ingredients in mixing bowl and refrigerate until ready to use. Brush salmon with olive oil and salt each fillet. Place salmon in broiler or on grill and cook until done (about 8-10 minutes). Ladle 1/4 cup salsa over top of cooked salmon and serve. (4 servings) CRAIG COMMON

From: The Connoisseur, Ann Arbor, MI

Baby Summer Salads with Calendula Petals

3	heads baby red oak leaf
3	heads lola rosa
2	heads frisee
1	cup pecan halves
2	cups maple syrup
1/4	cup balsamic vinegar
3/4	cup olive oil
1	teaspoon lime juice
	Salt and freshly-ground pepper
1/2	cup calendula petals
1/2	cup grated Asiago cheese

Preheat oven to 400°. In cold water gently wash greens, remove leaves and discard cores. By hand, tear greens into desired size, drain well and keep refrigerated. Place pecans and maple syrup in a small saucepan over low heat and simmer 20 minutes. Pour pecans and syrup into a colander and drain 5 minutes. Spread pecans on a teflon-coated cookie sheet and bake until caramelized. (Do not burn.) Let cool to room temperature. Place greens in a large salad bowl. Add vinegar, oil and lime juice. Add salt and freshly ground pepper to taste. Toss well and place on salad plates. Top with maple-glazed pecans and grated Asiago cheese. Sprinkle with calendula petals. (6 servings) ROBERT CREASEY, EXECUTIVE CHEF

Iced Passion Fruit Soup with Yogurt and Vanilla

1 0	fresh passion fruits
1/4	cup sugar
1	2-inch piece vanilla bean, split lengthwise
1	teaspoon unflavored gelatin
1/4	cup plain yogurt, whisked well
1/2	teaspoon freshly-ground espresso coffee
	Fresh mint leaves for garnish

Place a coarse sieve over a medium nonreactive saucepan. Working over the sieve, cut each passion fruit in half. With a teaspoon, scoop out the pulp. Push the pulp and juice through the sieve; discard the seeds. Add sugar, vanilla bean and 1 cup of water to the saucepan and bring just to a simmer over low heat, stirring. Remove from heat and sprinkle gelatin evenly over the mixture. Set aside to let gelatin thicken on the surface of the juice, about 3 minutes. Then whisk the mixture well to blend the gelatin. Set a fine sieve over a medium nonreactive bowl and strain mixture. Cool to room temperature, then place the bowl in a larger bowl filled with ice and water. Chill mixture over the ice, stirring frequently, about 5 minutes. (The recipe can be prepared to this point and refrigerated overnight, covered.) To serve, ladle chilled soup into 2 shallow soup dishes. Top each serving with 2 tablespoons yogurt, sprinkle ground espresso on top and garnish with mint leaves. (2 servings)

ROBERT CREASEY, CHEF DE CUISINE

Sautéed Fillet of Onaga (Hawaiian Red Snapper), Walnut Butter and Arugula Chiffonade

2	tablespoons walnut oil
2	6-ounce fillets of Onaga or Florida Red Snapper (boneless, scaled and skin on)
	Salt and cayenne pepper to taste
1/2	cup diced walnuts
1	teaspoon finely-minced shallots
1/4	cup dry white wine
1/2	cup fish stock
1/4	cup butter
	Lemon juice to taste
1 0	arugula leaves

Preheat oven to 350°. In sauté pan, bring walnut oil to medium high heat. Make 3 diagonal slits in the skin of the fish. Sprinkle with lemon juice and season with salt and cayenne pepper. Place skin-side down in the oil. Cook 2 minutes; turn and cook another minute. Remove fish and set aside. (Fillets should be about half-cooked.) Add walnuts to the pan with remaining oil and toss until golden brown. Remove nuts and set aside. Add shallots, white wine and fish stock to the pan and simmer until reduced by two-thirds. Strain the reduction through a fine sieve into a small saucepan. Place fish into the oven (skin side up) to finish cooking. Add walnuts to sauce and whisk in butter and a dash of lemon juice. Check sauce for seasoning. Julienne arugula leaves very fine at the last moment. Cover plates with sauce, place fish in the center of the plate, skin side up, and surround with arugula. Serve with fresh vegetables and rice pilaf. (2 servings) ROBERT CREASEY, CHEF DE CUISINE

Live Maine Lobster with Pernod Cream, Glazed with Cantal Cheese

2	1 1/4-pound live Maine lobsters
1	large pot boiling water
	Salt and cayenne pepper to taste
4	tablespoons butter
1	teaspoon finely-minced shallots
1/2	teaspoon finely-minced garlic
	Juice of 1 lime
2	tablespoons Pernod
1/2	cup fish stock
2	cups heavy cream
1	ripe tomato, peeled and diced
6	fresh basil leaves, chopped
1/2	cup finely-grated Cantal cheese

Place live lobsters in boiling water for one minute and remove. Detach the arms, claws and tail from the main body and remove all of the meat. Cut the main body lengthwise, not quite all the way through, and spread it apart gently to form a shell for serving in. Rinse out and put in low heat oven until dry. Cut lobster meat into bite-size pieces and season with salt and cayenne pepper. Bring 1 tablespoon butter to medium heat in sauté pan. Toss lobster in butter until two-thirds cooked. Remove and set aside. Sauté shallots and garlic in the same pan. Add lime juice, half of Pernod wine and fish stock and reduce by half. Add cream and simmer until desired sauce consistency. Add tomatoes, basil and lobster to the sauce. Whisk in remaining butter and Pernod and check for seasoning. Place dried lobster bodies in soup plates and ladle with equal amounts of sauce and lobster. Cover each one with Cantal cheese and glaze until golden brown. Serve with fresh vegetables and rice pilaf.

ROBERT CREASEY, CHEF DE CUISINE

Sautéed Breast of Muscovy Duck Pomegranate with Port Wine Sauce

2	Muscovy duck breast (skin on)
	Salt and freshly-ground white pepper to taste
1	tablespoon virgin olive oil
1	teaspoon finely-minced shallots
1	sprig fresh thyme
	Juice of 2 pomegranates
1/2	cup duck stock
1/2	cup port wine
4	tablespoons butter

Preheat oven to 400°. Season duck breasts with salt and white pepper. In a sauté pan, bring olive oil to medium high heat. Place duck breasts skin side up in the pan and sauté until golden brown, then turn and cook until skin is golden brown. Transfer the breasts to a baking dish and cook until the internal temperature is 130°. While the breasts are cooking, sauté shallots in the same pan with a sprig of thyme. Add pomegranate juice, duck stock and port wine and simmer until reduced by two-thirds. Whisk in butter and check for seasoning. Strain sauce through a fine sieve. When the duck is ready, remove from oven and carefully peel off the skin using a sharp knife. Slice the duck very thin against the grain and fan on plates. Cover with the finished sauce. Serve with fresh vegetables and wild rice. (2 servings) ROBERT CREASEY, CHEF DE CUISINE

Crème Brûlée

7	egg yolks
2/3	cup sugar
1	teaspoon cornstarch
1/2	pint milk
11/2	pints heavy cream
1	vanilla bean
2	tablespoons light brown sugar

Preheat oven to 250°. Combine egg yolks, sugar and cornstarch in a bowl and mix well. In a saucepan, combine milk, cream and vanilla bean pulp and bring to a boil. Add to the mixture and mix slowly until well blended. Fill 8-ounce capacity oven-proof crocks or cassoulets with mixture and bake in a waterbath for 11/2 hours. Remove from the waterbath and chill thoroughly. When ready to serve, sprinkle a thin layer of light brown sugar over each custard and cook on top oven rack underneath broiler until dark brown. Serve immediately. (4 servings)

ROBERT CREASEY, CHEF DE CUISINE

Chocolate Terrine with Sabayon Mousseline Sauce

PASTRY:

8	ounces semisweet chocolate
2	tablespoons espresso
1/2	teaspoon vanilla extract
6	eggs, separated
1/2	cup sugar

Preheat oven to 350°. Melt chocolate, espresso and vanilla over a double boiler, stirring constantly. Cool, then stir in egg yolks, blending well. In a separate bowl, whip egg whites and salt until frothy. Slowly add sugar and whip to a stiff peak. Fold egg whites into the chocolate mixture. Spread evenly onto a buttered sheet pan lined with parchment paper. Bake 20 minutes. Cool until warm. Cut rectangles of pastry to fit a terrine or bread loaf pan.

FILLING:

1	pound semisweet chocolate, chopped
2	cups heavy cream

Scald cream, then add chocolate and stir until blended. Cool to room temperature. To assemble the terrine, line terrine or bread loaf pan with parchment paper. Pour 1/4 of the chocolate into pan, place a piece of pastry on top and alternate until finished with a layer of chocolate on top. Chill for at least 3 hours. (8 servings)

NOTE: When chilled, carefully lift the Terrine out of the pan using the parchment paper. Slice to desired thickness using a sharp knife and serve with Sabayon Mousseline Sauce.

SABAYON MOUSSELINE SAUCE:

6	egg yolks
1/2	cup sugar
	Pinch salt
1	cup champagne
1	cup heavy cream

Mix egg yolks, sugar and salt. Add champagne. Whisk over a double boiler until thick and pale yellow in color. Put immediately over an ice bath and whisk until cold. In a separate bowl, whip cream to a soft peak and fold into the egg yolk mixture. MARY FRANZENBURG, PASTRY CHEF

From: Cottage Inn Cafe, Ann Arbor, MI

Cafe Cobb Salad

3	ounces smoked turkey, julienned
4	tomato slices, diced
1/4	cup diced red onions
2	boiled eggs, chopped
4	slices bacon, crisply cooked and crumbled
14	mandarin oranges

In a large bowl, arrange in order listed using half the turkey on bottom and top. BRAD BEACH, CORPORATE CHEF

Pasta Romanga

4	ounces chicken breast
1	ounce mushrooms
1/8	cup diced fresh tomatoes
1/8	cup red onions
2	ounces bacon, crumbled
1/2	cup heavy cream
1	ounce Romano cheese
2	tablespoons garlic butter (see recipe below)
6	ounces linguini, cooked al dente

GARLIC HERB BUTTER:

1/2	pound butter, room temperature
1/2	pound margarine, room temperature
1/4	cup minced fresh garlic
1/2	teaspoon black pepper

Blend ingredients for butter mixture with electric beaters or food processor until mixed well and no lumps appear. Keep chilled until ready to use.

While grilling chicken, sauté mushrooms, tomatoes and onions 1 minute in another pan. Add bacon, then cream, Romano cheese and garlic butter. Let thicken. Toss in linguini. Place on plate; cut chicken in 6 slices and put on top of pasta. BRAD BEACH, CORPORATE CHEF

oniditsa

nch pizza dough, or Boboli shell
1   ounce goat cheese
     Sun-dried tomato oil, to taste
2   ounces fresh spinach
1/2   ounce sun-dried tomato, diced or julienned
4   slices bacon, diced
3   ounces Mozzarella cheese
1   ounce pine nuts
     Pinch dill

Preheat oven to 500°. Sprinkle dough with goat cheese, then oil. Add spinach, sun-dried tomato, bacon, Mozzarella, pine nuts in this order. Add dill. Bake 4-5 minutes. BRAD BEACH, CORPORATE CHEF

From: Diamond Head Cafe, Ann Arbor, MI

Veggie Terrine

11/2 bunches of broccoli, blanched
4   eggs
1/2   cup heavy cream
     Fresh thyme, oregano and basil (optional)
8   Shiitake mushrooms, stems removed
6   medium-size carrots, blanched
     Salt and pepper to taste

Preheat oven to 300°. Puree broccoli with 2 eggs and 1/4 cup cream and half of the fresh herbs. Pour into a loaf pan lined with plastic wrap. Layer mushrooms on surface of broccoli, underside up. Puree carrots with remaining 2 eggs and 1/4 cup cream and remaining herbs. Pour over shiitake mushrooms, smooth. Cover with plastic wrap. Place loaf pan in a roasting pan with 2 inches of water. Bake 45 minutes or until internal temperature is 160°. LISA PAROLA MOORE

342

From: Dough Boys Bakery, Ann Arbor, MI

Glazed Apple Torte

1	cup crushed zwieback crumbs or graham cracker crumbs
2	tablespoons butter, melted
1	tablespoon sugar
1	teaspoon cinnamon

Preheat oven to 325°. Combine above ingredients and pat onto the bottom and sides of a 10-inch springform pan. Bake 8 minutes.

6	large tart apples (peeled and sliced into rings about 1/3-inch thick)
1/4	cup butter
3/4	cup sugar
6	eggs
2	cups sour cream
1/2	cup packed brown sugar
1 1/2	teaspoons grated lemon peel
1	teaspoon vanilla
	Sifted powdered sugar

Preheat oven to 350°. Melt butter in a large pan; add sugar and apple rings. Poach gently until sauce is reduced to a glaze. Arrange rings on baked crust, reserving 5 rings for top. In a bowl, beat eggs until light and beat in sour cream, brown sugar, grated peel and vanilla. Pour custard over apples and arrange reserved apples on top. Bake 40-45 minutes or until set. Remove from oven and let cool. Dust top with sugar. (8 servings)

DONI LYSTRA

Crêpes

11/2	**cups milk**
3	**eggs**
11/2	**cups flour**
1	**tablespoon sugar**
1	**teaspoon butter, melted**

Pour milk, eggs, flour, sugar and butter into blender (or beat by hand) until smooth and blended. Strain through sieve to get rid of lumps. If possible, let batter stand at room temperature 2 hours. Heat crêpe pan on medium heat about 2 minutes. With a pastry brush, brush pan with melted butter. Add just enough batter to barely cover bottom of pan. Brown on one side; turn crêpe and brown lightly on the other. Keep repeating process, adding melted butter to pan as needed.

STRAWBERRY FILLING:

1	**quart fresh or frozen strawberries, hulled and halved**
1/4	**cup sugar**
3	**tablespoons kirsch liqueur**
3	**tablespoons currant jelly**
2	**tablespoons water**
1	**pint heavy cream**
2	**tablespoons sugar**
1	**teaspoon vanilla or kirsch liqueur**

Place berries, sugar, kirsch, jelly and water in a deep skillet. Heat slowly and bring to boil; turn down and simmer, covered, about 3 minutes. Place 2-3 tablespoons of mixture in crêpe and roll closed. Lay crêpes in serving dish, seam side down. Repeat. Whip together cream, sugar and kirsch. Place a big spoonful on top of every crêpe. (12-14 crêpes, depending on size of crêpes) DONI LYSTRA

Basic Cream Puff Dough

1	cup water
1/2	cup butter
1/4	teaspoon salt
1	cup flour
4	eggs

Preheat oven to 400°. In a medium saucepan, combine water, butter and salt; bring to boiling point. Remove from heat. Immediately, with a wooden spoon, beat in flour all at once. Return to low heat and continue beating until mixture forms a ball and leaves the sides of the pan. Remove from heat. Add one egg at a time, beating hard after each addition, until smooth. Continue beating until mixture is shiny and forms "ribbons" when spoon is lifted from pan. Drop by rounded tablespoonfuls, 2 inches apart for cream puffs, on ungreased cookie sheet. Bake 45-50 minutes, or until golden brown. (12 large cream puffs) *"A very serviceable recipe that can be used in a variety of dessert and hors d'oeuvre dishes."*

FOR MADELEINES:
Above cream puff dough

1/4	cup powdered sugar
1	jar cherry preserves
1	cup heavy cream
1	teaspoon vanilla

Preheat oven to 400°. Prepare cream puff dough as directed above. Place dough in pastry bag with #6 star tip. Pipe, 2 inches apart, onto ungreased cookie sheets to make about 24 "S" shapes, each 3 inches long. Bake 25-30 minutes or until puffed and golden-brown. Remove to wire rack and cool completely. Whip cream, sugar and vanilla until stiff. Cover and refrigerate. Cut each cooled puff in half crosswise; scoop out any soft dough. Spoon 1 tablespoon preserves into each bottom half, then 1 tablespoon whipped cream. Replace top and sprinkle with powdered sugar. Refrigerate if not serving at once, but do not allow to stand too long as puffs get soggy.

RESTAURANT RECIPES

From: The Earle, Ann Arbor, MI

Pecan Tart

PASTRY SHELL:

3	cups flour
1/2	cup sugar
11/4	cups unsalted butter (cold, cut in 1-inch cubes)
1	egg and 1 egg yolk

Combine flour and sugar in a large bowl. Cut in cold butter. Mix until crumbly. Slowly add egg and yolk. Mix until combined. If dry, add a few drops of cold water. Do not overmix. Chill at least 1 hour before rolling out.

FILLING:

1/2	cup brown sugar
2	tablespoons flour
1	cup light corn syrup
3	tablespoons butter
3	large eggs
11/2	teaspoons vanilla
1/3	cup white rum
3	cups pecans, lightly toasted

Preheat oven to 350°. Mix sugar and flour together in a saucepan. Add corn syrup and butter. Put on low heat until butter is melted. Meanwhile, whip eggs and vanilla briefly in bowl. Set aside. Add rum to sugar/butter mixture (off the heat). Stir into egg mixture. Add nuts. Pour into unbaked tart shell and bake until golden brown.

SHELLEY CAUGHEY ADAMS, CHEF

From: Escoffier, Ann Arbor, MI

Charbroiled Flank Steak

2   pounds trimmed beef flank steak

MARINADE:
10   shallots, finely diced
2   dried red chile peppers, thinly sliced
2   cups olive oil
2   teaspoons Thai green curry paste
1/8   cup Szechwan peppercorns
1/8   cup white peppercorns
1/8   cup peeled and grated fresh ginger
1/8   cup brown sugar
2   cloves garlic, minced
1/4   bunch fresh thyme, chopped

Trim flank steak of any excess fat or cartilage. Combine all marinade ingredients. Place flank steak in a shallow pan and cover with marinade. (Flank steak is best when marinated for several days, but it should marinate at least overnight.) After marinating meat, charbroil to desired doneness and slice thinly against the grain. Arrange on a platter and serve.
(4 servings) *"A trip to an Asian market may be necessary for some of the ingredients."* MICHAEL HOULIHAN, EXECUTIVE CHEF

From: Food for All Seasons, Ann Arbor, MI

Asparagus-Pea Pod Salad

2	pounds fresh asparagus
1	pound fresh pea pods
1	English cucumber
1	head bibb lettuce, separated into leaves
4	navel oranges, peeled and cut into segments
1	cup roasted pine nuts
1	small red onion, cut into thin rings

HONEY VINAIGRETTE:

1	cup vegetable oil
1/3	cup rice vinegar
2	tablespoons walnut oil
1	teaspoon honey
	Salt and pepper to taste

Snap the woody ends off fresh asparagus. Cut into 2-inch pieces. Boil asparagus and cook until just tender, 1-2 minutes. Remove from boiling water; immediately plunge into ice water. Remove ends from pea pods. Repeat blanching procedure with pea pods. Peel cucumber; cut in half lengthwise. Remove seeds and cut into pieces 1/8-inch thick. Prepare the dressing. Whisk together all ingredients to combine. In a bowl, toss pea pods, asparagus and cucumber together with the dressing. Line a platter with lettuce leaves. Put asparagus mixture on top. Sprinkle with orange segments, pine nuts and onion rings. (16 servings)

TONI BENJAMIN AND MARY KATHRYN GENOVA

From: Fresh Cream Cafe, Ann Arbor, MI

Pineapple Cake

11/2	cups flour
11/2	teaspoons baking powder
11/2	teaspoons baking soda
1/2	teaspoon salt
2	cups sugar
1/2	cup long cooking oats
1	20-ounce can crushed pineapple, juice included
1/2	teaspoon vanilla extract
2	eggs, beaten
1/4	cup chopped walnuts

CREAM CHEESE FROSTING:

1	8-ounce package cream cheese, room temperature
1/2	cup butter or margarine, softened
2	cups powdered sugar
1/2	teaspoon lemon juice
1/2	teaspoon vanilla

Preheat oven to 350°. In a large mixing bowl, sift together flour, baking powder, baking soda and salt. Stir in sugar, oats, pineapple, juice and vanilla. Mix well. Stir in eggs and walnuts. Pour into a greased 9 x 13-inch baking dish and bake 35-40 minutes or until wooden pick comes out clean. Cool on wire racks. Combine cream cheese and butter; beat until fluffy. Gradually add sugar; beat until creamy. Mix in lemon juice and vanilla. Spread on cooled cake.

RESTAURANT RECIPES

From: Gandy Dancer Restaurant, Ann Arbor, MI

Maryland Crab Cakes

1/2	pound lump Maryland crabmeat, drained
1/2	pound deluxe crabmeat
1	egg, beaten
5	tablespoons mayonnaise
1	tablespoon finely-chopped parsley
2	teaspoons Worcestershire sauce
1	teaspoon prepared mustard
1	teaspoon salt
1/4	teaspoon white pepper
1/2	cup plain bread crumbs

Remove shells from crabmeat (do not break up crabmeat). In a stainless steel bowl, mix rest of ingredients except for bread crumbs. Combine with bread crumbs. Fold crabmeat in gently but thoroughly. (Be sure not to break up crabmeat.) Refrigerate 1 hour. Form into crabcakes. Broil both sides to a golden color. (7-8 servings) *"A stainless steel bowl allows for even mixture of all ingredients."* DOUG ROGOTZKE, CHEF

From: Golden Chef, Ann Arbor, MI

Cashew Shrimp

4-5	ounces white shrimp
1	egg white
1	teaspoon cornstarch
1/2	teaspoon salt
	Vegetable oil
1/4	cup raw cashew nuts
5-6	slices fresh ginger
10-12	green onions, 1-inch slices
1	teaspoon white wine
1/2	teaspoon salt
1	teaspoon sugar
1	teaspoon cornstarch (mixed with 1 teaspoon water)
1/2	teaspoon sesame oil

Clean shrimp and pat dry. Mix with egg white, cornstarch, salt and a little oil. Heat 1 tablespoon oil. Fry cashew nuts until brown. Remove and drain; put aside. Heat 1 teaspoon oil. Fry ginger slices and green onions. Add shrimp and white wine quickly. Mix with salt, sugar, cornstarch and water; stir until thoroughly mixed. Turn off heat. Add sesame oil, cashew nuts and serve immediately. (2 servings)

350

From: Gratzi, Ann Arbor, MI

Chicken with Wine and Mushrooms (Pollo al Marsala con Funghi)

1	chicken breast, boned and skinned (split in half)
1	tablespoon butter
1	tablespoon olive oil
	Salt and pepper to taste
	Flour
3/4	ounce pancetta (bacon)
1	teaspoon minced onions
3/4	ounce Porcini mushrooms
3/4	ounce marsala wine
2	tablespoons chicken stock
1/2	teaspoon chopped parsley
1	sprig parsley for garnish

Split chicken breast in half. Place butter and olive oil in sauté pan and heat until very hot. Season chicken with salt and pepper and dust with flour; shake excess off. Add chicken to pan and sauté until golden brown, approximately 2 minutes. Turn over and repeat. Add pancetta and render down until crispy but not burned. Add onions and sauté until translucent. Add mushrooms and sauté. Deglaze with marsala wine. Add chicken stock and parsley; mix well and reduce sauce to half the chicken. Remove from heat and place chicken on 12-inch round plate. Pour sauce over the breast and garnish with parsley. Serve immediately. (1 serving)

Pesto Sauce

2	quarts olive oil
1/2	cup minced garlic
21/2	cups pine nuts
2	cups freshly-grated Parmesan cheese
1	cup fresh basil leaves
1	cup fresh spinach leaves
4	teaspoons salt
2	teaspoons pepper

Place all ingredients into a 1-gallon blender and blend approximately 10 seconds. Mix well and push down spinach and basil leaves and blend again until smooth, approximately 10-20 seconds more. Pour sauce into plastic container making sure to scrape blender well with rubber spatula. Cover with Saran wrap and keep in refrigerator until needed.
(Makes 3 quarts)

Herbal Olive Oil

1	quart olive oil
1	cup extra-virgin olive oil
1	sprig fresh rosemary
1	sprig fresh oregano
1	sprig fresh thyme
1-2	leaves fresh basil
1/8	teaspoon crushed dry red peppers

Combine all ingredients. Cover and keep at room temperature at least 24 hours. (Makes 5 cups)

From: Katherine's Catering, Inc., Ann Arbor, MI

Black Bean Cakes with Cilantro Dipping Sauce or Salsa

2	cups black beans
1/2	teaspoon salt
1	bay leaf
1/2	teaspoon fresh thyme
1/2	cup chopped onions
1	clove garlic, minced
1	fresh jalapeño pepper, finely chopped
1	tablespoon chopped fresh parsley
1	egg
	Salt and pepper to taste
	Olive oil

EGGWASH:

2	eggs
1	tablespoon milk
1/4	cup cornmeal

Soak beans overnight. Boil with salt, bay leaf, thyme, 1/4 cup onions and garlic until beans are tender; drain. Purée beans. Sauté remaining 1/4 cup onions and jalapeño pepper; combine with bean purée. Add parsley, egg, salt and pepper. Shape bean cakes into 2-3-inch rounds; press flat. Dip in mixture of egg and milk, then cornmeal. Sauté cakes in a little olive oil; serve with choice of dipping sauces. (Makes 12-14 cakes)

DEBBIE KASTANIS, EXECUTIVE CHEF

Dipping Sauces for Bean Cakes

CILANTRO SOUR CREAM DIPPING SAUCE:
1/2   cup sour cream
1   tablespoon finely-chopped green onions
1   tablespoon chopped cilantro
1   teaspoon minced garlic
1   teaspoon fresh lemon juice
        Dash Tabasco sauce
        Salt and pepper to taste

RED ROMA SALSA:
1   pound ripe tomatoes (I prefer Roma), finely chopped
2   tablespoons minced red onions
1   tablespoon minced garlic
1   tablespoon finely-chopped fresh parsley
1   tablespoon finely-diced chile pepper
1   green pepper, finely diced
1   tablespoon fresh lemon juice

Combine ingredients for dipping sauce and combine salsa ingredients. Blend each well. Serve with bean cakes.

Vegetable Hearts Beet Fonder

1   beet
2   large carrots, peeled
1   white turnip, peeled
1   tablespoon unsalted butter
        Salt and white pepper to taste

Wash beet; boil approximately 20 minutes until tender. Allow to cool, then peel. Cut all vegetables into 1/4-inch thick rounds. Using a small heart-shaped cookie cutter, 1 or 1-1/2 inches, cut tiny hearts. (Two sizes of cookie cutters create a wonderful effect.) Blanch carrots and turnip vegetable hearts 1 minute, then place into an ice-water bath to cool quickly. Drain, cover and refrigerate. Wrap beet hearts separately. When ready to serve, melt butter in small pan. Sauté vegetables over medium heat until tender, about 6 minutes. Salt and pepper to taste. (2 servings)

DEBBIE KASTANIS, EXECUTIVE CHEF

Market Crudités with Balsamic Vinaigrette

VEGETABLES:

1/4	pound celery root, julienned
1/2	pound carrots, julienned
1/2	pound green beans
1/4	pound Brussels sprouts
2	plum tomatoes, sliced

VINAIGRETTE:

3	cups balsamic vinegar
1/4	cup Dijon mustard
3	cloves garlic, minced
1	tablespoon basil
1	tablespoon oregano
1	teaspoon pepper
3	tablespoons sugar
2	cups corn oil
2	cups olive oil

Clean vegetables; leave green beans and Brussels sprouts whole. Blanch all vegetables, except tomatoes, until tender. In a mixer bowl, combine all vinaigrette ingredients except oils; mix thoroughly. Slowly stream in oils. Marinate vegetables in balsamic vinaigrette. Arrange on plate contrasting shapes and colors. (6 servings) DEBBIE KASTANIS, EXECUTIVE CHEF

Grilled Salmon and Tomatillo Salsa

MARINADE:

2	tablespoons dry vermouth
	Juice of 1 lime
	Juice of 1 lemon
	Dash salt and pepper
6	7-ounce salmon fillets, skinned and deboned
	Lemon wedges

In a small bowl, combine vermouth, lime and lemon juices, salt and pepper; set aside. Rinse fillets under cold running water; pat dry. Lay fillets in oven-proof dish and cover with marinade 15 minutes. Preheat broiler. Strain and reserve marinade. Broil fillets approximately 3 inches below heat source, basting every 3 minutes with marinade until done, about 8-10 minutes. In warmer weather, grill fillets outdoors. Serve on chiffonade of lettuce topped with tomatillo salsa. Garnish with lemon wedges.

TOMATILLO SALSA:

1	pound fresh green tomatillos
3	tablespoons finely-chopped red onions
	Juice of 1 lime
2	cloves garlic, minced
1	bunch cilantro, chopped
1	jalapeño pepper, finely chopped

Husk tomatillos and dice. Add remaining ingredients and mix. Serve over salmon. (6 servings) DEBBIE KASTANIS, EXECUTIVE CHEF

Espresso Ice Cream

6	egg yolks
1/2	cup sugar
3	tablespoons brown sugar
3	cups heavy cream
1	cup instant espresso (dry)
3	tablespoons crème de cacao
2	tablespoons vanilla
1	teaspoon cinnamon
	Raspberry preserves (optional)

Beat egg yolks and sugars in a medium-size bowl just until blended. Heat cream in a medium-size saucepan until almost boiling. Pour cream in a thin stream into the egg yolk mixture, whisking constantly. Return mixture to saucepan and cook over medium-low heat to make a light custard, about 5-7 minutes. (Do not allow to boil.) Remove from heat. Dissolve instant espresso in a small amount of hot water. Stir in crème de cacao, vanilla and cinnamon; whisk into custard. Refrigerate, covered, until cold. Freeze in an ice cream maker, following manufacturer's instructions. Can be topped with raspberry preserves or served with raspberry shortbread hearts. (Makes approximately 1 quart) DEBBIE KASTANIS, EXECUTIVE CHEF

From: Kelly's 107, Saline, MI

Salmon, Cream and Shallots over Fettuccine Noodles

1 2	ounces fettuccine noodles
4	tablespoons butter
3	tablespoons minced shallots
1	tablespoon minced garlic
1	cup heavy cream
2	cups fresh cooked salmon
3	tablespoons chopped fresh dill
2	cups freshly-grated Parmesan cheese
	Salt and pepper to taste

Cook fettuccine noodles while preparing sauce. Drain well. Melt butter in a 10-inch sauté pan. Add shallots and garlic and sauté 2 minutes. Stir in cream. Bring to a boil and cook 3 minutes so the cream will begin to thicken. Add salmon, dill, Parmesan cheese, salt and pepper. Turn down heat and let simmer 3 minutes. Pour sauce over hot, well-drained fettuccine noodles. Serve immediately. (3 servings)

From: Kilwin's Chocolate Shoppe, Ann Arbor, MI

Fudge Nut Squares

COOKIE BASE:

1	cup butter
2	cups brown sugar
2	eggs
3	teaspoons vanilla
21/2	cups unbleached flour
1	teaspoon baking soda
1	teaspoon salt
3	cups rolled oats
1	cup chopped pecans

Preheat oven to 350°. Grease a 10 x 16-inch baking dish. Cream butter and brown sugar together. Add eggs and vanilla. Beat well. Sift together flour, soda and salt. Add to butter and sugar mixture. Add rolled oats. Press two-thirds of this cookie mixture into pan.

FILLING:

1 2	ounces Kilwin's semisweet bulk chocolate
1	15-ounce can sweetened condensed milk
3	tablespoons butter
3/4	cup chopped pecans
1	teaspoon vanilla

Melt chocolate, canned milk and butter in a double boiler over hot water. Add pecans and vanilla. Pour filling onto cookie mixture. Sprinkle remaining cookie mixture over filling and bake 20-25 minutes. (Do not overbake!) Cut into small squares. *"These are extra rich and delicious!"*

From: LaPinata Mexican Restaurant, Ann Arbor, MI

Guacamole

12	ripe avocados (we recommend Haas Avos)
1	tablespoon lemon juice
1	cup diced onions
11/4	cups diced tomatoes
1	teaspoon onion powder
1	tablespoon salt
1/2	teaspoon pepper
1	teaspoon garlic powder
1/4	cup jalapeño peppers
1	cup sour cream

Pit, scoop out and mash avocados. Add remaining ingredients and mix well. May be stored in refrigerator with plastic wrap pressed around rim of bowl. (8 cups)

Taco Salad Dressing

2	cups ketchup
11/2	cups vegetable oil
1	cup sugar
1/4	cup plus 1 tablespoon vinegar
1/4	cup mustard
1	teaspoon garlic powder

Mix all ingredients with a wire whisk or in blender. (5 cups)

From: The Lord Fox, Ann Arbor, MI

Pork and Wild Mushroom Strudel with Rosemary Mayonnaise

2	pounds pork loin
1	pound mushrooms
2	teaspoons orange zest
1/2	cup spinach (blanched)
1	tablespoon chopped basil
1	tablespoon toasted pine nuts
1	egg, beaten
2	teaspoons grated Parmesan cheese
	Salt and pepper
6	phyllo dough leaves
1/4	cup toasted bread crumbs

Shape pork loin into a tight roll; grill until rare and cool. Saute mushrooms; cool and combine with orange zest, spinach, basil, pine nuts, egg, cheese, salt and pepper. Lay out dough and brush with butter. Sprinkle with bread crumbs. Make mayonnaise mixture.

ROSEMARY MAYONNAISE:

1	cup mayonnaise
2	teaspoons orange juice
1 1/2	teaspoons orange zest
1 1/2	teaspoons rosemary
2	teaspoons heavy cream

Preheat oven to 350°. Spread mayonnaise mixture over phyllo dough. Wrap loin and seal. Place seam side down on a buttered sheet pan. Brush top of strudel with melted butter and bake 20 minutes.

From: The Marketplace, Dayton Hudson's, Ann Arbor, MI

Marinated Turkey Salad

11/2	pounds turkey breast, cooked
1	green pepper, julienne cut
1	red pepper, julienne cut
3/4	cup sliced black olives
1/2	pint cherry tomatoes, halved

DRESSING:

21/2	tablespoons Colavita olive oil
5	tablespoons Rothchild's raspberry vinegar
4	teaspoons sugar
4	teaspoons dried basil
2	teaspoons garlic powder
5	tablespoons vegetable oil

Julienne turkey 1/2 x 2 inches. Mix together dressing ingredients. Add to turkey and vegetables; toss to coat. Chill and serve.

Seafood Fettuccine

1/2	pound Colavita fettuccine
1/2	red onion
1/2	green pepper
1/4	pound Mrs. Friday's seafood flakes
2/3	pound small shrimp, cooked

DRESSING:

1/2	cup mayonnaise
2	tablespoons Kraft Gold Italian dressing
1/2	tablespoon lemon juice
1/4	bunch fresh parsley
1/2	tablespoon celery seed
1/4	teaspoon leaf oregano
	Salt and pepper to taste

Cook, drain and cool pasta. Dice vegetables. Pat dry seafood flakes and shrimp. In a small bowl, blend mayonnaise, dressing, lemon juice and spices. Mix all together. Chill and serve. (6 servings)

Greek Feta Salad

1	pound pasta shells (medium size)
1	cup chopped celery
3/4	cup sliced black olives
1/2	pound Greek feta cheese, crumbled
1/2	cup grated Parmesan cheese
2	ripe tomatoes, coarsely chopped

DRESSING:

1	cup mayonnaise
3/4	cup Golden Italian dressing
1	tablespoon oregano
1	teaspoon black pepper

Cook pasta in plenty of water until al dente. Drain and rinse well with cold water. Whisk dressing ingredients together in a small bowl. Toss dressing with all ingredients (except tomatoes). Gently fold tomatoes into salad. (8 servings)

Torte alla Andrew

1 1/2	pounds Colavita spaghetti
2	tablespoons Colavita extra-virgin olive oil
1	onion, finely diced
1	tablespoon minced garlic
1/2	bunch parsley, minced
1 1/2	tablespoons lemon juice
2	teaspoons basil
2	teaspoons oregano
1/2	teaspoon black pepper
6	tablespoons grated Parmesan cheese
1 1/3	cups cottage cheese
1	egg plus 1 egg yolk
1	teaspoon garlic salt
3	tomatoes, sliced
1 1/2	cups shredded Mozzarella cheese

Grease and flour 10-inch springform pan. Cook spaghetti (omit salt in water). Preheat oven to 350°. Heat oil in skillet and sauté onions and garlic (5 minutes). Add to pasta. Add parsley, lemon juice, basil, oregano, pepper, half Parmesan, cottage cheese, egg and garlic salt to pasta. Assemble half pasta mixture, then half sliced tomatoes, then half Mozzarella (pressing into pan). Repeat. Top with remaining Parmesan. Bake 45 minutes.

: **Maude's Restaurant, Inc., Ann Arbor, MI**

Gazpacho Soup

1 2	quarts cucumbers, peeled and coarsely chopped
1 2	quarts green pepper, coarsely chopped
4	pounds onions, coarsely chopped
2/3	gallon Wishbone Italian dressing (with top 1/3 of oil drained off gallon container)
2	#10 cans diced tomatoes
1	#5 can tomato juice
1	#5 can V-8 juice
1	16-ounce can diced red pepper
1	teaspoon white pepper
2	teaspoons salt
1	cup finely-chopped parsley

GARNISH:
1	cucumber spear (fresh)
1	tablespoon sour cream
1	tablespoon croutons

Place chopped cucumber, green pepper and onions in large bowl. Put diced tomatoes through chopper one turn only. Add to chopped vegetables. Add dressing and mix well. Add remaining ingredients and mix very well. Refrigerate. Serve garnished with spear of cucumber, croutons and sour cream. (5 gallons)

MARIA CONSUELO SANTACOLOMA T, KITCHEN MANAGER

Chicken and Artichoke Pasta

1	4-ounce chicken breast, skinned and boned, 2-inch cubes
2	tablespoons butter
	Salt to season
	Flour for dusting
1/4	cup mushrooms, sliced 1/8-inch thick
1	tablespoon red peppers, cut into fine julienne
2	tablespoons sherry wine
1/4	cup primavera sauce
6	tablespoons heavy cream
1	tablespoon herb butter
1	teaspoon finely-chopped parsley
2	ounces artichoke hearts, quartered
6	ounces fettuccine, cooked al dente

Place butter in a skillet and heat. Season chicken with salt and dust in flour mix lightly. Shake off excess flour. Place chicken breast strips in skillet and sauté for 30 seconds. Add mushrooms and red peppers and continue to sauté all together for an additional 30 seconds. Add sherry wine and cook for ten seconds. Add primavera sauce, cream, herb butter, half the parsley, artichoke hearts and fettuccine. Stir well and cook until pasta is well heated. Place on plate and sprinkle with remaining parsley. Serve immediately. (1 serving)

MARIA CONSUELO SANTACOLOMA T, KITCHEN MANAGER

German Potato Salad

2	pounds potatoes, preferably Michigan
1	teaspoon salt
1/4	teaspoon fine black pepper
1/2	cup finely-chopped onions
1/4	cup apple cider vinegar
1/4	cup corn oil
3/4	cup hot beef or chicken broth

Boil potatoes with skins on until tender. Peel while hot and allow to cool but only enough to be able to slice about 1/8-inch thick. Add salt, pepper, onions, vinegar and oil. Pour hot broth over potatoes. Mix together gently in order not to break up potatoes. Let stand at room temperature at least 1 hour. Mix again just before serving. (4 servings)

Homemade German Noodles (Spätzle)

21/2	cups flour
1/2	teaspoon salt
2	eggs
1/2	cup water (approximately)

Combine flour and salt in mixing bowl. Make a well in the center. Add eggs and 1/4 cup water. Beat until stiff dough forms, adding more water until consistency is thick and firm and coming away easily from sides of bowl. Knead until smooth. Let stand 15 minutes. Dampen pastry board with water and place dough on it. Flour a rolling pin and roll dough to 1/8-inch thick or less. Heat a pan of salt water to boiling. With a sharp knife, cut off very thin slivers of dough and push directly into boiling water. Spätzle will rise to surface when done. Remove with slotted spoon. Drain in colander.

364

Red Cabbage Rotkohl

1/4	cup goose fat or corn oil
1	onion, diced
3	tart apples, diced
1	large head red cabbage, shredded
3/4	cup red wine vinegar
1	whole clove
1	small bay leaf
	Salt and pepper
	Sugar
1/2	cup water
1/2	cup red wine

In a saucepan, melt fat or corn oil. Add onions; sauté. Add apples, cabbage, then vinegar, clove, bay leaf, salt, pepper, sugar and water. Bring to a boil. Reduce heat; simmer until cabbage is tender. Add water from time to time to prevent sticking. Then, add red wine. (4 servings)

Rouladen

4	slices beef top round, 1/4-inch thick
	Salt and pepper to taste
	Prepared mustard
4	dill pickle spears
4	slices bacon
3	onions, chopped
1	teaspoon tomato paste
1	cup beef stock
1	tablespoon flour
1/2	cup red wine

Preheat oven to 300°. Season beef with salt and pepper. Thinly spread each piece with mustard. Place pickle and bacon slices lengthwise on meat. Sprinkle heavily with diced onions. Roll up lightly. Secure with toothpicks. Using a whisk, combine tomato paste, beef stock, flour and red wine. Place beef rolls in baking dish. Pour tomato mixture on top. Cover and cook about 1 hour and 15 minutes.

RESTAURANT RECIPES

From: Monahan's Seafood Market, Ann Arbor, MI

Monahan's Pompano en Papillote

2	pieces parchment paper
3/4	pound Amber Jack Fillet (3/4-inch thick), skin removed*
1	tablespoon butter, melted (or extra-virgin olive oil)
1	tablespoon dry white wine
1	tablespoon slivered San Remo sun-dried tomatoes
2	teaspoons chopped fresh chives
2	teaspoons chopped fresh basil

Preheat oven to 350°. Crease parchment paper, dividing it in half. Lightly brush center of one side with olive oil. Brush all the edges of the paper to improve the seal when it's folded. Place one portion of the fillet on the oiled half. Baste with butter (or oil) and sprinkle with white wine. Loosely arrange tomatoes and herbs over each portion. Fold parchment over and tightly crimp edges around fish to form a pouch. *(Mike Monahan always goes around a second time with an extra crimp for good measure!)* Repeat with remaining fillet portions. Make sure to give fish enough room inside to steam. Place pouches on baking sheet. Bake 14 minutes or until fillets are opaque. Open one pouch to check for doneness, watching out for the steam inside. If done, reseal and serve immediately in the pouches. (2 servings) **"We'll custom cut the fillet to appropriate thickness, if needed. At Monahan's we wrap all our fish in pure vegetable parchment paper. We'll gladly supply you with the parchment for all your seafood papillotes! Call if you have a question!"*

Sautéed Skate with Brown Butter

3/4-1	pound skate fillet
1/4	cup flour
3	tablespoons butter
2	tablespoons olive oil
1	tablespoon capers
1	tablespoon raspberry vinegar (or any other fruit vinegar)

Dust skate fillets in flour. In a sauté pan on a medium-high setting, melt 1 tablespoon butter with 2 tablespoons olive oil and heat until bubbling, but not smoking (fillets should sizzle when placed in pan). Sauté about 3 minutes per side or until fillets are opaque to the center. Remove skate from pan and turn temperature setting down to medium. Add remaining 2 tablespoons of butter. When butter just begins to brown, add capers and fruit vinegar, stir and immediately drizzle brown butter over skate portions. (This brown butter can also be served over poached skate.) (2 servings)

366

Maine Shrimp and Sun-Dried Tomatoes with Fettuccine

4-6	ounces dried fettuccine*
3	tablespoons extra-virgin olive oil*
2	tablespoons butter or margarine*
1	pound peeled Maine shrimp
1 1/2	tablespoons slivered San Remo marinated sun-dried tomatoes
1	teaspoon finely-chopped fresh parsley
1	tablespoon dry white wine
1	tablespoon fresh lemon juice
	Freshly-ground black pepper to taste

Cook pasta according to package directions; drain. Toss with 1 tablespoon olive oil; keep warm. Heat 2 tablespoons olive oil and butter in sauté pan on medium-high heat. When a test shrimp sizzles vigorously, oil is hot enough. Add shrimp, turning gently and constantly 3 minutes. In the last minute, add remaining ingredients. Serve immediately over pasta. Add freshly-ground pepper to taste. (2 servings)

*CHEF'S TIP: Al Dente brand squid ink pasta makes a dramatic black bed for the scarlet ambrosia of shrimp and tomatoes. May substitute the olive oil from the sun-dried tomato container for more flavor. The shell of this shrimp just slips off; no need for a utensil; no need to devein.

Steamed Whole Walleye Shanghai-Style

11/2-2 pounds whole walleye, cleaned
1   clove garlic, minced
2   teaspoons grated fresh ginger
3   scallions, sliced lengthwise
3   tablespoons black bean sauce (available at Monahan's)
1   tablespoon chopped cilantro (Chinese parsley)

Score fish on one side with diagonal slices at 1-inch intervals, just deep enough to pierce the skin. To steam, bring 2 inches of water to a full boil. Position the "steaming rack" over the water. Place scored fish on rack and coat with black bean sauce. Sprinkle with garlic and ginger. Cover and steam 15-20 minutes or until fish is opaque at its thickest part. Place whole fish on serving platter, garnish with scallions and cilantro. (2 servings) *"Steaming is one of the simplest and gentlest methods of fish preparation. It allows the fish's natural flavor to take center stage, enhanced by only subtle seasoning. Great low-cal potential since steaming imparts no calories on the fish whatsoever."*

COOK'S TIP: An optional flair for this dish: Prepare a hot garlic oil by heating 1/4 cup vegetable oil, and adding 2 cloves crushed garlic. Cook 1 additional minute, then remove garlic with a slotted spoon. Add 2 tablespoons sesame oil at the end. At this point, the oil should be hot and the fish should have just finished steaming. Put whole fish on serving platter, carefully pour hot oil over it, then garnish as above and serve.

Steaming equipment: Use a bamboo steamer placed in a wok. Or improvise with a disposable aluminum roasting pan punched full of holes over a pot. (Mike Monahan broke the center post off his vegetable steamer and it works great!) A good steamer is anything that accommodates the fish, keeps it above the water, and has a tight-fitting lid to keep the steam from escaping.

Baked Whole Red Snapper Veracruz

2	pounds whole Red Snapper, cleaned and scaled*
1	teaspoon salt
2	tablespoons fresh lime juice

SAUCE:

1	medium onion, chopped
1/4	cup extra virgin olive oil
2	cloves garlic, peeled and sliced
1	pound fresh or canned plum tomatoes, chopped
2	tablespoons capers
1 0	Ionian green olives, halved and pitted (available at Zingerman's), or substitute 20 jarred Spanish green olives
1	bay leaf
2	teaspoons dried oregano (with fresh herb, use 6 times more than dried)
1	4-ounce can of chopped green chiles
2	tablespoons Tiger Sauce (a fabulous, spicy seafood sauce available at Monahan's)

Preheat oven to 375°. To prepare fish: Place in an oiled baking dish. Prick the fish, rub with salt and lime juice, then set aside to marinate. To prepare sauce: Sauté onions in olive oil until soft; add garlic, then add all remaining ingredients and simmer 10 minutes. Pour sauce over fish and bake uncovered. Baste with the sauce after 15 minutes. Bake 30 minutes, or until opaque at the thickest part. (2 servings)

COOK'S TIP: Reminder: 10 minutes cooking time per 1 inch of fish thickness. Adjust time for different types and thicknesses of fish.

*Possible substitutions: Whole Yellowtail Snapper, Grouper, Progy or Striped Bass. About substituting fillets: Although not as dramatic of a presentation, this piquant and colorful sauce will flatter a fine snapper fillet. Do not prick the fillet, and reduce salt to 1/2 teaspoon and baking time to 20 minutes.

From: The Moveable Feast, Ann Arbor, MI

Sauté of Shrimp Madagascar

FISH FUMET:

2	pounds fish heads and bones, rinsed and broken
1	onion, diced
2	carrots, diced
1	leek, diced
2	bay leaves
2	sprigs each thyme and fresh parsley
2	cups dry white wine

SAUCE:

2	cups fish fumet
1	cup dry white wine
1/2	cup heavy cream
2	teaspoons crushed green peppercorns
	Salt and pepper to taste

MAIN INGREDIENTS:

6	tablespoons clarified butter
1	pound monkfish, 1-inch chunks and dredged with flour
1	pound shrimp (21-25 size), peeled and deveined

Combine all fumet ingredients with 8 cups water in a non-reactive pot. Bring to a boil and skim off the scum. Lower heat; simmer, uncovered, 30 minutes. Strain through a colander lined with cheesecloth. Return to pan; reduce to 2 cups. Whisk together all sauce ingredients; set aside. Heat butter in sauté pan. Add monkfish. Cook slightly and add shrimp. When shrimp are half cooked, pour off butter and add sauce. Season with salt and pepper and simmer until heated through. Serve with Basmati Rice.

BASMATI RICE:

2	cups Basmati rice
2	cups fish stock
1	cup white wine
1	teaspoon salt
2	leeks, white part only, chopped
3	tablespoons butter, melted
1/2	cup chopped sun-dried tomatoes
1/2	cup freshly-grated Parmesan cheese

Combine rice, stock, wine and salt in saucepan. Bring to a boil. Reduce heat, cover and allow to simmer 20 minutes. Turn off heat and allow to steam for another 15 minutes. Combine rest of ingredients; toss with rice mixture. PATRICIA J. POOLEY

From: Olive Garden Italian Restaurant, Ann Arbor, MI

Shrimp Primavera

6	tablespoons butter or margarine
1	tablespoon freshly-minced garlic
1	1-ounce package Knorr Newburg sauce mix (or similar)
1	32-ounce can crushed tomatoes
1 1/2	tablespoons fresh lemon juice
1/4	teaspoon crushed red pepper (or to taste)
1/2	teaspoon basil
1/4	teaspoon marjoram
1/2	teaspoon black pepper
2	tablespoons butter
1/2	pound mushrooms, halved (or quartered if large)
1	cup green bell peppers, cut into 1-inch squares
1	cup red bell peppers, cut into 1-inch squares
1/2	cup yellow onion, cut into 1-inch squares
1	pound fresh Olive Garden linguine (or quality dry pasta)
1	pound medium-to-large cooked shrimp (thawed and drained)
	Grated Parmesan cheese

Melt butter in 3-quart saucepan over medium heat. Add garlic and cook one minute. Add remaining spices and tomato ingredients, stir well and simmer 10 minutes. Meanwhile, in a large sauté pan, melt 2 tablespoons butter. Sauté vegetables about 3 minutes until crisp-tender. Add to the sauce and simmer 5 minutes more. Cook pasta according to directions. When pasta is almost done, stir shrimp into sauce to heat through. Do not boil. Spoon Shrimp Primavera over hot linguine. Sprinkle with Parmesan cheese. (4-6 servings)

Peaches 'n Cream Cheesecake

BASE:

1	egg
1/3	cup sugar
1/4	cup flour
2	tablespoons water
1/4	teaspoon vanilla
1/4	teaspoon baking powder
	Pinch salt

Preheat oven to 375°. Lightly grease base of 10-inch springform pan. Beat egg in 1 1/2 quart bowl with mixer on high speed (4 minutes) to a thick yellow foam. Mix in sugar on low speed until smooth. Add flour, water, vanilla, baking powder and salt. Mix on low speed until fully blended. Pour into springform pan, rolling around until level. Bake 16-18 minutes on lowest oven rack. Cool to room temperature.

FILLING:

4	8-ounce packages cream cheese, room temperature
1	cup sugar
4	eggs
1	teaspoon flour
1	teaspoon vanilla
1	cup sour cream
1/4	cup peach liqueur, peach schnapps or reserved peach juice from canned or fresh peaches
2	cups canned or firm, ripe, fresh peaches (sliced, well drained)

Preheat oven to 325°. Mix cream cheese, sugar, eggs and flour with electric mixer on high until smooth. Add vanilla, sour cream and peach flavoring, and mix on medium speed to a smooth thick consistency. Fold in peach slices carefully and distribute evenly. Pour cheesecake filling onto cooled sponge cake base. Bake 70 minutes on lower oven rack, turn off oven, open oven door to broil position and let cake remain 40 minutes. Cool to refrigerated temperature.

TOPPING:

1	pint whipped cream (or equivalent)

Top with fresh whipped cream and serve. Can be stored up to 2 days in refrigerator.

372

Raspberry Mousse Cheesecake

1   9-inch chocolate crumb crust

FILLING:
2   8-ounce packages cream cheese, room temperature
1/2 cup sugar
2   eggs
1/2 teaspoon vanilla

Preheat oven to 325°. Mix cream cheese, sugar, egg and vanilla with mixer on medium speed until thoroughly blended (about 3-4 minutes). Pour mixture into prepared chocolate crumb crust. Place on baking sheet. Bake 25 minutes. Cool to refrigerated temperature.

MOUSSE:
11/2 teaspoons gelatin
11/2 tablespoons cold water
1/2   cup raspberry preserves
2   tablespoons sugar
1   cup heavy cream

Sprinkle gelatin over cold water; stir. Let stand 1 minute. Microwave on high for 30 seconds or until gelatin dissolves. (Or, heat on stove with 1 additional tablespoon of water.) Combine gelatin with raspberry preserves. Chill 10 minutes. Whip cream until soft peaks form. Add 2 tablespoons sugar. Continue whipping until stiff peaks form. Measure 11/2 cups of whipped cream for mousse; set aside. Refrigerate remainder of cream for topping. Gently fold raspberry mixture into measured whipped cream. Spread raspberry mousse on top of cheese filling, mounding slightly in the center. Chill 1 hour before serving. To serve, top each piece with a dollop of reserved whipped cream.
(6 generous servings)

From: Paesano's, Ann Arbor, MI

Gorgonzola Pear Salad

4	ounces Romaine lettuce, torn
2	ounces red mustard greens
1	head radicchio, core removed and torn
1	pear, quartered
1/2	cup walnuts
1/4	cup walnut oil
1/4	cup balsamic vinegar
2	ounces Gorgonzola cheese, crumbled

Preheat oven to 350°. Mix greens in a bowl; then divide on 4 plates. Wedge each pear quarter in 3 and top greens. Place walnuts on cookie sheet and bake 10 minutes. Allow to cool; then finely chop. Mix half the walnuts with oil and vinegar. Sprinkle remaining walnuts and cheese over salads. Drizzle vinegar and oil mixture over salads. Serve immediately. (4 servings)

Spaghetti alla Carbonara

2	tablespoons olive oil
8	strips bacon, cut into 1/2-inch pieces
6	large cloves garlic, minced
1/2	teaspoon red pepper
12	mushrooms, quartered
1	medium red onion, julienned
1	cup finely-grated Romano cheese
2	pounds spaghetti
1	tablespoon freshly-ground black pepper
6	eggs

Heat pan on medium heat; add oil and bacon. Add garlic, red pepper, mushrooms and onions; sauté 1-2 minutes. While vegetables are sautéing, mix together eggs and cheese in a large bowl. Slowly pour bacon grease and vegetables into egg mixture while whipping vigorously to emulsify. Cook pasta until al dente; drain and toss with egg/vegetable mixture. Top with pepper and serve immediately. (4 servings)

CHEF'S TIP: When bacon grease is whipped into egg and cheese mixture, it should emulsify to form a sort of mayonnaise. CHRIS THOMAS

374

Linguine with Shrimp in Spicy Ginger-Garlic Sauce

3	tablespoons vegetable oil
24	(16-20 count) shrimp, peeled and deveined
1	tablespoon red pepper flakes (or to taste)
1	tablespoon minced ginger
1	tablespoon minced garlic
3/4	cup sake
3/4	cup shrimp stock
4	green onions, 3/4-inch slices
1/2	cup butter, 1/2-inch cubes
2	pounds linguine

Heat pan on high 20-30 seconds; add oil. Sauté shrimp 30-40 seconds on each side. Add red pepper flakes, ginger and garlic. Continue to sauté just until garlic starts to turn brown. Remove from heat and deglaze with sake and shrimp stock. Return to medium heat and reduce liquid by half. Remove from heat and add green onions. Stir in butter, one cube at a time. Cook pasta until al dente. Toss mixture with pasta and serve. (4 servings)

CHRIS THOMAS

Veal Saltimbocca

4	leaves fresh sage, minced
4	2-ounce veal scallopines
4	slices prosciutto, sliced thin enough to see through
1	cup flour
4	eggs, beaten
2	cups bread crumbs
1/4	cup olive oil
1/2	teaspoon minced garlic
1	tablespoon minced green onions
6	tablespoons white wine
1/2	cup veal stock
4	tablespoons fresh lemon juice
1	tablespoon capers
1	tablespoon finely-chopped parsley
1/2	cup butter, cut into 1/2-inch cubes

Sprinkle sage on top of veal scallopines. Place slices of prosciutto over veal. Cover with plastic wrap and pound prosciutto into veal with meat mallot until approximately 1/4-inch thick. Dredge veal in flour, dip in eggs, then coat with bread crumbs. Heat sauté pan on high heat; add oil. Sauté veal 40-50 seconds on each side. Remove from pan. Sauté garlic and green onions until garlic starts to turn brown. Deglaze with wine, stock and lemon juice. Add capers and parsley. Reduce liquid by half. Remove pan from heat and stir in butter one cube at a time. Pour sauce over veal and serve. (2 servings) CHRIS THOMAS

Veal Marsala

4	2-ounce veal scallopines (pounded to 1/4-inch thickness)
1/2	cup flour
1/4	cup olive oil
1	teaspoon minced garlic
2	tablespoons minced shallots
6	mushrooms (sliced to 1/4-inch thickness)
3/4	cup marsala wine
1/2	cup veal stock
2	tablespoons cornstarch
	Salt and pepper to taste

Dredge veal in flour. Heat sauté pan over high heat. Add oil. Sauté veal 20-25 seconds on each side. Remove from pan. Sauté garlic, shallots and mushrooms until garlic starts to turn brown. Deglaze with marsala and stock. Dissolve cornstarch in a small amount of water and stir into sauce until desired thickness. Season with salt and pepper. Pour sauce over veal. (2 servings) CHRIS THOMAS

Lemon Chicken

8	3-4 ounce chicken breast halves (pounded to 3/8-inch thick)
1/2-1	cup flour
6	cloves garlic, minced
1/2	cup olive oil
4	green onions, minced
3/4	cup white wine
3/4	cup chicken stock
1/4	cup lemon juice
3	tablespoons brown sugar
2	tablespoons cornstarch
	Salt and pepper to taste
2	tablespoons finely-chopped parsley

Dredge chicken in flour. Heat sauté pan on high; add oil. Sauté chicken until brown on both sides and cooked through. Remove from pan. Add garlic and green onions; sauté until they just start to turn brown. Deglaze with wine, stock and lemon juice. Add sugar and reduce liquid by half. Dissolve cornstarch in a small amount of water and stir into sauce until desired thickness. Season to taste with salt and pepper. Stir in parsley. Pour sauce over chicken and serve. (4 servings) CHRIS THOMAS

From: Palio, Ann Arbor, MI

Linguine alla Viareggina

1 0	little neck clams
3/4	cup white wine
1	teaspoon chopped fresh thyme
1/2	teaspoon minced fresh garlic
1/4	cup olive oil
	Juice from clams
1/2	teaspoon chopped fresh oregano
1/2	teaspoon chopped fresh thyme
1/4	cup white wine
1/2	teaspoon chopped parsley
1/4	cup diced fresh tomato
1	tablespoon butter
	Salt and pepper
8	ounces linguine, cooked al dente

Place clams, wine, thyme and garlic in pot. Cover and steam clams. Drain juice into sauté pan. Add remaining ingredients and reduce to desired consistency. Serve over pasta. Garnish with cooked clams. (1 serving)

Rigatoni Strasckate alla Lucchese

2	ounces Italian sausage links
2	ounces ground Italian sausage
6	tablespoons heavy cream
1/4	cup chicken broth
1/4	teaspoon crushed Italian red peppers
1/2	teaspoon chopped fresh rosemary
2	tablespoons butter
1	medium fresh tomato, peeled, seeded and diced
3	ounces green peas, frozen
2	tablespoons dry white wine
1/2	teaspoon minced garlic
	Pinch salt and pepper
8	ounces rigatoni pasta, cooked

Cook sausage links and cut on bias. Cook and drain ground sausage. In sauté pan, add all ingredients except pasta and simmer to desired consistency. Stir in cooked pasta. (1 serving)

From: Park Avenue Delicatessen, Ann Arbor, MI

Amaretto Bangors (Low-Fat Brownies)

11/4	cups flour
1/4	teaspoon baking soda
1/8	teaspoon baking powder
1/8	teaspoon salt
11/2	cups cocoa
11/2	cups sugar
1	cup Kraft-Free mayonnaise
1/4	cup light corn syrup
1/4	cup amaretto
3	egg whites, chilled
1	tablespoon vanilla extract
1/4	cup toasted chopped almonds
2	ounces frozen Lindt Swiss white confectionary bar (chopped in 1/4-inch pieces)

Preheat oven to 325°. Lightly grease a 9 x 13-inch baking dish with olive oil. Mix dry ingredients except sugar. In another bowl, mix sugar, mayonnaise, corn syrup, amaretto, egg whites and vanilla. Add dry ingredients to wet ingredients; mix well. Pour into baking dish. Gently fold in nuts and white chocolate. Bake 25-30 minutes. Cool in refrigerator 2 hours before slicing. (24 brownies) "*3.25 grams of fat each.*"

MARY DIXON

From: Pastabilities, Ann Arbor, MI
Linguine al Angela

1/3	cup sun-dried tomatoes
1/2	cup olive oil
2	cloves (or more) garlic, sliced
1/4	pound fresh shrimp, peeled
1/4	pound fresh sea scallops (if large, cut in half)
1/3	cup pitted black olives (all-cured Greek olives)
1/2	cup white wine
1/4	cup chopped fresh parsley
1	pound fresh linguine, cooked (while sauce is being made)

Soak tomatoes in 1/2 cup water and microwave until soft. When cool, slice and keep the water they were soaked in; set aside. Heat oil in pan. Add garlic and stir. Add shrimp and scallops; cook about 3-4 minutes (or until cooked through). Add sliced tomatoes and olives; stir about a minute. Add white wine, parsley and 1/2 cup water from microwaved sun-dried tomatoes. Boil pasta at the same time you're making sauce. Serve linguine on plate and add sauce. MARGUERITE OLIVER

378

Asparagus-Prosciutto Lasagna

BÉCHAMEL SAUCE OR WHITE SAUCE:
2	tablespoons butter
2	cloves garlic, sliced thin, then minced
1	tablespoon flour
1	cup chicken stock (no chicken stock if making white sauce)
1	cup milk (2 cups milk if making white sauce)

Preheat oven to 375°. Prepare Béchamel or White Sauce. Melt butter. Add minced garlic, then stirring add flour. Add stock and milk, (or just milk if making white sauce), stirring constantly. Cook and stir until thickened. Set aside.

LASAGNA:
1/2	pound fresh asparagus
1/4	pound thinly-sliced prosciutto
1	pound fresh lasagna sheets
1/4	cup shredded Mozzarella cheese
1/4	cup freshly grated Parmesan cheese

Save tips of asparagus. Cut off tough end pieces. Slice remaining stalk and steam until tender. Process until smooth. Add to the béchamel sauce. Shred prosciutto into very small pieces and add to sauce. To build lasagna, take a small amount of sauce and spread on 9 x 13-inch baking dish. Then layer lasagna sheets. Then more sauce until you have 3-4 layers. Sprinkle sauce over top sheet of lasagna, then Mozzarella. Sprinkle with Parmesan and arrange asparagus tips on top. Bake about 45 minutes.

MARGUERITE OLIVER

ı: Prickly Pear Cafe, Ann Arbor, MI

Guacamole

3	large ripe avocados
1/2	pound fresh tomatoes, chopped
11/4	cups chopped green chiles
1/4	cup grated onions
2	tablespoons lime juice
1/4	cup lemon juice
2	teaspoons salt
1/8	teaspoon pepper or hot sauce
	Garlic to taste

Peel avocados and break up with fork to a lumpy consistency. In separate stainless steel bowl, combine tomatoes, green chiles, onions, lime and lemon juice. Season to taste. Combine with avocado and chill well. (A further seasoning adjustment may be required prior to eating after flavors have blended. The mixture should be spicy but not uncomfortably hot.)

Gazpacho

1/2	pound onions, peeled
1/2	pound green peppers
3/4	pound cucumbers
3/4	pound tomatoes
1	tablespoon minced garlic
1	teaspoon salt
1/8	teaspoon pepper
1/8	teaspoon cayenne pepper
	Dash thyme, tarragon and savory
1/2	cup tomato purée
1/4	cup wine vinegar
3/4	cup olive oil
2	tablespoons lemon juice
3	eggs
11/2	cups tomato juice
	Consommé or clam juice as needed

Place all ingredients, except tomato juice, in food processor or blender. Chop very fine. (Ingredients should be well blended.) Add tomato juice and blend only until mixed with other ingredients. Adjust seasoning and refrigerate, covered, until soup is well chilled. Make a garnish of diced tomatoes, cucumbers and green peppers. Place a heaping teaspoon of garnish in each cup or bowl before serving. (12 servings)

Warm Chicken Salad

1	head Boston bibb lettuce
1	tomato, diced
1/2	cup crumbled Anejo cheese
1	red onion, sliced 1/4-inch thick, grilled
2	chicken breasts, grilled and julienne sliced

DRESSING:

1	cup heavy cream
1/4	cup shredded Monterey Jack cheese
1/4	cup crumbled Anejo cheese (or Monterey Jack cheese with 1/2 teaspoon paprika)
	Salt and pepper

Make dressing first. In a saucepan, reduce heavy cream to a half cup; add cheeses. Season to taste with salt and pepper. Keep dressing warm. Place lettuce on two chilled plates; top with tomatoes and cheese. Top with grilled onions, chicken and 1/4 cup dressing. HEAD CHEF GARY PIERCE

Seviche Del Peru

2	pounds scallops, sliced
1/4	cup lime juice
1/2	cup lemon juice
2	cloves garlic, minced
	Hot sauce to taste
	Salt and pepper to taste

GARNISH:

2	tablespoons julienned green onions
2	tablespoons julienned green pepper
1/4	cup julienned tomato
2	tablespoons julienned pimentos
1	tablespoon each julienned ripe olives and green olives
1	cup avocado balls
10	sprigs parsley for garnish

Combine scallops with lime and lemon juice, garlic and hot sauce. Marinate at least six hours or overnight in a covered earthen container. Turn over several times during this period. Add salt and pepper. Carefully fold in garnish. Add avocado balls. Allow to chill well before serving. Put into glass cups. Garnish with vegetables and parsley. *"Seviche is a popular South American appetizer. Any firm-flesh fish such as bass, halibut, red snapper, etc., may be cut into strips and substituted for scallops. Ingredients for the garnish and seasonings may vary as well."*

From: The Produce Station, Ann Arbor, MI

Guacamole

9   ripe avocados, peeled and pitted
11/2   teaspoons minced garlic
1   small jalapeño pepper, seeded and minced
1/3   cup lime juice
1/4   pound Roma tomatoes, chopped
11/2   teaspoons ground cumin
1/2-1   tablespoon Clancy's fancy hot sauce

Chop avocados and garlic together in blender or food processor. Add jalapeño pepper, lime juice, tomato and cumin. Blend well. Carefully add hot sauce, a quarter tablespoon at a time, as it is quite hot; add to taste.

Sesame Noodles

1   pound linguine, cooked
4   teaspoons sesame seeds, toasted
1   tablespoon black sesame seeds
4   teaspoons sesame oil
1-2   tablespoons Eden tamari
1   bunch green onions, cut at an angle

Combine all ingredients in a large bowl; toss well. (6-8 servings as a side dish)

382

From: Raisin River Cafe, Saline, MI

Sour Cream Coffee Cake

1	cup butter
2	cups sugar
2	eggs, beaten
2	cups sour cream
1	tablespoon vanilla extract
2	cups unbleached flour
1	tablespoon baking powder
1/4	teaspoon salt

WALNUT MIXTURE:

2	cups chopped walnuts
3/4	cup sugar
1	tablespoon cinnamon

Preheat oven to 350°. Cream together butter and sugar. Add eggs, then sour cream and vanilla. Sift together dry ingredients. Fold dry mixture into wet mixture. Grease and flour 10-inch Bundt pan. Pour half the mixture into pan. Sprinkle half of nut mixture into pan. Repeat with mixture and nuts. Bake 1 hour. Serve warm. WENDY WELLER

From: The Real Seafood Company, Ann Arbor, MI

Sautéed Whitefish with Michigan Cherries

1	7-ounce whitefish fillet, lightly dusted in flour
2	tablespoons clarified butter
2	tablespoons white wine
1/2	cup Michigan dried cherries
1/4	cup Shiitake mushrooms
1	tablespoon butter
2	tablespoons clear chicken broth
	Pinch fresh basil

Sauté whitefish fillet in butter until golden brown. Deglaze pan with white wine. Add cherries and mushrooms and toss. Add butter, chicken broth and basil. Reduce until thick. (1 serving)

From: Red Lobster Restaurant, Ann Arbor, MI

Langostino Nachos

6-8	ounces nacho chips
6	ounces shredded Mozzarella cheese (or any cheese of your choice)
4	ounces chopped langostinos (small Chilean lobster)
1/4	cup chopped onions
1/4	cup chopped tomatoes
	Jalapeño peppers, optional

Layer ingredients in order given. Microwave or heat in oven until cheese melts. Serve with salsa and sour cream.

From: Thano's Lamplighter

Honey Puffs (Louroumades)

2	cups flour
1	package dried yeast
1	teaspoon salt
2	tablespoons sugar
2	cups warm water
	Hot oil for frying
	Cinnamon and nuts
	Powdered sugar
	Honey

Blend flour, yeast, salt, sugar and water in a bowl with a fork. Cover and set overnight in refrigerator. Next day, take 1 teaspoon of dough and drop into hot oil. Fry several at a time until golden. Drain on paper towels. Serve hot with honey, cinnamon, powdered sugar and nuts. (3 dozen)

Pastitsio

1	pound macaroni
1	cup milk
3	eggs, beaten
1	large onion, chopped
2	tablespoons butter
3	pounds ground chuck
1	tablespoon parsley
1/2	teaspoon cinnamon
	Salt and pepper
1	8-ounce can tomato sauce
1	cup grated Parmesan cheese

Cook macaroni al dente; drain. Add milk and eggs; set aside. Preheat oven to 350°. Sauté onions in butter. Add meat, parsley, cinnamon, salt and pepper. Add tomato sauce and bring to a boil. Butter a 13 x 17-inch baking dish. Pour half of the macaroni into pan. Sprinkle some cheese, then layer meat mixture. Add rest of macaroni and cheese. Top with Béchamel.

KREMA BÉCHAMEL:

2	tablespoons butter or margarine
1/4	cup flour mixed with 1/4 cup farina
6	cups milk
3	eggs, beaten

In a small saucepan, melt butter. Add flour and stir constantly. Whisk in milk. Continue to cook until mixture thickens. Add eggs to sauce. Spread on macaroni layer. Bake 1 hour.

From: Travis Pointe Country Club

Mediterranian French Salad à la Carte

9	ounces mixed greens
3	tablespoons Dijon vinaigrette
1 0	pieces mandarin orange segments
1	tablespoon julienned sun-dried tomato
1/2	tablespoon chopped walnuts

Toss mixed greens in vinaigrette. Place in a deep bowl. Garnish with mandarin orange segments around the outside, tomato in the center and walnuts around the top. (1 serving)

Steak au Poivre

1	12-ounce New York Strip steak
1	tablespoon black peppercorns
3	tablespoons clarified butter or vegetable oil
1/4	cup dry white wine
1/2	cup heavy cream

Preheat oven to 375°. Trim excess fat from steak. Using a rolling pin, crack the peppercorns. Press the cracked pepper firmly into both sides of steak. Heat oil in a sauté pan, then add steak. Sear both sides well. Place in a pan and finish in the oven to desired temperature. Allow the oil in the sauté pan to cool, then add wine and cream. Reheat and reduce by 2/3 or until desired consistency. Place steak on a plate and pour the sauce over.

COOK'S TIP: Be sure not to add wine to hot oil or it will burst into flames and splatter. PAUL NIMMO

Chicken Breast Wellington

1	10-ounce can button mushrooms
3	tablespoons heavy cream
1/4	teaspoon salt
1/4	teaspoon black pepper
1	teaspoon clarified butter
6	2-ounce chicken breasts, skinned and boned
1/2	teaspoon salt
1/2	teaspoon poultry seasoning
6	puff pastry sheets, 10 x 7 inches
1	egg, beaten
1/4	cup Madiera wine
1 1/4	cups brown sauce

Preheat oven to 300-400° depending on oven. Puree mushrooms and sauté. Add cream, salt and pepper and reduce a little. Cool the mushroom purée. Pound chicken with salt and poultry seasonings. Fold the breasts in half and steam in a covered pan to 170° internally. Cool the chicken, then place onto puff pastry so that a little egg wash can be brushed around the edge. Fold the pastry over and crimp shut with a fork. Egg wash the outside and bake 15 minutes until golden brown. Reduce Madiera wine and add to brown sauce. Serve the pastry-wrapped chicken breast on top of the sauce. (6 servings)

Salmon en Papillote

1	salmon fillet
	Parchment Paper
1/4	cup minced carrots
1/2	tablespoon minced shallots
1/4	cup sliced mushrooms
1/2	tablespoon lemon juice
1/2	tablespoon white wine
1/4	teaspoon basil
1/4	teaspoon oregano
1/4	teaspoon salt
1	lime twist
2	tablespoons butter

Using 1/2 sheet of parchment paper and a rectangle of parchment paper to go under the fillet, fold the half sheet in half. Place salmon inside and top with a mixture of carrots, shallots and mushrooms, seasoned with lemon juice, white wine and seasonings. Place a lime twist on top and a little butter and seal by crimping the edges. Brush with butter and bake until done. Place on large oval plate with rice pilaf and vegetable. (1 serving)

Hummer

2	tablespoons Puerto Rican rum
2	tablespoons Kahlua
1	tablespoon Créme de Cacao
2	cups vanilla Häagen Dazs ice cream
	Whipped cream
	Kahlua

Blend liquor with ice cream until smooth and creamy. Top with a dollop of whipped cream and a splash of Kahlua. (2 servings) LUANNE HAAS

Black Magic

1	tablespoon Amaretto di Saronno
1	tablespoon Bailey's Irish Cream
1	tablespoon Kahlua
	Coffee
	Whipped Cream

Combine ingredients with fresh piping hot coffee and finish with freshly-whipped cream. (1 serving) DICK HASELSCHWERDT

From: Trellis Cafe & Tea Room, Ann Arbor, MI

Kansas City Steak Soup

3	cups water
2	small onions, chopped
3	stalks celery, chopped
2	carrots, sliced
1	pound coarsely-ground beef
1	teaspoon pepper
1	10-ounce package frozen mixed vegetables
1	16-ounce can tomatoes
2	beef bouillon cubes
1/2	cup margarine, melted
1/2	cup flour

Put water and all ingredients, except margarine and flour, into a large soup pot and simmer on low 3 hours. Before serving, thicken with margarine and flour mixture, stirring with a whisk. Simmer 5 minutes. *"This can be made in a crockpot and cooked on low, 8-10 hours. Turn to high to thicken before serving."* CARROLL THOMSON

Carroll's Crunchies

1	cup margarine, softened
3/4	cup brown sugar
3/4	cup sugar
1	tablespoon salad oil
1	tablespoon molasses
1	tablespoon honey
2	eggs
2	tablespoons milk
2	teaspoons vanilla
2	cups flour
1/2	teaspoon salt
1/2	teaspoon cinnamon
1	teaspoon each baking powder and baking soda
21/2	cups oats
11/2	cups raisins
2	cups chocolate chips
11/2	cups chopped nuts

Preheat oven to 325°. Cream margarine with sugars, oil, molasses and honey. Add eggs, milk and vanilla. Beat well. Stir in flour and seasonings. Add remaining ingredients. Drop by large packed scoops (I use ice cream scoop) onto a greased cookie sheet. Bake 12-15 minutes.

CARROLL THOMSON

388

From: Uncle Frank's Chicagos & Coneys
Ann Arbor, MI

Creole Gumbo

3	pounds cooked turkey, diced
	Flour
	Salt and Pepper
	Vegetable oil or margarine (enough to cover bottom of pan)
4	pounds okra, sliced
3	large onions, chopped
3	tomatoes, chopped
5	cups tomato sauce
3/4	cup beef base
1/4	cup minced garlic
12	bay leaves
	Cayenne pepper to taste
	Hot sauce to taste
2	cups margarine, melted (or vegetable oil)
4	cups flour

Dredge turkey in flour, salt and pepper. Sauté turkey in oil until slightly browned. Add okra, onions, tomatoes and tomato sauce. Whip beef base in a small amount of hot water until dissolved and add to above mixture. Add garlic, bay leaves, cayenne pepper and hot sauce. Add water to within a few inches of the top of the pot and mix well. Heat through and stir often until simmering point. Make a roux with margarine and flour. Blend in well and allow to simmer approximately 1/2 hour. Remove bay leaves before serving. (Makes approximately 20 quarts)

From: Village Kitchen, Ann Arbor, MI

Vegetable Lasagna

1	1-pound box lasagna noodles
1	head broccoli, chopped
1	small onion, finely diced
1	large zucchini, sliced
1	small green pepper, diced
1	large yellow squash, sliced
1	tablespoon garlic powder
1	teaspoon oregano
1	teaspoon basil
1	teaspoon dill
1	teaspoon lemon pepper
	Dash salt
1	egg
1	1-pound carton (2 cups) cottage cheese
1	pound shredded Provolone cheese
1	pound shredded Mozzarella cheese
1	cup tomato sauce
1	pound sliced Swiss cheese
	Grated Parmesan cheese

Boil noodles and drain well. Preheat oven to 400°. Steam veggies for 1-2 minutes, drain well, let cool. Put all spices and egg into cottage cheese, mix well. Put a layer of noodles in a greased 9 x 11-inch baking dish. Add half of the steamed veggies, top with 1 cup cottage cheese, 1 cup Provolone and 1 cup Mozzarella. Pour 6 tablespoons of tomato sauce evenly over cottage cheese. Add layer of noodles and repeat; cover with Swiss cheese. Top with remaining tomato sauce and sprinkle with Parmesan. Cover with foil and bake 1 hour and 10 minutes, removing foil the last 15 minutes. SIDNEY M. MCBRIDE, CHEF/KITCHEN MANAGER

From: Weber's Inn, Ann Arbor, MI

Cider-Basted Chicken

8	boneless chicken breasts
1	cup apple cider
1/2	cup brown sugar
1/4	cup soy sauce
1	tablespoon Worcestershire sauce
1	teaspoon ground ginger
1	clove garlic, minced
	Juice from 1/2 lemon
1	cup olive oil
1/2	cup chopped parsley
1	bay leaf
	Salt and pepper to taste

Mix all of above ingredients, except chicken, together in stainless steel or glass bowl. Place chicken breasts in mixture. Marinate overnight. Prepare outdoor grill. Remove marinated chicken from mixture. Cook chicken over medium-hot coals about 5 inches from source of fire. Grill 5 minutes. Turn chicken and brush with original mixture. Grill 5 minutes more until chicken is cooked thoroughly. CHEF MATT PARENT

Chicken Marsala

1	7-ounce chicken breast, skinned and boned
	Seasoned flour (salt, pepper, garlic salt, paprika)
	Olive oil
	Salt and pepper
1	large green onion, minced
4	mushrooms, sliced
1	shot marsala wine
1/3	cup beef broth
1	teaspoon butter
1 1/2	cups cooked fettuccine
	Romano cheese, grated

Place skillet on medium high heat. Dredge chicken in seasoned flour, shake off excess. Add olive oil to sauté in skillet, let get hot. Add chicken breast. Brown on one side, turn over and season with salt and pepper. Add green onions and mushrooms. Cook two minutes, add marsala wine. (Be careful of flames!) Let marsala evaporate. Add beef broth, let reduce two minutes. Whip in butter. Place on warm plate, pour sauce over chicken. Season warm pasta with butter, salt, pepper. Place on plate, top with grated Romano cheese. LINDA WEBER

Wild Mushroom Sauté

1	tablespoon olive oil
1/4	cup sliced Shiitake mushrooms (stems removed)
1/4	cup sliced oyster mushrooms
1	tablespoon minced shallots
11/2	tablespoons Madeira wine
	Seasoning salt to taste
1/4-1/2	cup heavy cream
	Chopped parsley for garnish

Heat a nonstick skillet and add olive oil and mushrooms; sauté 3 minutes. Add shallots and sauté 30 seconds more (be careful not to burn shallots). Add wine, seasoning salt and cream. Reduce heat until sauce is thickened, about 2-3 minutes. Divide onto two plates. Sprinkle with chopped parsley and serve with French bread. (2 appetizer servings) CHEF MATT PARENT

Pecan Whiskey Tart

CRUST:

1	cup sugar
1	pound butter
1	egg plus 1 egg yolk
7	cups cake flour

FILLING:

4	eggs
1	cup brown sugar
1/4	cup light corn syrup
1/4	cup molasses
1/2	teaspoon salt
1/2	teaspoon vanilla
1/4	cup whiskey
11/4	cups chopped pecans
2	tablespoons butter
	Melted chocolate for top
	Garnish: Whipped cream and pecan halves

Preheat oven to 350°. To make crust: Grease an 11-inch tart pan. Cream butter and sugar. Add egg and egg yolk. Add flour and mix well. Chill. Line tart pan with dough. Whisk eggs to break up. Mix in sugar, corn syrup, molasses, salt, vanilla and whiskey. Stir in pecans and butter. Pour over dough. Bake 35 minutes or until set. When cool, top with lattice of chocolate. Garnish with rosettes of whipped cream and pecan halves.

From: Zingerman's Deli, Ann Arbor, MI

Bulgarian Cucumber Soup

2	pounds cucumbers, peeled, seeded and cut into chunks
1	cup milk
21/2	cups sour cream
1	cup plain, low-fat yogurt
11/2	cups finely-chopped walnuts
2	tablespoons chopped fresh dill
3	tablespoons olive oil
2	teaspoons salt
1/2	teaspoon white pepper
1/4	teaspoon garlic powder

Place half the cucumbers in a food processor or blender. Add a little milk and blend until cucumber is puréed. Transfer purée to a large bowl; add sour cream and yogurt and stir until thoroughly mixed. Stir in remaining milk. Cut the remaining cucumber into small cubes. Add chopped cucumber and remaining ingredients to the puréed mixture; stir well. Cover and refrigerate until cold. Before serving, stir well, then ladle into bowls or mugs. Sprinkle with additional chopped dill, if desired. (8-10 servings)

Noodle Kugel

1/2	pound egg fettuccine
1/2	pound farmer's cheese, crumbled
6	tablespoons butter, melted
1	cup sour cream
1/2	cup sugar
1	tablespoon vanilla
1/2	teaspoon cinnamon
1/4	teaspoon salt
6	large eggs
1	cup raisins

Cook fettuccine in boiling salted water by package directions until tender but still firm. Drain in a colander and rinse under cold water. Set aside to drain. Preheat oven to 325°. Combine farmer's cheese, butter, sour cream, sugar, vanilla, cinnamon and salt in a food processor. Blend until smooth. In a large bowl, combine cheese mixture with eggs and beat until mixed. Stir in raisins and then add cooled fettuccine. Toss to mix thoroughly. Grease a 9 x 13-inch baking dish. Add the contents of the bowl pressing it into the dish so that the noodles are covered with cheese mixture. Bake 35 minutes or until kugel is set and the top is golden. Remove to a rack and let cool in the dish. (Makes 8-12 pieces)

RESTAURANT RECIPES

Lentil-Feta Salad

1	cup lentils, rinsed
1/4	medium red onion, plus 3 tablespoons minced
1	clove
1	bay leaf
1	tablespoon salt, plus 1/4 teaspoon
1 1/2	teaspoons Dijon mustard
1	clove garlic, minced
1/2	teaspoon ground cumin
1/4	teaspoon oregano
1/4	teaspoon black pepper
1/2	cup olive oil
	Juice of 1/2 lemon
3	tablespoons grated carrot
1/2	pound (1 cup) feta cheese, crumbled
2	tablespoons chopped parsley

Pour 1 quart of cold water into a medium saucepan. Add lentils, onion stuck with the clove, bay leaf and 1 tablespoon salt. Bring water to boil, lower heat to simmer and cook about 20 minutes. Lentils should be tender but not mushy. Drain in a colander (do not rinse) and transfer to a shallow bowl. Cool in the refrigerator. In a mixing bowl, combine mustard, garlic, cumin, oregano, remaining 1/4 teaspoon salt and pepper. Slowly stir in olive oil, then lemon juice to make a dressing. Add cooled lentils, minced red onions, carrots, most of the feta and most of the parsley. Toss gently to mix. Serve in a festive bowl garnished with remaining feta and parsley. (6 servings)

Index

INDEX

INDEX

INDEX

INDEX

405

INDEX

INDEX

407

411

INDEX

Ann Arbor's Cookin' II
c/o Ronald McDonald House
1600 Washington Heights
Ann Arbor, MI 48104

Please send me _____ copies of Ann Arbor's Cookin II @ $15 each _____
Postage and handling in Continental U.S. @ $2.00 each _____
Sales tax @ .60 per cookbook (MI residents) _____
TOTAL ENCLOSED _____

Please make checks payable to Arbor House.
Name _____
Street _____
City _____ State _____ Zip _____

- -

Ann Arbor's Cookin' II
c/o Ronald McDonald House
1600 Washington Heights
Ann Arbor, MI 48104

Please send me _____ copies of Ann Arbor's Cookin II @ $15 each _____
Postage and handling in Continental U.S. @ $2.00 each _____
Sales tax @ .60 per cookbook (MI residents) _____
TOTAL ENCLOSED _____

Please make checks payable to Arbor House.
Name _____
Street _____
City _____ State _____ Zip _____

- -

Ann Arbor's Cookin' II
c/o Ronald McDonald House
1600 Washington Heights
Ann Arbor, MI 48104

Please send me _____ copies of Ann Arbor's Cookin II @ $15 each _____
Postage and handling in Continental U.S. @ $2.00 each _____
Sales tax @ .60 per cookbook (MI residents) _____
TOTAL ENCLOSED _____

Please make checks payable to Arbor House.
Name _____
Street _____
City _____ State _____ Zip _____